Breaking the News

ALSO BY JAMES FALLOWS

The Water Lords
National Defense
More Like Us
Looking at the Sun

BREAKING THE NEWS

*How the Media Undermine
American Democracy*

James Fallows

Pantheon Books, New York

Library of Congress Cataloging-in-Publication Data
Fallows, James M.
    Breaking the news : how the media undermine American democracy / James Fallows.
        p.   cm.
    ISBN 0-679-44209-X
    1. Press—United States—Objectivity.   2. Mass media—United States—Objectivity.   3. Press and politics—United States.   4. n-us.   I. Title.
PN4888.O25F35   1996
302.23'.0973—dc20   95-31467
                                                                              CIP

BOOK DESIGN BY LAURA HOUGH
Manufactured in the United States of America

    6   8   9   7   5

For Charles Peters

and William Whitworth

Contents

Breaking the News

Introduction

Americans have never been truly fond of their press. Through the last decade, however, their disdain for the media establishment has reached new levels. Americans believe that the news media have become too arrogant, cynical, scandal-minded, and destructive. Public hostility shows up in opinion polls, through comments on talk shows, in waning support for news organizations in their showdowns with government officials, and in many other ways. The most important sign of public unhappiness may be a quiet consumers' boycott of the press. Year by year, a smaller proportion of Americans goes to the trouble of reading newspapers or watching news broadcasts on TV. This is a loss not only for the media but also for the public as a whole. Ignoring the news leaves people with no way to prepare for trends they don't happen to observe themselves, no sense of what is happening in other countries or even other parts of their own town, no tools with which to make decisions about public leaders or policies. Evidently many people feel that these losses represent a smaller sacrifice than being exposed to what the news offers.

The big American institutions that have failed in the recent past often wasted years blaming others for their problems. The U.S. military was near collapse in the immediate aftermath of the Vietnam War. Many members of the military felt stabbed in the back and blamed their problems on weak political leaders and ungrateful fellow citizens. The Big Three automakers of Detroit, with their dinosaurlike vehicles, were unprepared in the 1970s for the sudden rise in world oil prices or for competition from Japan. They complained about the unfairness of oil producers in the Middle East, regulators in Washington, and car makers in Japan.

There was some truth in such complaints. But the larger truth is that these institutions reversed their decline only when they recognized and corrected defects in their own internal values. In the early 1970s, control of the auto companies had passed from "car men," who had been trained to design and build automobiles, to "money men," who knew all about quarterly profits and stock options but very little about making cars. In the face of Japanese competition, the Big Three floundered until they put "car men" back in charge. The American military of the same era was damaged by an ethic of careerism directly at odds with its older tradition of service. Officers bucked for promotion by being yes-men to their superiors and helping get defense contracts approved. In the field in Vietnam, enlisted men often limited their goal to surviving their 365 days "in country" and officers tried mainly to get a combat-command ticket punched. Then, during the decade after Vietnam, the military examined its ethics more deeply and honestly than any other American institution, and it corrected much of what was wrong.

The media establishment is still in the denial stage. Many of today's journalists are all too aware of the pressures pushing their profession in a direction they don't want to go. But they have not been able to deal with outside complaints honestly enough to begin the process of reform. In response to suggestions that the press has failed to meet its public responsibilities, the first instinct of many journalists is to cry "First Amendment!," which is like the military's reflexive use of "national security" to rebut outside criticism of how it does its work.

Criticize reporters or editors for their negativity, and you will be told that they are merely reflecting the world as it is. Objecting to news coverage, they say, is merely "blaming the messenger"; the press claims no responsibility for the world that it displays. Accuse a publication of left-wing bias, and its editors will reply that they are often accused of being right-wing, too—or of being pro-black, or anti-black, or pro-business, or nuttily pro-environment, or of being biased in every other conceivable way. If people are complaining from all sides, the editors reason, it must mean that they've got the balance just about right. Say that coverage is shallow or sensationalistic, and reporters will reply that they are already serving up more extensive, thoughtful news analysis than a lazy public will bother to read. If they don't feature crime and gore on the local TV news or run celebrity profiles in the paper, they'll lose their audience to competitors that do. Complain that reporters are insulated and elitist, being more committed to the values of the powerful politicians they cover than to the interests of the audience they supposedly serve, and journalists will say that even if the charge were accurate it would be irrelevant. They are "insulated," they feel, only in the sense that research scientists are, devoting all their effort to understanding an exotic subject. They can better serve the public by getting a close-up view of power than by artificially keeping their sources at arm's length.

There is some truth in journalism's complaints and excuses. But the larger truth is that the most influential parts of the media have lost sight of or have been pushed away from their central values. This book is an attempt to explain why the values of journalists have changed, how their current practices undermine the credibility of the press, and how they affect the future prospects of every American by distorting the processes by which we choose our leaders and resolve our public problems. Many journalists have noted the crisis in their profession, and a number of them have begun reform efforts. This book describes the efforts they have made.

Everyone knows that big-time journalists have become powerful and prominent. We see them shouting at presidents during White House press conferences. We hear them offering instant Thumbs Up/Thumbs Down verdicts a few seconds after a politician completes a speech. We know that they swarm from one hot news event to the next—from a press conference by Gennifer Flowers, to a riot site in Los Angeles, to congressional hearings on a Supreme Court nominee, to the arraignment of Tonya Harding.

Yet from outside the business it may be hard to understand the mixture of financial, social, and professional incentives that have produced this self-aggrandizing behavior. Some of the changes have been underway for decades, and others have taken effect in the last three or four years. Together they have turned the internal values of elite journalism upside down.

Any organization works best when the behavior that helps an individual get ahead is also the behavior that benefits the organization as a whole. Any organization suffers when what is good for the individual is bad for the group. As journalism has become more star-oriented, individual journalists have gained the potential to command power, riches, and prestige that few of their predecessors could have hoped for. Yet this new personal success involves a terrible bargain.

The more prominent today's star journalists become, the more they are forced to give up the essence of real journalism, which is the search for information of use to the public. The effects of this trade-off are greatest at the top of the occupational pyramid, which is why the consequences are so destructive. The best-known and best-paid people in journalism now set an example that erodes the quality of the news we receive and threatens journalism's claim on public respect.

The harm actually goes much further than that, to threaten the long-term health of our political system. Step by step, mainstream journalism has fallen into the habit of portraying public life in America as a race to the bottom, in which one group of conniving, insincere politicians ceaselessly tries to outmaneuver another. The great problem for American democracy in the 1990s is that people barely trust elected leaders or the entire legislative system to accomplish anything of value. The politicians seem untrustworthy while they're running, and they disappoint even their supporters soon after they take office. By the time they leave office they're making excuses for what they couldn't do.

Deep forces in America's political, social, and economic structures account for most of the frustration of today's politics, but the media's attitudes have played a surprisingly important and destructive role. Issues that affect the collective interests of Americans—crime, health care, education, economic growth—are presented mainly as arenas in which politicians can fight. The press is often referred to as the Fourth Branch of Government, which means that it should provide the information we need so as to make sense of public problems. But far from making it easier to cope with public challenges, the media often make it harder. By choosing to present public life as a contest among scheming political leaders, all of whom the public should view with suspicion, the news media help bring about that very result.

While creating new obstacles for American politics, today's media outlets have also put themselves in an impossible position. They increasingly present public life mainly as a depressing spectacle, rather than as a vital activity in which citizens can and should be engaged. The implied message of this approach is that people will pay attention to public affairs only if politics can be made as interesting as the other entertainment options available to them, from celebrity scandals to the human melodramas featured on daytime talk programs. In attempting to compete head-to-head with pure entertainment programs, the "serious" press locks itself into a competition it cannot win. Worse, it increases the chances of its own eventual extinction. In the long run, people will pay attention to journalism only if they think it tells them something they must know. The less that Americans care about public life, the less they will be interested in journalism of any form.

This book mainly describes the media from the outside, assessing the way journalists' behavior affects our public life. But since I have spent more than twenty years as a reporter, it naturally also reflects my own concerns about the institution of which I am a part.

I got into journalism by accident and stayed because I liked it. I liked many of the incidental aspects of the business—the craftsmanship required to tell a story in limited space with limited time, the thousands of decisions and feats of teamwork necessary to make a newspaper appear each morning or a broadcast begin on time. I enjoyed the chance to learn about a variety of subjects without having to tie myself permanently to any one of them.

I also believed that journalism mattered. Journalists have rarely been loved, but their work has often been valued. Through what they find out, they give other people tools for understanding the world beyond their immediate experience. Few Americans know firsthand about China or Bosnia, about the conditions in Mexico that affect immigration or those in Japan that affect trade policy. Few know about life on aircraft carriers or life inside the White House or even life on the far side of their own town. Yet Americans are asked to have opinions on these subjects or at least to choose among potential officeholders with opinions. As much or as little as we know about these subjects depends on what journalists tell us.

Tremendous potential power comes with being a reporter. You have the negative power to say things about other people, in public, to which they can never really respond in kind. You have the positive power to expand other people's understanding of reality by bringing new parts of the world to their notice. Taking this power seriously means taking your calling seriously, which in turn means recognizing the impact of the tool or weapon in your hands.

Like teachers, soldiers, nurses, or parents, journalists perform a job whose full value is not represented in their pay. When they do their jobs well, many people benefit. When they do their jobs poorly, when they are irresponsible about their power, the damage spreads further than they can see.

The institution of journalism is not doing its job well now. It is irresponsible with its power. The damage has spread to the public life Americans all share. The damage can be corrected, but not until journalism comes to terms with what it has lost.

Chapter 1

Why We Hate the Media

Why, exactly, has the media establishment become so unpopular with so many people? Here are just a few examples of what provokes American anger. They suggest that the public has good reason to think that the news media are not doing their job.

Washing Their Hands of Responsibility: "North Kosan"

In the late 1980s, public television stations aired a talking head series called *Ethics in America.* For each show, more than a dozen prominent thinkers sat around a horseshoe-shaped table and tried to answer troubling ethical questions posed by a moderator.

From the respectability of the panelists to the super-seriousness of the topics, the series might have seemed a good bet to be paralyzingly dull. But the drama and tension of at least one show made that episode absolutely riveting.

This episode was sponsored by Montclair State College, in Boston, in the fall of 1987. Its title was "Under Orders, Under Fire," and most of the panelists were former soldiers talking about the ethical dilemmas of their work. The moderator was Charles Ogletree, a professor at Harvard Law School, who moved from expert to expert asking increasingly difficult questions in the law school's famous Socratic style.

During the first half of the show Ogletree made the soldiers squirm about ethical tangles on the battlefield. The man getting the roughest treatment was Frederick Downs, a novelist who as a young Army lieutenant in Vietnam had lost his left arm when a mine blew up.

Ogletree asked Downs to imagine that he was a young lieutenant again. He and his platoon were in the nation of "South Kosan," advising South Kosanese troops in their struggle against invaders from "North Kosan." (This scenario was apparently a hybrid of the U.S. role in the wars in Korea and Vietnam.) A North Kosanese unit had captured several of Downs's men alive—but Downs had captured one of the North Kosanese. Downs did not know where his men were being held, but his prisoner did.

And so Ogletree put the question: How far will Downs go to make the prisoner talk? Will he order him tortured? Will he torture the prisoner himself? Suppose Downs has a big knife in his hand. Where will he start cutting the prisoner? When will he make himself stop, if the prisoner just won't talk?

Downs did not shrink from the questions. He wouldn't enjoy doing it, he told Ogletree. He would have to live with the consequences for the rest of his life. But, yes, he would torture the captive. He would use the knife. He would do the cutting himself. He would listen to the captive scream. He would do whatever was necessary to try to save his own men. While explaining his decisions Downs sometimes gestured with his left hand for emphasis, except that the hand was a metal hook.

Ogletree worked his way through the other military officials, asking all how they reacted to Frederick Downs's choice. Retired general William Westmoreland, who had commanded the whole American force in Vietnam when Downs was serving there, deplored Downs's decision. After all, he said, even war has its rules. An Army chaplain wrestled with what he'd do if Downs came to him privately and confessed what he had done. A Marine Corps officer juggled a related question, of what he'd do if he came across an American soldier who, like Downs in the hypothetical case, was about to torture or execute a bound and unarmed prisoner.

The soldiers disagreed among themselves. Yet in describing their decisions, every one of them used phrases like "I hope I would have the courage to . . ." or "In order to live with myself later I would . . ." The whole exercise may have been set up as a rhetorical game, but Ogletree's questions clearly tapped into serious discussions the soldiers had already had about the consequences of choices they made.

Then Ogletree turned to the two most famous members of the evening's panel, better known than William Westmoreland himself. These were two star TV journalists: Peter Jennings of *World News Tonight* and ABC, and Mike Wallace of *60 Minutes* and CBS.

Ogletree brought them into the same hypothetical war. He asked Jennings to imagine that he worked for a network that had been in contact with the enemy North Kosanese government. After much pleading, the North Kosanese had agreed to let Jennings and his news crew into their country, to film behind the lines and even travel with military units. Would Jennings be willing to go? Of course, Jennings replied. Any reporter would—and in real wars reporters from his network often had.

But while Jennings and his crew are traveling with a North Kosanese unit, to visit the site of an alleged atrocity by American and South Kosanese troops, they unexpectedly cross the trail of a small group of American and South Kosanese soldiers. With Jennings in their midst, the northern soldiers set up a perfect ambush, which will let them gun down the Americans and Southerners, every one.

What does Jennings do? Ogletree asks. Would he tell his cameramen to "Roll tape!" as the North Kosanese opened fire? What would go through his mind as he watched the North Kosanese prepare to ambush the Americans?

Jennings sat silent for about fifteen seconds after Ogletree asked this question. "Well, I guess I wouldn't," he finally said. "I am going to tell you now what I am feeling, rather than the hypothesis I drew for myself. If I were with a North Kosanese unit that came upon Americans, I think that I personally would do what I could to warn the Americans."

Even if it means losing the story? Ogletree asked.

Even though it would almost certainly mean losing my life, Jennings replied. "But I do not think that I could bring myself to participate in that act. That's purely personal, and other reporters might have a different reaction."

Immediately Mike Wallace spoke up. "I think some other reporters *would* have a different reaction," he said, obviously referring to himself. "They would regard it simply as a story they were there to cover."

"I am astonished, really," at Jennings's answer, Wallace said a moment later. He turned toward Jennings and began to lecture him:

"You're a *reporter.* Granted you're an American"—at least for purposes of the fictional example; Jennings has actually retained Canadian citizenship. "I'm a little bit at a loss to understand why, because you're an American, you would not have covered that story."

Ogletree pushed Wallace. Didn't Jennings have some higher duty, either patriotic or human, to do something rather than just roll film as soldiers from his own country were being shot?

"No," Wallace said flatly and immediately. "You don't have a higher duty. No. No. You're a reporter!"

Jennings backtracked fast. Wallace was right, he said. "I chickened out." Jennings said that he had gotten so wrapped up in the hypothetical questions that he had lost sight of his journalistic duty to remain detached.

As Jennings said he agreed with Wallace, everyone else in the room seemed to regard the two of them with horror. Retired Air Force general Brent Scowcroft, who had been Gerald Ford's national security advisor and would soon serve in the same job for George Bush, said it was simply wrong to stand and watch as your side was slaughtered. "What's it *worth?*" he asked Wallace bitterly. "It's worth thirty seconds on the evening news, as opposed to saving a platoon."

Ogletree turned to Wallace. What about that? Shouldn't the reporter have said *something?*

Wallace gave his most disarming grin, shrugged his shoulders and spread his palms wide in a "Don't ask me!" gesture, and said, "I don't know." He was mugging to the crowd in such a way that he got a big laugh—the first such moment of the discussion. Wallace paused to enjoy the crowd's reaction. Jennings, however, was all business, and was still concerned about the first answer he had given.

"I wish I had made another decision," Jennings said, as if asking permission to live the last five minutes over again. "I would like to have made his decision"—that is, Wallace's decision to keep on filming.

A few minutes later Ogletree turned to George M. Connell, a Marine colonel in full uniform. Jaw muscles flexing in anger, with stress on each word, Connell looked at the TV stars and said, "I feel utter . . . *contempt.*"

Two days after this hypothetical episode, Connell said, Jennings or Wallace might be back with the American forces—and could be wounded by stray fire, as combat journalists often had been before. The instant that happened, he said, they wouldn't be "just journalists" any more. Then they would expect American soldiers to run out under enemy fire and drag them back, rather than leaving them to bleed to death on the battlefield.

"We'll do it!" Connell said. "And that is what makes me so contemptuous of them. Marines will die going to get . . . a couple of journalists." The last few words dripped with disgust.

Not even Ogletree knew what to say. There was dead silence for several seconds. Then a square-jawed man with neat gray hair and aviator glasses spoke up. It was Newt Gingrich, looking a generation younger and trimmer than when he became Speaker of the House in 1995. One thing was clear from this exercise, he said: "The military has done a vastly better job of systematically thinking through the ethics of behavior in a violent environment than the journalists have."

That was about the mildest way to put it. Peter Jennings and Mike Wallace are just two individuals, but their reactions spoke volumes about the values of their craft. Jennings was made to feel embarrassed about his natural, decent human impulse. Wallace was completely unembarrassed about feeling no connection to the soldiers in his country's army or considering their deaths before his eyes as "simply a story." In other important occupations people sometimes face the need to do the horrible. Frederick Downs, after all, was willing to torture a man and hear him scream. But Downs had thought through all the consequences and alternatives, and he knew he would live with the horror for the rest of his days. When Mike Wallace said he would do something horrible, he didn't bother to argue a rationale. He did not try to explain the reasons a reporter might feel obliged to remain silent as the attack began—for instance, that in combat reporters must be beyond country, or that they have a duty to bear impartial witness to deaths on either side, or that Jennings had implicitly made a promise not to betray the North Kosanese when he agreed to accompany them on the hypothetical patrol. The soldiers might or might not have found such arguments convincing, but Wallace didn't even make them. He relied on charm and star power to win acceptance from the crowd.

Mike Wallace on patrol with the North Kosanese, cameras rolling while his countrymen are gunned down, recognizing no "higher duty" to interfere in any way and offering no rationale beyond "I'm with the press"—this is a nice symbol for what Americans hate about their media establishment in our age.

Confusing the Issue: The Talk Shows

A generation ago, political talk programs were sleepy Sunday-morning affairs. The secretary of state or the majority leader of the Senate would show up to answer questions from Lawrence Spivak or Bob Clark, and after thirty minutes another stately episode of *Meet the Press* or *Issues and Answers* would be history.

Everything in public life is "brighter" and more "interesting" now. Driven by constant competition from the weekday trash-talk shows, anything involving political life has had to liven itself up. Under pressure from the Saturday political-talk shows—*The McLaughlin Group* and its many disorderly descendants—even the Sunday morning shows have put on rouge and push-up bras.

Meet the Press, moderated by Tim Russert, is probably the meatiest of these programs. High-powered guests discuss serious topics with Russert, who worked for years in politics, and with veteran reporters. Yet the pressure to keep things lively means that squabbling replaces dialogue, as in "discussions" like the one below.

In March 1995, the guests on *Meet the Press* were Laura d'Andrea Tyson, President Clinton's main economic advisor;

Representative John Kasich, a Young Turk Republican from Ohio who had just become chairman of the House Budget Committee; and Senator Bill Bradley, a Democrat from New Jersey, who among his other accomplishments had long specialized in tax policy. The reporter joining Russert in asking questions was David Broder of the *Washington Post*.

More "issues"-minded people than these five would be difficult to find, even in Washington. And yet this is how they ended up talking about the federal deficit, budget cuts, and Medicare:

REP. KASICH: OK. I'm going to show you a chart. If we cut—first of all, in the private sector, health-care costs last year went up by about 3 percent. You know Medicare went up? It's going bankrupt. Did you know Medicare's going bankrupt? Do you know next year it's going to run a deficit? Let me show you. If you are in a position of trying to slow the growth of Medicare to just half the increase, let me show you what you get. Do you think the government can create a program that spends that much more and still provide security to our senior citizens and provide quality? The issue is we're not going to cut Medicare. We're going to slow the growth to keep the system from going bankrupt.

MR. RUSSERT: I'm not—I haven't suggested—all—Dr. Tyson, I beg you to get in here, because the president . . .

DR. TYSON: All right. Well . . .

REP. KASICH: Let's talk about Medicaid. You want to talk about Medicaid?

MR. RUSSERT: This is the president's status quo. And, Senator Bradley, you've called for deficit reductions. The fact is the Democrats and Republicans, unless we deal with Medicare, Medicaid . . .

REP. KASICH: But we're going to. We're going to. I'm telling you we're going to slow the growth.

DR. TYSON: Excuse me. Can I say something? What we have said—first of all, let me tell you two things about us. Number one, just slowing the growth of Medicare and Medicaid—let's be serious here. If you say, "I'm going to have it grow at 3 percent between now and 2002," that is equivalent to a 38 percent reduction in spending on Medicare, projected spending, and a 37 percent projected spending increase in Medicaid. There is inflation in both of these programs. There are increases in beneficiaries in both of these programs.

REP. KASICH: 1.8 percent.

DR. TYSON: Three percent is not enough to cover the rate of inflation, and it's not enough to cover the increase in beneficiaries.

REP. KASICH: Laura, I'm sorry. Those numbers are wrong.

DR. TYSON: So what we have said—they are absolutely . . .

REP. KASICH: Make up any numbers you want.

DR. TYSON: They are absolutely not correct. You know what? You should have . . .

REP. KASICH: Caseload goes up 1.8 percent.

DR. TYSON: You should have on this program someone to do fact checking because I'm telling you . . .

REP. KASICH: Yeah, we should. That would be a good idea.

DR. TYSON: . . . the 3 percent growth per year . . .

REP. KASICH: You're right.

SEN. BRADLEY: Just a minute. Just a minute. Let me just . . .

DR. TYSON: Now let me say something else; second point: We have said again and again, and let me repeat again so that everybody hears it very clearly, we believe we have made substantial progress on the deficit. We have brought it down significantly. We have cut it in half both absolutely and relative to GDP. But . . .

MR. RUSSERT: Doctor . . .

REP. KASICH: The deficit's going up $30 billion this year.

DR. TYSON: But—but, but, but we think more should be done. Now, how do we think more should be done?

MR. RUSSERT: But Dr. Tyson, wait. In terms of fact checking . . .

DR. TYSON: OK.

MR. RUSSERT: Just a second. Out of the Clinton deficit reduction, over 60 percent was from tax increases, not from spending cuts. Let me finish.

DR. TYSON: Look, the point is the deficit—we're not talking here—you are not talking about what . . .

MR. RUSSERT: Your budget plan—excuse me.

REP. KASICH: You need a referee.

MR. RUSSERT: I'm being a fact checker; I'm being a fact checker. The budget you put forward . . .

DR. TYSON: You are.

MR. RUSSERT: . . . puts together $200 billion deficits. David, you jump in here about . . .

DR. TYSON: We agree. We agree with that.

MR. RUSSERT: Please, David.

DR. TYSON: I agree with that.

MR. BRODER: Yeah.

DR. TYSON: I did not say that was not true, did I?

MR. RUSSERT: Robert Reich, on this program said . . .

DR. TYSON: I did not say that was not true.

MR. RUSSERT: . . ."A balanced budget is not his goal."

DR. TYSON: Look, what I said is, we have—are bringing down—look, if you have a company . . .

REP. KASICH: Your deficit's going up by $30 billion of your budget, Doctor.

Meet the Press is one of the most thoughtful, "in-depth" talk shows. You can imagine a transcript from *Crossfire* or *The Capital Gang.* The discussion shows that are supposed to add to public understanding may actually reduce it, by hammering home the message that "issues" don't matter except as items for politicians to squabble about. Some politicians in Washington may indeed view all issues as mere tools to use against their opponents. But far from offsetting this conception of public life, the national press often encourages it. As Washington-based talk shows have become more popular in the last decade, they have had a trickle-down effect in cities across the country. In Seattle, in Los Angeles, in Boston, in Atlanta journalists become more noticed and influential through regular seats on talk shows—and from those seats they mainly talk about the game of politics.

Who Cares About Real Issues? What Reporters Want to Know

In the 1992 presidential campaign, candidates spent more time answering questions from "ordinary people"—citizens in town hall forums, callers on radio and TV talk shows—than in previous years. During and after the campaign, several observers noticed how different these questions were from the ones reporters posed at press conferences. The citizens asked overwhelmingly about the *what* of politics. What are you going to do about the health care system? What can you do to reduce the cost of welfare? The reporters asked almost exclusively about the *how*. How are you going to try to take away Perot's constituency? How do you answer charges that you have flip-flopped?

After the 1992 campaign, the contrast between the questions from citizens and those from reporters was widely discussed in journalism reviews and postmortems on campaign coverage. Reporters acknowledged that they should try harder to ask questions their readers and viewers seemed to care about—that is, questions about the difference political choices would make in people's lives.

In January 1995, there was a chance to see how well the lesson had sunk in. In the days just before and just after President Clinton delivered his State of the Union address to the new Republican-controlled Congress, he answered questions in a wide variety of forums in order to explain his plans.

On January 31, four days after the speech, the president flew to Boston and took questions from a group of teenagers there. The teenagers asked him seven questions, nearly all of which concerned the effects of legislation or government programs on their communities or schools. These were the questions (paraphrased in some cases):

1. "We need stronger laws to punish those people who are caught selling guns to our youth. Basically, what can you do about that?"
2. "I noticed that often it's the media that is responsible for the negative portrayal of young people in our society." What could political leaders do to improve the way young people think of themselves?

3. Apprenticeship programs and other ways to provide job training have been valuable for students not going to college. Can the administration promote more of these programs?

4. Programs designed to keep teenagers away from drugs and gangs often emphasize sports and seem geared mainly to boys. How could such programs be made more attractive to teenaged girls?

5. What is it like at Oxford? (This was from a student who was completing a new alternative-school curriculum in the Boston public schools, and who had been accepted at Oxford.)

6. "We need more police officers that are trained to deal with all the other cultures in our cities." What could the government do about that?

7. "In Boston, Northeastern University has created a model of scholarships and other supports to help inner-city kids get to and stay in college. As president, can you urge colleges across the country to do what Northeastern has done?"

Earlier in the month the president had taken questions, in three separate sessions, from the three network news anchors: Peter Jennings of ABC, Dan Rather of CBS, and Tom Brokaw of NBC. There was no overlap whatsoever between the questions the students asked and those raised by the anchors. None of the questions from these news professionals concerned the impact of legislation or politics on people's lives. Nearly all the questions concerned the pure game of politics—the struggle among candidates interested mainly in their own advancement.

Peter Jennings, who met Clinton early in the month as the Gingrich-Dole Congress was getting underway, asked questions centering on the theme that Clinton had been eclipsed as a political leader by these two Republicans. His first question was whether Newt Gingrich had become "the new pivotal figure in American politics," and his last question, based on indications of the president's declining popularity, was, "You don't think you have a deaf ear?"

Dan Rather did interviews through January with prominent politicians—Senators Edward Kennedy, Phil Gramm, and Bob Dole—building up to a long profile of President Clinton on the day of the State of the Union address. Every question he asked was about popularity or political tactics. He asked Phil Gramm to guess whether Colin Powell would enter the race (No) and whether Bill Clinton would be renominated by his party (Yes). He asked Bob Dole what kind of mood the president seemed to be in, and whether Dole and Gingrich were, in effect, the new bosses of Washington. When Edward Kennedy began giving his views about the balanced-budget amendment, Rather steered him back on course:

> Senator, you know I'd like to talk about these things the rest of the afternoon, but let's move quickly to politics. Do you expect Bill Clinton to be the Democratic nominee for reelection in 1996?

The CBS *Evening News* profile of Clinton, which was narrated by Rather and was presented as part of its "Eye on America" series, contained no mention whatsoever of Clinton's economic policy, his tax or budget plans, his failed attempt to pass a health care proposal, his successful attempt to ratify NAFTA, his efforts to "reinvent government," or any substantive aspect of his proposals or plans in office. Its subject was exclusively Clinton's "handling" of his office— his "difficulty making decisions," his "waffling" at crucial moments. "The public grew uneasy," Rather said:

> Whitewater deepened people's doubts about the president. After Vince Foster's suicide, it took the Clinton

administration five months to admit it had removed
Whitewater-related papers from Foster's office. Now, it
seemed, the president didn't talk straight. He was covering up. Criticism intensified.

In wrapping up his analysis, Rather said that the significance of the State of the Union speech was, again, how it
would position the president politically: "President Clinton's friends and aides say that he is now, again, reaching
deep down inside and is finding anew his character." If
Rather or his colleagues had any interest in the content of
Clinton's speech, rather than its political effect, none of their
questions revealed it.

Tom Brokaw's questions were more substantive, but
even he concentrated mainly on the politics of the event.
How did the president feel about a poll showing that 61 percent of the public felt he had no "strong convictions" and
could be "easily swayed"? What did Bill Clinton think
about Newt Gingrich? "Do you think he plays fair?" How
did he like it when people kept being arrested for shooting
at the White House?

When ordinary citizens have a chance to pose questions
to political leaders, they rarely ask about the game of politics. They mainly want to know how the reality of politics
will affect them—through taxes, programs, scholarship
funds, wars. Journalists justify their intrusiveness and excesses by claiming that they are the public's representatives,
asking the questions their fellow citizens would ask if they
had the privilege of meeting with presidents and senators. In
fact they ask questions no one but their fellow political
professionals cares about. And they often do so with a dis-
courtesy and rancor, as at the typical White House news conference, that represents the public's views much less than it
reflects the modern journalist's belief that being independent boils down to acting hostile.

Reductio ad Electum: The One-Track Mind

The limited curiosity that elite reporters display in their questions is evident in the stories they write once they have received answers. They are interested mainly in pure politics and can be coerced only as a last resort into examining the substance of an issue. The subtle but steady result is a stream of daily messages that the real meaning of public life is the struggle of Bob Dole against Newt Gingrich against Bill Clinton, rather than our collective efforts to solve collective problems. For example:

Through the summer of 1995, the Clinton administration edged steadily closer toward restoring diplomatic relations with Vietnam. Since 1975, when North Vietnamese troops captured the southern capital of Saigon, the U.S. government had forbidden its citizens or companies to trade with Vietnam. Through the mid-1980s, when Vietnamese troops were occupying Cambodia, a number of Western and Asian governments joined the United States in imposing trade and diplomatic sanctions. But in the late 1980s, as the Vietnamese government withdrew its troops from Cambodia and liberalized its own economy, other nations expanded their commercial, cultural, and political ties with Vietnam. By the time Bill Clinton took office, the United States was virtually alone in its pretense that the existence of modern Vietnam could be ignored. Outside the United States, this stance was seen as an indication that Americans still had not come to terms with their emotions and resentments about the war.

In the first months of the Clinton administration, business groups, Asia scholars, Vietnamese-American organizations, and even many Vietnam-veterans groups recommended that the new president change the old policy and allow normal dealings with Vietnam. The administration resisted, partly because several small but vocal groups claimed that the Vietnamese government was still concealing the truth about American POWs and MIAs. (Retired general John Vessey, former chairman of the Joint Chiefs of Staff, disagreed. Vessey led negotiations with the Vietnamese on this issue, and publicly said that they were cooperating.) The administration's strategists were also aware that the POW groups that opposed the move would be all the more upset if it were enacted by a man who had been at Georgetown and Oxford when their loved ones were being shot down or captured.

Nonetheless, in 1994 the president ordered an end to the trade embargo, and in 1995 his administration prepared the groundwork for the inevitable return to normal relations.

On June 26, 1995, a few weeks before the president announced that full diplomatic relations would be restored, the *New York Times* ran a front-page story about this process. Its headline was, "Clinton on Spot on Vietnam Issue." The subhead said, "He Hesitates on Recognition Despite Urgings of Aides." The story began:

> Twenty-six years after he agonized over avoiding service in a war he "opposed and despised," President Clinton is moving toward the end of another agonizing deliberation over Vietnam: how and when to grant the former enemy full diplomatic recognition.

What is unusual about this approach, in which the significance of the Vietnam decision was reduced to the political problems it created for the president? Very little, which is the point. The natural instinct of newspapers and TV is to present every public issue as if its "real" meaning were political in the narrowest and most operational sense of that term—the attempt by parties and candidates to gain an advantage over their rivals. Reporters do of course write stories about political life in the broader sense and about the substance of issues—the pluses and minuses of recognizing Vietnam, the difficulties of holding down the Medicare budget, whether immigrants help or hurt the nation's economic base. But when there is a chance to use these issues as props or raw material for a story about pure political tactics, most reporters leap at it. It is sexier and easier to write about Bill Clinton's "positioning" on the Vietnam issue, or how Newt Gingrich is "handling" the need to cut Medicare, than to look into the issues themselves.

Examples of this preference occur so often that they're difficult to notice, like individual grains of sand on the beach. But every morning's newspaper, along with every evening's newscast, reveals this pattern of thought.

- In February 1995, when the Democratic president and the Republican Congress were fighting over how much federal money would go to local law enforcement agencies, one network news broadcast showed a clip of Gingrich denouncing Clinton, and another of Clinton standing in front of a sea of uniformed policemen while making a tough-on-crime speech. The correspondent's sign-off line was: "But the White House likes the sound of 'cops on the beat.'" That is, the president was pushing the plan because it would sound good in his campaign ads. Whether or not that was Clinton's real motive, nothing in the broadcast gave the slightest hint of where the extra policemen would go, how much they might cost, whether there was reason to think they'd do any good. Everything in the story suggested that the crime bill mattered *only* as a chapter in the real saga, which was the struggle between Bill and Newt.

- In April 1995, after the explosion at the Murrah Building in Oklahoma City, discussion changed quickly from the event itself to politicians' "handling" of the event.

On the weekend after the blast, President Clinton announced a series of new antiterrorism measures. The
next morning, on National Public Radio's *Morning Edition,* Cokie Roberts was asked about the prospects for
his proposals taking effect. "In some ways, it's not even
the point," she replied. What mattered was that Clinton "looked good" by taking the tough side of the issue.
No one expects Cokie Roberts or other political correspondents to be experts on controlling terrorism, or
negotiating with the Syrians, or the other specific measures on which presidents make stands. But all issues
are shoehorned into the expertise the most prominent
correspondents do have, which is the struggle for one-
upmanship among a handful of political leaders.

- When health care reform was the focus of big political
battles between Republicans and Democrats, it was on
the front page and the evening newscast every day.
When the Clinton administration declared defeat in
1994 and there were no more battles to be fought,
health-care news coverage virtually stopped too—even
though the medical system still represented one-
seventh of the economy, even though HMOs and corporations and hospitals and pharmaceutical companies
were rapidly changing policies in the face of ever-rising
costs. Health care was no longer *political* news, and
therefore it was no longer interesting news.

- After California's voters approved Proposition 187 in
the 1994 elections, drastically limiting benefits available to illegal immigrants, the national press ran a
trickle of stories on what this would mean for California's economy, its school and legal systems, even its relations with Mexico. A flood of stories examined the
political impact of the immigration "issue"—how the
Republicans might exploit it, how the Democrats

might be divided by it, whether it might propel Pete Wilson to the White House.

On August 15, 1995, Bill Bradley announced that after representing New Jersey in the Senate for three terms he would not run for a fourth term, in 1996. In his press statement revealing the decision and the news conferences he conducted afterward, Bradley did his best to talk about the deep problems of public life and economic adjustment that had left him frustrated with the normal political process. Each of the parties had locked itself into rigid positions that kept them from dealing with realistic concerns of ordinary people, he said. American corporations were doing what they had to do for survival in international competition: they were "downsizing" and making themselves radically more efficient and productive. But the result was to leave "decent, hard-working Americans" more vulnerable to layoffs and loss of their careers, medical coverage, pension rights, and social standing than they had been in decades. Somehow, Bradley said, we had to move past the focus on short-term political maneuvering and determine how to deal with the forces that were leaving Americans frustrated and insecure.

That, at least, was what Bill Bradley said. What turned up in the press was almost exclusively speculation about what this move meant for the presidential race of 1996 and the party line-up on Capitol Hill. Might Bradley challenge Bill Clinton in the Democratic primaries? If not, was he preparing for an independent run? Could the Democrats come up with any other candidate capable of holding onto Bradley's seat? Wasn't this a huge slap in the face for Bill Clinton and the party he purported to lead? In the immediate aftermath of Bradley's announcement, leading TV and newspaper reporters competed to come up with the shrewdest analysis of the political impact of the move. None of the country's major papers or networks used Bradley's announcement as a "news peg" for an analysis of the real issues he had raised.

Two days after his announcement, Bradley was interviewed by Judy Woodruff on the CNN program *Inside Politics*. Woodruff is a widely respected and knowledgeable reporter, but her interaction with Bradley was like the meeting of two beings from different universes. Every answer Bradley gave concerned the substance of national problems that concerned him. Every question she asked was about short-term political tactics. Woodruff asked about the reaction to this move from Bob Dole, or Newt Gingrich, or Bill Clinton. Bradley replied that it was more important to concentrate on the difficulties both parties had in dealing with real national problems.

Near the end of the interview Bradley gave a long answer about how everyone involved in politics had to get out of the rut of converting every subject or comment into a political "issue," used for partisan advantage. Let's stop talking, Bradley said, about who will win what race and start talking about the challenges we all face.

As soon as he finished, Judy Woodruff asked her next question: "Do you want to be president?" It was as if she had not heard a word he had been saying—or *couldn't* hear it, because the media's language of political analysis is so separate from the terms in which people describe real problems in their lives.

Every day's paper and every night's broadcast news gives further examples. The habit of emphasizing partisan consequences is so ingrained that it's hard to realize that it's not a law of nature.

What's the harm? This style of coverage implies that there is only one real story behind the many, varied events of each day. That is the story of who has the most political power, as exemplified by who will win the next presidential race. The effect is as flattening and mind-shrinking as if the discussion of every new advance in medicine boiled down to speculation about whether its creator would win the Nobel Prize that year. Regardless of the tone of coverage, medical research will still go on. But a relentless emphasis on the cynical game of politics threatens public life itself, by implying day after day that the political sphere is mainly an arena in which ambitious politicians struggle for dominance, rather than a structure in which citizens can deal with worrisome collective problems.

Pointless Prediction: The Political Experts

On Sunday, November 6, 1994, two days before the congressional elections that would sweep the Republicans to power, the *Washington Post* published the results of its "Crystal Ball" poll. Fourteen prominent journalists, pollsters, and all-around analysts made their predictions about how many seats each party would win in the House and Senate and how many governorships each would take.

One week later, many of these same experts would be saying on their talk shows that the Republican landslide was "inevitable" and "a long time coming" and "a sign of deep discontent in the heartland." But before the returns were in, how many of the fourteen experts predicted that the Republicans would win both houses of the Congress and that Newt Gingrich would be Speaker?

Exactly three. Morton Kondracke, of *Roll Call* magazine and *The McLaughlin Group* talk show; John McLaughlin, founder of the same show; and Mary Matalin, the Bush campaign strategist and host of the *Equal Time* talk show, all guessed that the Republicans would take the Senate and, by a small margin, the House. (Matalin predicted that the Republicans would have a three-vote majority in the House; McLaughlin, four votes; Kondracke, fourteen votes. The actual margin was twenty-two.) All the other experts predicted that the Democrats would hold onto the House with a reasonable margin—twenty-two seats, according to Eleanor Clift of *Newsweek*; eighteen seats, according to William Schneider of CNN; ten seats, according to Christopher Matthews of the *San Francisco Examiner*.

What is interesting about this event is not that so many experts could be so wrong. Immediately after the election, even Newt Gingrich seemed dazed by the idea that the forty-year reign of the Democrats in the House had actually come to an end. Rather, the episode said something about the futility of political prediction itself, a task to which the big-time press devotes enormous effort and time. *Two days* before the election, many of the country's most admired analysts had no idea what was about to happen. Yet in a matter of weeks these same people, unfazed, would be writing articles and giving speeches and being quoted about who was "ahead" and "behind" in the emerging race for the White House in 1996.

As with medieval doctors who applied leeches and trepanned skulls, the practitioners cannot be blamed for the limits of their profession. But we can ask why reporters spend so much time directing our attention toward what is not much more than guesswork on their part. It builds the impression that journalism is about spectacles and diversions—guessing what might or might not happen next month—rather than inquiries that might be useful, such as extracting lessons of success and failure from events that have already occurred. Competing predictions add almost nothing to our ability to solve public problems or make sensible choices among complex alternatives. Yet this useless distraction has become a speciality of the political press. Predictions are easy to produce, they allow the reporters to act as if they possess special inside knowledge, and there is no consequence for being wrong.

Spoon-feeding: The White House Press Corps

In the early spring of 1995, when Newt Gingrich was dominating news from Washington and the O.J. Simpson trial was dominating news as a whole, the *Washington Post* ran an article about the pathos of the White House pressroom. Nobody wanted to hear what the president was doing. So the people who cover the president could not get on the air. Howard Kurtz, the *Post*'s media writer, described the human cost of this political change:

> Brit Hume is in his closet-size White House cubicle, watching Kato Kaelin testify on CNN. Bill Plante, in the adjoining cubicle, has his feet up and is buried in the *New York Times*. Brian Williams is in the corridor, idling away the time with Jim Miklaszewski.
>
> An announcement is made for a bill-signing ceremony. Some of America's highest-paid television correspondents begin ambling toward the pressroom door.
>
> "Are you coming with us?" Williams asks.
>
> "I guess so," says Hume, looking forlorn.

The White House spokesman, Mike McCurry, told Kurtz that there was some benefit to the enforced silence: "Brit Hume has now got his crossword puzzle capacity down to record time. And some of the reporters have been out on the lecture circuit."

The deadpan restraint with which Kurtz told this story is admirable. But the question many readers would want to scream at the unfortunate, idle correspondents is: *Why don't you go out and do some work?*

What might these well-paid, well-trained correspondents have done, while waiting for the O.J. trial to become
boring enough that they'd get back on the air? They could
have tried to learn something that would be of use to their
viewers, when the emergency-of-the-moment went away.
Without leaving Washington, without going more than a
ten-minute taxi ride from the White House (so they would
be on hand, if a sudden press conference were called), they
could have prepared themselves to discuss the substance of
issues that would affect the public.

For example, two years earlier, Vice President Gore had
announced an ambitious plan to "reinvent" the federal government. Had it made any difference, either in improving
the performance of government or in reducing its cost, or
was it all for show? Republicans and Democrats were sure to
spend the next few months fighting about cuts in the capital
gains tax. Capital gains tax rates were higher in some countries and lower in others. What did the experience of these
countries show about whether cutting the rates helped an
economy grow? The rate of immigration was rising again,
and in California and Florida it was becoming an important
political issue. What was the latest evidence on the economic and social effect of immigration? Should Americans
feel confident or threatened that so many foreigners were
trying to make their way in? Soon both political parties
would be advancing plans to reform the welfare system.
Within a two-mile radius of the White House were plenty of
families living on welfare. Why not go see how the system
had affected them, and what they would do if it were
changed? The federal government had gone further than
most private industries in trying to open opportunities to
racial minorities and women. The Pentagon had gone furthest of all. What did people involved in this process—men
and women, blacks and whites—think about its successes

and failures? What light did their experience shed on the impending "affirmative action" debate?

The list could go on for pages. With a few minutes' effort—about as long as it takes to do a crossword puzzle—the correspondents could have drawn up lists of other subjects they had never "had time" to investigate before. They had the time now. What they lacked was a sense that their responsibility involved something more than their standing up to rehash the day's announcements when there was room for them again on the news.

Journalists Living in Glass Houses: Financial Disclosure

Half a century ago, reporters knew but didn't say that Franklin Roosevelt was in a wheelchair. A generation ago, many reporters knew but didn't write about John Kennedy's insatiable appetite for women. For several months in the early Clinton era, reporters knew about but didn't disclose Paula Jones's allegation that, as governor of Arkansas, Bill Clinton had exposed himself in front of her, in a hotel room to which he'd dragooned her, and said, "Kiss it." Eventually this claim found its way into all major newspapers, thereby proving that there is no longer any such thing as an accusation too embarrassing to be printed, if it seems to bear on a politician's "character."

It is not just the president who has given up his privacy, in the name of the "public right to know." Over the last two decades, officials whose power is tiny compared to the president's have had to reveal embarrassing details about what most Americans consider very private matters: their income and wealth. Each of the more than two thousand people appointed by the president to executive branch jobs must re-

veal previous sources of income and summarize his or her financial holdings. Congressmen have changed their rules to
forbid themselves to accept "honoraria" for speaking to interest groups or lobbyists. The money that politicians do
raise from individuals and groups must all be disclosed to
the Federal Election Commission. The data they disclose is
available to the public and appears often in publications,
most prominently the *Washington Post*.

No one even contends that every contribution makes
every politician corrupt. But financial disclosure has become
commonplace on the "better safe than sorry" principle. If
politicians and officials are not corrupt, the reasoning goes,
they have nothing to fear in letting their finances be publi-
cized. And if they are corruptible, public disclosure is a way
to stop them before they do too much harm. The process
may be embarrassing, but this is the cost of public life.

How different the "better safe than sorry" calculation
seems when journalists are involved! Reporters and pundits
hold no elected office, but they are obviously public figures.
The most prominent TV talk show personalities are better
known than all but a handful of congressmen. When politicians and pundits sit alongside each other and trade opinions
on Washington talk shows, they underscore the essential
similarity of their political roles. The pundits have no vote in
Congress, but in overall political impact a word from George
Will, Ted Koppel, William Safire, or their colleagues who run
the major editorial pages, dwarfs anything a third-term congressman could do. If an interest group did have the choice of
buying the favor either of one prominent media figure or of
two junior congressmen, it wouldn't even have to think about
the decision. The pundit is obviously more valuable.

If they were writing about backdoor campaign financing, journalists would instantly see through the fog of
legalisms to say: prominent journalists have tremendous
power, and therefore their sources of money are relevant. Yet

the analysts who are so clear-eyed in seeing the conflict of interest in Newt Gingrich's book deal or Hillary Clinton's cattle trades claim that they see no reason, none at all, why their own finances might be of public interest.

In 1993, Sam Donaldson, of ABC, described himself in an interview as being in touch with the concerns of the average American. "I'm trying to get a little ranching business started in New Mexico," he said. "I've got five people on the payroll. I'm making out those government forms." Thus, he understood the travails of the small businessman and the difficulty of government regulation. Donaldson, whose base pay from ABC is approximately $2 million per year, did not point out that his several ranches in New Mexico together covered some 20,000 acres. When doing a segment attacking farm subsidies on *Prime Time Live* in 1993 he did not point out that "those government forms" allowed him to claim nearly $97,000 in sheep and mohair subsidies over two years. When William Neuman, a reporter for the *New York Post*, tried to take pictures of Donaldson's ranch house, Donaldson had him thrown off his property. ("In the West, trespassing is a serious offense," he explained.)

Had this behavior involved a politician or even a corporate executive, Donaldson would have felt justified in the most aggressive reportorial techniques. When these techniques were turned on him he complained that the reporters were going too far.

In May 1995, Donaldson's colleague on *This Week With David Brinkley*, George Will, wrote a column and delivered on-air comments ridiculing the Clinton administration's plan to impose tariffs on Japanese luxury cars, notably the Lexus. On the Brinkley show he said that the tariffs would be "illegal" and would merely amount to "a subsidy for Mercedes dealerships."

Neither in his column nor on the show did Will disclose that his wife, Mari Maseng, had been paid some $200,000 as a registered foreign agent for the Japan Automobile Manufacturers Association, nor that the duty for which she was hired was to get American commentators to criticize the tariff plan. When Will was asked why he had said nothing, he replied that it was "just too silly" to think that his views might have been affected by his wife's contract.

Will had, in fact, espoused such views for years, long before Mari Maseng worked for the JAMA and even before she was married to George Will. Few of his readers would leap to the conclusion that Will was serving as a mouthpiece for his wife's employers. But most would have preferred to have learned this information from Will himself, a disclosure indicating his awareness that journalists have to work to maintain the public's trust.

A third member of the regular Brinkley panel, Cokie Roberts, is, along with Will and Donaldson, a frequent and highly paid speaker to corporate audiences. Like the others she has made a point of not disclosing what interest groups she speaks to, nor for how much money. She has criticized the Clinton administration for its secretive "handling" of controversies surrounding Hillary Clinton's lucrative cattle-future trades and the Whitewater affair, yet like the other pundits she refuses to acknowledge that secrecy about financial interests undermines journalism's credibility too.

Seeing Ourselves as Others See Us: Term Limits

As soon as the Democrats were routed in the 1994 elections, commentators and TV analysts said it was obvious that the American people were tired of seeing the same old faces in Washington. Those who lived inside the Beltway forgot what it was like in the rest of the country. They didn't get it. They were out of touch. The only way to jerk the congressional system back to reality was to bring in new blood.

A few days after the new Congress was sworn in, CNN began running an updated series of promotional ads for its *Crossfire* program. (The previous ads had featured shots of locomotives colliding head-on and rams crashing into each other with their horns, to symbolize the meeting of minds on the show.) Everything has been shaken up in the capital, the ad began. New faces. New names. New people in charge of all the committees.

"In fact," the announcer said, in a tone meant to indicate whimsy, "only one committee hasn't changed. The *welcoming* committee."

The camera pulled back to reveal the three hosts of *Crossfire*—Pat Buchanan, John Sununu, and Michael Kinsley—standing with arms crossed on the steps of the Capitol building, blocking the path of the new arrivals trying to make their way in. "Watch your step," one of the hosts said.

Talk about "not getting it"! The people who put together this ad must have imagined that the popular irritation with "inside the Beltway" culture was confined to Members of Congress—and not to Members of the Punditocracy, many of whom had held their positions much longer than the typical congressman had. The difference between the "welcoming committee" and the congressional committees headed by fallen Democratic titans like Dan Rostenkowski and Jack Brooks is that the congressmen could be booted out.

"Polls show that both Republicans *and* Democrats felt better about the Congress just after the 1994 elections," a Clinton administration official said in 1995. "They had 'made the monkey jump'—they were able to discipline an institution they didn't like. They could register the fact that they were unhappy. There doesn't seem to be any way to do that with the press, except to stop watching and reading, which more and more people have done."

Out of Touch with America: The State of the Union

On January 24, 1995, Bill Clinton kicked off his dealings with a Republican Congress with his State of the Union address. In the week leading up to a State of the Union address, White House aides always leak word to reporters that this year the speech will be "different." No more long laundry list of all the government's activities, no more boring survey of every potential trouble spot in the world. This time, for a change, the speech is going to be short, punchy, and "thematic." When the actual speech occurs, it is never short, punchy, or "thematic." It is long and detailed, like all its predecessors, because as the deadline nears every part of the government scrambles desperately to have a mention of its activities crammed somewhere into the speech.

In the days before the 1995 speech, Bill Clinton's assistants said that, no matter what had happened to all those other presidents, this time the speech really would be short, snappy, and thematic. The president understood the situation, he recognized his altered role, and he saw this as an opportunity to set a new theme for his third and fourth years in office.

That evening, the predictions once again proved wrong. Bill Clinton gave a speech that not only failed to be short and snappy but was also enormously long even by standards of previous State of the Union addresses. The speech had three or four apparent endings, it had ad-libbed inserts, it covered both the details of policy and the president's theories of what had gone wrong with America. One hour and twenty minutes after he took the podium, the president stepped down.

Less than one minute later, the mockery from commentators began. For instant analysis NBC went to Peggy Noonan, who had been a speechwriter for presidents Reagan and Bush. She grimaced and barely tried to conceal her disdain for such an ungainly, sprawling speech. Other commentators soon mentioned that congressmen had been slipping out of the Capitol building before the end of the speech, that Clinton had once more failed to stick to an agenda, that the speech probably would not give the president the new start he sought. The comments were virtually all about the tactics of the speech, and they were virtually all thumbs down.

A day and a half later, the first newspaper columns showed up. They were even more critical. On January 26 the *Washington Post*'s op-ed page consisted mainly of stories about the speech, all of which were witheringly harsh. "All Mush and No Message" was the headline on a column by Richard Cohen. "An Opportunity Missed" was the more statesmanlike judgment from David Broder. Despite the difference in headlines the two columns began with identical complaints. Broder's said:

> If self-discipline is the requisite of leadership—and it is—then President Clinton's State of the Union address dramatized his failure. It was a speech about everything, and therefore about nothing. It was a huge missed opportunity—and one he will regret.

Cohen's version was:

> Marshall McLuhan said the medium is the message. If so, Bill Clinton's medium was his State of the Union address, and its message was that he still lacks discipline. In an incredible one hour and 20 minutes, he managed to obscure his themes, trample on his rhetorical high spots and weary his audience. Pardon me if I thought of an awful metaphor: Clinton at a buffet table, eating everything in sight.

What a big fat jerk that Clinton was! How little he understood the obligations of leadership! Yet the news section of the same day's *Post* had a long article based on discussions with "focus groups" of ordinary citizens around the country who had watched the president's speech. "For these voters, the State of the Union speech was an antidote to weeks of unrelenting criticism of Clinton's presidency," the article said:

> "Tonight reminded us of what has been accomplished," said Maureen Prince, who works as the office manager in her husband's business and has raised five children. "We are so busy hearing the negatives all the time, from the time you wake up on your clock radio in the morning . . ."
>
> The group's immediate impressions mirrored the results of several polls conducted immediately after the president's speech.
>
> ABC News found that eight out of 10 approved of the president's speech. CBS News said that 74 percent of those surveyed said they had a "clear idea" of what Clinton stands for, compared with just 41 percent before the speech. A Gallup Poll for *USA Today* and Cable News Network found that eight in 10 said Clinton is leading the country in the right direction."

Nielsen ratings reported in the same day's paper showed that the longer the speech went on, the more people tuned in to watch.

The point is not that the pundits are necessarily wrong and the public necessarily right. It is the gulf between the two groups' reactions that is significant. The very aspects of the speech that had seemed so ridiculous to the professional commentators—its detail, its inclusiveness, the hyperearnestness of Clinton's conclusion about the "common good"—seemed attractive and valuable to most viewers.

"I'm wondering what so much of the public heard that

our highly trained expert analysts completely missed," Carol Cantor, a software consultant from California, posted in a discussion on the WELL, a popular on-line forum, three days after the speech. What they heard was, in fact, the whole speech, which allowed them to draw their own conclusions rather than being forced to accept the expert "analysis" of how the president "handled" the occasion. In most cases the analysis goes unchallenged, since the public has no chance to see the original event the pundits are describing. In this instance, viewers had exactly the same evidence about Clinton's performance as the "experts" did, and from it they drew radically different conclusions. Carol Cantor's comment on the WELL continued:

> I never have a greater sense of two Americas than when I'm watching public opinion, the whole possibility of public thought, being swamped by pundit opinion. That other America is very tiny, it has only a few inhabitants, they all live in Washington, and they never shut up.

In 1992 political professionals had laughed at Ross Perot's "boring" and "complex" charts about the federal budget deficit—until viewers seemed to love them. And for a week or two after this State of the Union speech, there were little jokes on the weekend talk shows about how out-of-step the pundit reaction had been with opinion "out there." But after a polite chuckle at the jokes the talk shifted to how the president and the Speaker and Senator Dole were "handling" their jobs.

Lost Credibility

"When movie officials come in here to talk about the question of violence in films, they are no longer in the denial stage," Reed Hundt, the chairman of the Federal Communications Commission said early in 1995. "They know there is a problem. The difference with the press is that they still *are* in denial. When I met [a famous TV reporter], all she could talk about was how much more good news was on the air than ever before."

As with the reaction to President Clinton's State of the Union speech, there is an astonishing gulf between the way journalists—especially the most prominent ones—think about their impact and the way the public does.

"I'd like to dip the McLaughlin Group and the Capitol Hill Gang in cajun-style batter and deep fry them all so I could sell them as Pundit McNuggets," Patrick Lopez, who lives in Austin, Texas, wrote in a WELL on-line discussion group titled "Pundicide" in 1995. "Low on nutrition, but they taste great cuz there's such a high fat content!"

In movies of the 1930s, reporters were gritty characters, instinctively siding with the Common Man. In the 1970s, Robert Redford and Dustin Hoffman, starring as Woodward and Bernstein in *All the President's Men,* were better paid but still gritty reporters not afraid to challenge big power. Even the local TV news crew featured on *The Mary Tyler Moore Show* had a certain down-to-earth pluck. Ted Knight, as the pea-brained news anchor Ted Baxter, was a ridiculously pompous figure but not an arrogant one.

Since the early 1980s, the journalists who have shown up in movies have been portrayed, on average, as more loathsome than the lawyers, politicians, or business moguls who are the traditional bad guys in films about the white-collar world. In *Absence of Malice,* made in 1981, the ambitious newspaper reporter (Sally Field) ruined the reputation of a businessman (Paul Newman) by rashly publishing articles accusing him of murder. In *Broadcast News,* released in 1987, the anchorman (William Hurt) is still an airhead, like Ted Knight; but unlike Ted he works in a business that is systematically hostile to anything except profit and bland good looks. The only sympathetic characters in the movie, an overeducated reporter (Albert Brooks) and a hyperactive and hyperidealistic producer (Holly Hunter), would have triumphed as heroes in a newspaper movie of the 1930s. In this one they are ground down by the philistines at their network.

In the *Die Hard* series, starting in 1988, a TV journalist (William Atherton) is an unctuous creep who will lie and push helpless people around in order to get on the air. In *The Bonfire of the Vanities* (1990), the tabloid-writer Peter Fallow (Bruce Willis) is a disheveled British sot who will do anything for a free drink. In *Rising Sun* (1993), a newspaper reporter known as "Weasel" (Steve Buscemi) is an out-and-out criminal, accepting bribes to influence his coverage. As Antonia Zerbisias pointed out in 1993 in the *Toronto Star*, movies and TV shows offer almost no illustrations of journalists who are not full of themselves, shallow, and indifferent to the harm that they do. During Operation Desert Storm, *Saturday Night Live* ridiculed the buffoons from the American press corps asking briefers questions like, "Can you tell us exactly when and where you are going to launch your attack?"

Even real-life members of the Washington pundit corps make their way into movies—Eleanor Clift, Morton Kondracke, the *Crossfire* hosts in 1990s movies like *Dave* and *Rising Sun*. Significantly, their role in the narrative is specifically as buffoons. The joke in each movie is how rapidly they leap to conclusions, how predictable their reactions are, how automatically they polarize the debate without any clear idea of what has really occurred. That real-life journalists are willing to keep appearing in these movies, knowing how they will be cast, says something about the source of self-respect in today's media. Celebrity, on whatever basis, matters more than being taken seriously.

Movies do not necessarily capture reality but they suggest a public mood—in this case, a contrast between the media celebrities' apparent self-satisfaction and the contempt in which its best-known representatives are held by the public. "The news media has a generally positive view of itself in the watchdog role," said the authors of an exhaustive survey of public attitudes toward the press, released in May 1995. But "the outside world strongly faults the news media for its negativism. . . . The public goes so far as to say that the press gets in the way of society solving its problems, an opinion that is even shared by many leaders." According to the survey, "two out of three members of the public had nothing or nothing good to say about the media." As American institutions in general have lost credibility, few have lost it as fully as the press.

The media establishment is beginning to get at least a dim version of this message. Through the last decade, newspaper conventions have been a litany of woes. Fewer readers. Lower "penetration" rates, as a decreasing share of the public pays attention to news. A more and more desperate search for ways to attract the public's interest. In the short run these challenges to credibility are a problem for journalists and journalism. In the longer run they are a problem for democracy.

Chapter 2

What Changed

Charles Prestwich Scott was editor of England's *Manchester Guardian* for more than half a century, from 1872 to 1929. During that time he experimented greatly with journalism, attracting writers like John Maynard Keynes and Arnold Toynbee to his pages. He also laid down aphorisms about the role of the press, including this central principle:

> The function of a good newspaper and therefore of a good journalist is to see life steady and see it whole.

"To see life steady and see it whole" may have an antique sound to contemporary readers, but it is still the essence of what people want from journalism. Seeing life steady means keeping the day's events in proportion. Seeing it whole means understanding the connections among the causes and consequences of varied happenings.

Some of today's media figures have become popular because of the way they superficially appear to honor the "steady and whole" principle. The politically oriented radio talk shows spawned by the success of the *Rush Limbaugh Program* illustrate the pattern. When listeners tune into Limbaugh each day, they know that he will fit the varied events of the preceding hours into the same dramatic structure he had established for them before. This is the struggle of good versus bad, conservatives versus liberals, spokesmen for common sense against enviro-wackos. Pat Robertson has a whole picture of good and evil into which he can fit any event. So does Louis Farrakhan. So does Jesse Jackson, and so did Ronald Reagan during his years as a broadcast commentator and as president.

It is harder to give events some context if you are trying to avoid following a political, religious, or other party line. But the task is not impossible. Nearly 150 years ago, American newspapers tried to make this transition in going from party-sponsored publications to "independent" newspapers. At the time of the American Revolution and for several decades afterward, it was taken for granted that newspapers would be the mouthpieces of politicians and political parties. The *Philadelphia Aurora* was the voice of Thomas Jefferson and his "Republicans" (forebears of today's Democrats). The *Gazette of the United States* was a steadfast supporter of Alexander Hamilton—Jefferson's great rival—and his Federalist-party plans for the new nation. When the First Amendment to the Constitution was drafted, outlawing any restrictions on freedom of the press, the assumption was that newspapers would necessarily be partisan. Protecting the papers was a corollary of protecting free political organization.

By the time of the Civil War publishers and editors were declaring their independence of political parties. The *New York Herald,* founded by James Gordon Bennett in the 1830s, and the *New York Tribune,* founded by Horace Greeley in the 1840s, attempted to provide a less partisan view of public affairs. Since that time papers have always been accused and have often been guilty of favoritism and partisanship, but their official goal has been to provide coherence and meaning to the news without representing any political party.

Today's newspapers, newsmagazines, and network news operations attempt to continue the experiment begun by Bennett and Greeley: providing context for the news without hewing to a settled political line. Many members of the public are suspicious of this effort, but perhaps for the wrong reason. The main public complaint is that too many reporters are political liberals, and that therefore they twist the news to fit their own preconceived views.

It is true that in several ways the reportorial elite—those based in large cities and working for large news organizations—have an outlook different from that of average Americans. Polls have shown for years that elite reporters are less religious than the statistically representative American, more supportive of gun control, more opposed to the death penalty, more accepting of abortion and homosexuality, and in other ways more "culturally liberal" than most of their fellow citizens. Especially on these "cultural" issues, the reporters' own beliefs may affect the tone of their coverage—for instance, the relative lack of serious coverage of religion on TV or in mainstream papers, or the instinct to portray anti-abortion groups as "religious extremists" in contrast to "principled" opponents of capital punishment.

But concentrating on this "cultural politics" gap conceals a larger source of bias in the press. For one thing, the supposed "liberalism" of the elite press is more limited than many people believe. On economic issues—taxes, welfare, deficit control, trade policy, attitudes toward labor unions—elite reporters' views have become far more conservative over the last generation, as their incomes have gone up. It is very rare for a major paper to publish an article or even op-ed piece that is enthusiastic about labor unions.

The jerky, up-and-down coverage of the Clinton administration illustrates the limits of a "liberal conspiracy" theory of press coverage. On form it would have seemed that Bill Clinton was the dream candidate for liberal members of the press corps. During his campaign he advanced the "New Democrat" positions that many liberal columnists had been advocating. (National service, welfare reform, expanded education, and so on.) He was of the same generation as many bureau chiefs and commentators, and despite living in Arkansas he knew most of them through his nationwide network of well-educated friends.

Nonetheless, coverage of Clinton was both more hostile and more volatile than that of any president since at least Harry Truman. During the ill-starred administration of Jimmy Carter, the first *Time* and *Newsweek* covers with titles like "Can Carter Cope?" did not appear until the president had been in office for nearly a year. Clinton encountered a *Time* cover on "The Incredible Shrinking Presidency" and a *Newsweek* cover asking "What's Wrong?" four months after he was sworn in. Even before Clinton took office, in December 1992, the humor columnist Dave Barry published an article about the "failed Clinton presidency," but at least he was being ridiculous on purpose.

Just after Clinton's election, *Time* published an adoring profile of George Stephanopoulos, the president's all-purpose advisor, whose youth, edge, and intensity (the article said) portended similar virtues for the administration as a whole. "Self-effacing George Stephanopoulos is one of the savviest communicators in the business," a caption announced. The story explained: "This brooding, dark presence has a quiet authority. His power whisper makes people lean into him, like plants reaching toward the sun." A few months later, when Stephanopoulos had moved out as head White House communicator and David Gergen had moved in, the author of the profile, Margaret Carlson, said on a Washington talk show that Gergen's arrival was a godsend, since "the discourse in the press room was as uncivilized as it could get. . . . We wanted the boil to pop because it couldn't get any worse." (In 1995 Carlson explained that such coverage of Stephanopoulos had followed the "classic honeymoon pattern," in which the press inflates the reputations of those who have engineered a big electoral victory only to deflate them later on. The process was extreme for Stephanopoulos, she said, because he had stood out for his glamour and approachability during the campaign, but then had seemed humorless and uninformative when conducting White House press briefings.)

Partisan differences may have played some role in these mood swings—specifically, a greater tendency among liberal reporters than conservatives to attack politicians they basically agree with. During the 1992 elections, the semi-liberal magazine the *New Republic* had beaten the drum for the Clinton campaign. But even before Clinton took office the magazine inaugurated a "Clinton Suck-Up Watch" feature, in which reporters were ridiculed for cozying up to Clinton too much. It is inconceivable that a comparable conservative publication—the *Wall Street Journal*'s editorial page, the *National Review,* the *American Spectator*—would have published a "Reagan Suck-Up Watch" during the 1980s. "In the first months of the administration, there was certainly peer pressure not to seem too close to Clinton," says Walter Shapiro of *Esquire* magazine, who had worked in the Carter administration. "I don't think that the concept of being 'too close' to Newt exists for conservative writers."

But the more important factor, both in coverage of Bill Clinton and in the press's larger presentation of public life, has little to do with party bias. It reflects instead the instincts, pressure, and incentives of the modern news business. C. P. Scott of the *Manchester Guardian* was calling for a panoramic approach to the news—journalism as a large-format camera that captured sharp details but also showed their place in a broader setting. Today's press often resembles a hand-held camera in an MTV video, lurching from a quick shot of the floor to a close-up of a singer's knees.

Financial, technological, political, and cultural changes have made today's journalism what it is. They include the many-faceted influence of TV; the modern style of political campaigning; the altered role of the American presidency itself; and the financial fundamentals of the business.

News as Spectacle: The Rise of TV in General and 60 *Minutes* in Particular

Since we can't imagine the modern world without TV, it's pointless even to try. In a commencement speech at Harvard in 1995, Vaclav Havel, national hero and president of the Czech Republic, manfully tried to balance the overall good and bad effects of TV on modern life. On the good side, he said, it allowed people to learn that their fellowmen were suffering in distant countries like Rwanda. On the bad side, it distorted their view of their immediate neighbors and indeed of themselves. "I never fail to be astonished at how much I am at the mercy of television directors and editors, at how my public image depends far more on them than it does on myself," Havel said. "I know politicians who have learned to see themselves only as the television camera does. Television had thus expropriated their personalities, and made them into something like television shadows of their former selves. I sometimes wonder whether they even sleep in a way that will look good on television."

Two of TV's many impacts on modern life have been particularly harmful for journalism.

One is a strange equivalence of spectacles. For TV purposes, the ideal world is one in which whatever is on the screen at this moment is entirely engrossing. One event is not necessarily more important than another, because they all are supposed to claim our attention in the brief *now* during which they exist. It could be the NBA finals. It could be live scenes from the explosion in Oklahoma. It could be Kato Kaelin's first network interview. It could be the election returns that give us a new president. It could be Michael Jackson and Lisa-Marie Presley. It could be Al Gore debating Ross Perot. They are all spectacles, and to TV they are all the same. The O.J. Simpson trial symbolized the convergence of "news" and "entertainment," but the convergence was inevitable as long as athletes, politicians, movie stars, and murderers had to compete for space in the same small box.

This flattening effect is natural to TV but is at total odds with some of journalism's fundamental roles. In the real world, events have a history. Part of the press's job is to explain that history, although that goes against TV's natural emphasis on the *now*. In real life, events have proportions. Kato Kaelin and a presidential election are both interesting, but it is the election that will still matter ten years from now. Part of the press's job is to keep things in proportion. TV's natural tendency is to see the world in shards. It shows us one event with an air of utmost drama, then forgets about it and shows us the next.

The jumbling together of events into one big spectacle arises from the technology of TV. But the TV age affected journalism in a second way, by altering the internal incentives of journalism in a profound but underappreciated fashion. It demonstrated that the way to become most successful as a "journalist" was to give up most of what was involved in being a "reporter."

These two terms can be synonymous, and "journalism" is the only sensible name for the activity that reporters, writers, editors, broadcasters, and others engage in. But behind the term "reporter" is the sense that the *event* matters most of all. Your role as a reporter is to go out, look, learn—and then report on what you've found.

The connotations of "journalist" are hazier, and in practice this is the label chosen by most TV figures whose own personalities are the real subject of whatever story they "report." When Dan Rather travels to Afghanistan, the subject of the broadcast is not Afghanistan, it is Rather-in-Afghanistan. Afghanistan becomes important because a U.S. anchorman is there. When Diane Sawyer conducts a high-profile interview, the real story is the interaction between two celebrities. One of them is a politician or movie star or athlete, but the other is a particular sort of TV "journalist."

The creation of journalistic celebrities has a long history. Charles Dickens reported from the American frontier for his British readers. In the late 19th century the *New York World* promoted the exploits of plucky "girl reporter" Nellie Bly, who raced around the world by ship, train, horseback, and rickshaw in seventy-two days to beat the eighty-day record set by the fictional Phileas Fogg. World War II necessarily drew American attention outside the country's borders and created a class of star war correspondents, based mainly in Europe. Edward R. Murrow broadcast from Czechoslovakia as it was occupied and London as it was bombed. Eric Sevareid, Charles Collingwood, Howard K. Smith, Walter Cronkite, and other wartime reporters became famous themselves. But there was a difference between them and most of today's TV celebrity correspondents: they carried with them a sense of authority, based mainly on their on-the-scene wartime reporting, rather than sheer celebrity or the spillover importance they got by being assigned to a major beat like the White House. Their audience could assume that whatever these figures turned their attention to was important and worthy of attention by the public as a whole.

The first early warning of what was to come occurred a decade after the war's end, when Edward R. Murrow conducted interviews with celebrities for CBS television's new *Person to Person* series. But the shift from authority to celebrity in TV news was ratified in the 1970s, thanks largely to the effects of 60 *Minutes.*

60 *Minutes* changed TV journalism for one simple reason: it made money. Before the program's rise to popularity in the early 1970s, network news operations had been "loss leaders." It was prestigious for William Paley's CBS to have the Murrows, Sevareids, and Cronkites on its news staff, as it was for Sarnoff's NBC to have Huntley and Brinkley. (ABC, until at least the late 1970s, could take no prestige from its news operation, because its news team was so weak.) CBS's documentaries made little money for the network but enhanced its reputation for seriousness. Government licensing regulations required networks and local stations to devote a certain number of hours each week to public service programing, which was the origin of Sunday programs like *Meet the Press.* Through this period the news divisions were subsidized by the rest of the network. Their nonprofit existence meant that they always lacked money, but with the money they did have they were more or less free to do as they chose.

"Back in those days the news division would go to the network with tin cup in hand and would get three or four million dollars for the whole year," Ted Koppel of ABC has noted.

> They would say, "Don't come to us for any more!" The concomitant was a great freedom. They didn't care if you did a documentary on the closing of shoe factories in New England. No one in those days from the network would ever have said, "Do you think you are going to get a good rating?" By contrast, these days each of the network news divisions spends approximately half a billion dollars on news.

And those news shows, of course, are expected to bring in more than they spend, as 60 *Minutes* first showed was possible.

Part of the program's success was thanks to its scheduling, right after the Sunday pro football games. But it also made news entertaining, by making it like everything else on TV. The most popular TV series brought us a familiar cast of characters facing new adventures each week. 60 *Minutes* did the same. There were Mike, Morley, Ed, and their successors, doing familiar things in new locales. The audience's knowledge of the characters, with their quirks and histories, and its desire to see what high jinks they'd get up to this time, played a large part in desire to tune in for each new episode.

Through this format, 60 *Minutes* presented a lot of "real" news with an interesting veneer. But it also presented a lot of merely "interesting" material as if it were real news. Producer Don Hewitt was the creative force behind the show. "In the past, the definition of a great editor was of someone who knew how to draw the fine line between what people needed to know and what they wanted to know," David Halberstam, who wrote about CBS in his book *The Powers That Be,* has said. "He knew that special balance."

> But at 60 *Minutes* there is an almost pathological fear of being boring, which reflects Hewitt's obsession with ratings, and therefore a comparable lack of proportion or balance. But the real challenge for talented journalists has always been to take subjects which are seemingly boring and make them interesting and thereby show ordinary people their stake in something complex. Almost anyone can take a crime or a petty corruption piece and make it sexy, or at least semi-sexy.
>
> So you quickly get to a formula. Some hyped-up piece on a petty crime where the bad guys are trying to

stonewall Mike Wallace gets as much play as a story on industrial decline which is a transcending national story, and which gets 15 minutes and then is kissed off for ten years. . . . The talent level is very high, and the package is very skillfully put together, but the driving force has always seemed to me more about entertaining then informing.

In fact, of the nearly 500 stories that 60 *Minutes* aired between 1990 and 1994, more than one-third were celebrity profiles, entertainment-industry stories, or exposés of what Halberstam called "petty scandals." Barely one-fifth of the stories concerned economics, the real workings of politics, or any other issue of long-term national significance. Except for a flurry of stories after the Rodney King episode in Los Angeles, 60 *Minutes* averaged only one program per year touching on the effects of race in America.

"When they do their promotional ads at CBS they like to use Mike Wallace as a signature figure," Halberstam said. "But I think Mike Wallace's instinct, when he looks at a story and thinks of drawing a line, is not whether something which happened is right or wrong, or moral or immoral, which is crucial for a signature journalist. It is whether it will entertain or not, and how he can cast himself—that's very important in shows like this, how you cast your stars."

The success of 60 *Minutes* also reinforced the concept that you could be a celebrated broadcast "journalist" while neglecting the most vital functions of the traditional "reporter."

The legwork for 60 *Minutes* and other newsmagazine shows is done by squadrons of producers and researchers whose faces the viewers never see. They follow up leads from the newspapers, they collect tips, they camp in small towns for two weeks to line up the right sources for the filmed interviews. When everything is in place, but not until then, the stars are brought in to ask questions with the cameras turned on. To the viewer it looks as if Diane or Ed or Mike has been on the story from the start, since we see them in the basic journalistic act of interviewing. But these "journalists" have usually arrived only a day or two earlier, and they will fly out as soon as the shooting is done so they can jump into another story someplace else.

Why does this matter? Because for reporters *the* fundamental act is the interview. It is possible, of course, for reporters to overdo their reliance on interviews—to believe that unless something is said during an interview it isn't real. This cuts them off from the vast range of stories that could be developed by reading books, documents, or academic research reports, and makes them overemphasize certain facts merely because they came from an interesting or hard-to-arrange interview. Still, "interviewing" in the broadest sense involves a reporter's immersion in new information that will shape his views. Through the process of listening, learning, testing assumptions, and letting themselves be surprised by new evidence, reporters decide what they think is true enough to write.

This cannot be done with the assembly-line interviews of the newsmagazine shows. The shows' unsung producers can act as reporters and follow unexpected leads, but that is not quite the same. The star journalist who is working from briefing papers and a set of proposed questions is an actor rather than a real interrogator. He lacks the background to ask the right follow-up question or to recognize when the person being interviewed has said something surprising and new. Yet the celebrities who fly in for canned interviews and cut themselves off from the reportorial process have set the standard for fame, wealth, and power as broadcast "journalists." The more successful you are as a TV star, the less you can be a reporter. To succeed on TV you have to be on the air. To succeed as a reporter you have to be "off the air"—or at least on the road.

In the 1980s, retired general William Westmoreland sued CBS News over an allegation that Westmoreland had been at the center of a campaign to deceive Lyndon Johnson about prospects in Vietnam. David Halberstam had spent years on this subject, leading to his 1972 book *The Best and the Brightest*. As the trial began, Morley Safer asked him whether he would go down to the courthouse as a sign of solidarity for his journalistic brethren. Halberstam thought that the story was accurate in its description of how Westmoreland and his people manipulated statistics but unfortunate in the way that Wallace had ambushed Westmoreland. He told Safer no; this was more solidarity than he was capable of.

> The next day, the phone rang. It was one of America's most recognizable voices. Mike Wallace was asking me, Did you say it?
>
> I said, You bet your ass, I did. He seemed puzzled. Is it something personal between us? he asked. I said, No, it was the carelessness of what you did on the Westmoreland piece, on something that was a very large part of my life, taking a story that big and giving it the 60 *Minutes* technique, the quick parachute jump in, and then the equally quick departure. That's the kind of story you have to devote weeks to.
>
> He said, That's what you have to do when you do 37 pieces a year.
>
> I told him, Mike, *do fewer.*

The age of TV and of TV "journalism" has made it hard for anyone to "do fewer." TV itself has a natural drive to create more, not fewer, spectacles. News operations cannot get along with fewer profitable shows. And TV journalists cannot accept fewer on-air appearances or fewer segments per show. These imperatives all make sense, according to the logic of TV.

From "The Making" to "The Selling" of a President

At the same time as television was changing the underpinning of media success, giving the greatest rewards to those who were willing to abandon journalism's most fundamental role, there was also a shift in the way the media portrayed the process of democracy and public action of any sort. Coverage became far more querulous and skeptical, in a way that made it harder for public officials to explain their positions or for citizens to believe what they heard.

Theodore White deeply changed political journalism with his book *The Making of the President, 1960.* Before that time, readers knew almost nothing about the mechanics and "spin" of a political campaign. By bringing campaign advisors into the spotlight, by explaining how Nixon and Kennedy prepared for their momentous debates, White took advantage of a huge gap in public awareness of politics. White was a skillful narrator who liked to talk about the "mood of the nation" and the sweep of historic events. His book cast a heroic light on the great pageant of democracy that was a presidential campaign.

Ten years later, Joe McGinnis changed political journalism in the opposite way. McGinnis, then still in his twenties, covered the 1968 Nixon campaign and published a book called *The Selling of the President, 1968.* The structure was the same as in Theodore White's book—backstage views of the strategists and candidates as they planned for public events—but the tone was as irreverent and debunking as White's had been respectful. McGinnis described advertising men who might as well have been promoting shampoo as a political candidate. He revealed an offstage Nixon who scorned the public he appealed to in his speeches. He showed the campaign choosing positions not because Nixon had ever thought about them but because they would be useful jabs at his opponent, Hubert Humphrey.

In short, Joe McGinnis showed us presidential politics as we have come to think of it ever since. After the appearance of McGinnis's book, the idea expressed in Theodore White's work—that presidential candidates were sincere, serious men presenting different visions of the future—seemed out-of-it and naive. Indeed, White was ridiculed for his 1972 *Making of the President* book because he seemed to have taken the Nixon campaign at face value rather than lampooning it, in the fashion of Hunter S. Thompson, or exposing it because of Watergate. White never wrote another installment in the *Making* series. Many other writers appeared to fill his gap as campaign chronicler, but most of them emphasized the gap between politicians as they hoped to be seen and the real, conniving figures of the back room. One exception proving the rule was Richard Ben Cramer. His book about the 1988 campaign, called *What It Takes*, was written in a jazzy style like that of Tom Wolfe but shared Theodore White's perspective that the candidates were decent people usually trying their best.

Twenty-five years after *The Selling of the President*, the day-in, day-out coverage of politics owes much more to McGinnis's model than to Theodore White's. TV reports during a presidential campaign usually end with a "kicker" contrasting what the politician says with what the reporter thinks is really true. "A problem in our business is that everyone wants to be a pundit in the last fifteen seconds of their piece," Tom Brokaw has said. "Everyone wants to put a little spin in there, which may not deal at all with the facts of the day." Newspaper and newsmagazine stories during the

campaign emphasize the chess game that strategists are
playing as they choose issues to emphasize and create attractive photo opportunities. None of the coverage puts much
weight on the possibility that the candidate really believes
what he says.

The resulting "cynical" and "negative" coverage is one
of the main reasons people complain about the press, according to several recent opinion polls. Reporters know that they
sound cynical, and they know that people blame them for it.
But they say it's not their fault. They are simply reflecting
the world they see. They say that their cynical tone is justified—even required—by the relentless "spin" of the politicians they write about.

The modern history of spin-ology is usually traced to
an encounter in 1984 between Lesley Stahl, of CBS, and an
official from the Reagan White House. Stahl had produced a
piece designed to show the contradiction between what
Ronald Reagan said and what he did. She included footage
of Reagan speaking at the Special Olympics competition, for
children with mental disabilities, and then pointed out that
his administration had cut funding for mental health. She
showed him at ceremonies opening a nursing home, and
then pointed out that he had opposed public-health funding too.

Soon after the piece aired on CBS, Stahl got a call from
a White House official. She was expecting to be chewed out
and was amazed when the official praised her. Why? she
asked, adding: "Did you hear what I said? I killed you." The
official explained the reality to her this way (as Stahl later recalled it):

> You television people still don't get it. *No one* heard
> what you said. Don't you people realize that the pic-
> ture is all that counts. A powerful picture drowns out
> the words.

This anecdote comes up frequently in discussions of cynicism and the press. The reporters who retell it are trying to explain why they might sound as jaded as they do. Their experience of recent politics, as they understand it, is of being endlessly manipulated and "spun" by politicians who care about appearance rather than substance, and who win elections by concealing their substantive views. Campaign aides say that every speech was wonderful and give assurances that the candidate is locked into a policy—which he changes the next day. On election night, 1994, George Stephanopoulos gave the general public a glimpse of what spinning could be like when, with Democrats falling all around him, he told TV interviewers it had been "a pretty good night" so far. "They'll look you straight in the eye and tell you things they don't believe," Joe Peyronnin, vice president of CBS News, has said.

The strictures of journalism make it hard for reporters to fight back directly. Under the existing rules of sourcing, reporters can't begin a story by saying: "The president's campaign manager called me today and, while shielding himself by saying 'This is on deep background,' planted rumors about his opponent that he and I both know are not true." The reporter's remaining outlet is an all-purpose sneer, which vents his frustration and sends the viewers a warning that politicians are trying to hoodwink them too.

The result is an arms race of "attitude," in which reporters don't explicitly argue or analyze what they dislike in a political program but instead sound sneering and supercilious about the whole idea of politics. Public officials become more manipulative and cunning to try to get their message past the hostile press—and the press becomes even more determined to point out how insincere the politicians are. As in a real arms race, neither side feels it can safely disarm.

Maureen Dowd, a tart and witty writer for the *New York Times*, has found herself cited in almost every article about excess cynicism in the press. The most famous illustration from her work is the first sentence from her story about President Clinton's visit to Oxford, which ran on the front page of the *Times* in June 1994: "President Clinton returned today from a sentimental journey to the university where he didn't inhale, didn't get drafted and didn't get a degree."

Yet Dowd herself sees this tone as a necessary reaction to government chicanery. "The Reagan press corps was pilloried for not being tough enough," she has said.

> Critics claimed that many reporters had been so snowed by Ronald Reagan's charm that they missed huge stories about astrology and Iran-Contra.
>
> During the Bush years, Democrats continued to want tough, vigilant coverage of the White House— and they loved it when I did irreverent stories that tweaked George Bush for being out-of-touch or inarticulate.
>
> But when reporters gave the same scrutiny to President Clinton, Democrats acted betrayed. The Clinton crowd assumed that most reporters were liberals who would help them succeed, and they never really accepted the idea of a skeptical press as a legitimate part of the democratic process.
>
> Attacking the press is a cheap way to throw the spotlight off a politician who is stumbling. The vigilance demanded by Democrats in the coverage of Reagan and Bush is the "cynicism" they complain of now.

It doesn't matter, for the moment, whether the Clinton administration is complaining about the same treatment it wished on George Bush. Both have been sneered at and treated as if everything they did was a ruse, and this is because of a change in the press's attitude in the last twenty years. The working assumption for most reporters is that most politicians and handlers will mislead them most of the time. The coverage we see is a natural result—which aggravates today's prevailing despair and cynicism about public life.

The Berlin Wall Comes Down, Taking the "Leader of the Free World" with It

The president of the United States is still first among equals of the world's political figures. But from 1933 until 1991—from the inauguration of Franklin Roosevelt until the collapse of the Soviet Union—he was something more. During the New Deal, Roosevelt brought the presidency to the center of American life in a way that none of his predecessors since Abraham Lincoln had done. Once the United States entered World War II, Roosevelt became the "Leader of the Free World," a title his successors held for nearly fifty years. The term was often used with irony, but it expressed a literal truth. Each American president, like each of his counterparts atop the Soviet system, actually had the power of life and death for the world in his hands. Each day might be *the* day on which the president had to order missiles launched from the silos in North Dakota and from the submarines in the deep. The hair-trigger nature of life in the nuclear age was a common theme of movies and novels through the late 1960s, at which point they were edged off center stage by the real war in Vietnam. Still, through the 1970s and 1980s the military aide with the "football" was always there, no more than a few steps from the president, ready to give him the codes to launch a nuclear strike if the dreaded moment came.

Coverage of presidents was not always positive during this era. Lyndon Johnson and Richard Nixon, in their different ways, felt excoriated by the press, and Gerald Ford and Jimmy Carter felt condescended-to and mocked. Yet even at their most judgmental, White House correspondents acted as if they were watching a game played for major stakes. The mental picture shared by presidents and correspondents alike was of the Cuban Missile Crisis: big men making tough decisions on which the fate of billions turned. So while reporters might consider Gerald Ford an oaf, Jimmy Carter a weakling, and Ronald Reagan an ignoramus, they knew that the presidency itself represented power so awesome that it could not be ridiculed.

In the late 1990s, the nuclear weapons are still in their silos, the man with the football still has the codes, and an American president still has the theoretical power to unleash devastation upon mankind. But since the collapse of the Soviet Union early in the decade, the concept of "Leader of the Free World" has had a hollow sound. Leader against what, now that the Russian Republic is trying to join NATO? Leader of whom? George Bush skillfully led a six-month wartime alliance to oppose Saddam Hussein, but its members could agree on little except their desire to keep oil flowing normally from the Persian Gulf. Post–Cold War presidents must make life-and-death decisions, but these concern episodic dramas—invading Haiti, keeping troops in Somalia, devising a response to regional crises in the Balkans and elsewhere—rather than being part of the decades-long Cold War drama of clashing ideologies backed by ultimate weapons.

The easing of nuclear tensions and disappearance of the Soviet state constitute mankind's great step forward in the late twentieth century. In diminishing the majesty surrounding the "Leader of the Free World," this change may merely be restoring the U.S. presidency to the lesser role it occupied through most of the country's history. In principle, reporters should now be able to present a balanced vision of the positives and negatives of government, since their accounts need not be skewed by the background awareness of the president's Zeus-like might. But in practice, as the president has lost the august aura that came with his Cold War role, many reporters have started thinking that he has no truly vital jobs left to do. None of them would put it quite that baldly, of course. But the assumption comes through in their treatment of health reform, budget-cutting trade negotiations, and the other challenges of the modern presidency as if they were fundamentally boring, and worth notice only as arenas in which politicians try to trick each other and the public too.

The Decline of Local Newspapers, *Life,* and Network News; the Rise of Gannett, *Yachting,* Court TV, and the Journalist as Entrepreneur

Newspapers and TV stations routinely report on the "profound economic and technological shifts" that have transformed life for the steel and textile industries, or for unionized workers, or for other groups affected by changes they cannot control.

The news business itself has struggled to cope with similar changes. The afternoon newspaper is virtually gone, a victim of television and the automobile. Afternoon papers thrived when people could read them on the bus or subway on the way home from work, or when they could settle down with the paper at home, before or after dinner—in the hours now filled by TV. The cellular phone and talk radio fit the car-commuting age. The afternoon paper does not. Newspapers in general have been fighting a losing business battle for decades. Their most obvious enemy has been television, which gets the news out faster and sops up potential readers' time. But papers across the country have also been weakened by the same demographic shifts that have killed off big department stores and eroded historic downtown shopping centers.

The big community-wide paper, the big department store, and the big, concentrated downtown shopping district are artifacts of a lost era of marketing to a broad American middle class. Over the last three decades, retailing and publishing alike have steadily narrowed and refined their focus, to reach more carefully selected subgroups of a more segmented American population. The big, traditional downtown retailers—the Broadway stores in Los Angeles, Filene's in Boston, Macy's in New York, Wanamaker's in Philadelphia, Woodward and Lothrop in Washington, and Sears from coast to coast—have either declared bankruptcy or been gravely weakened. Specialized shops—Williams-Sonoma, Crate and Barrel—have taken off customers at the top end of the market, and huge volume discounters, from Wal-Mart to TrakAuto, have removed them at the bottom. As the traditional retailers have suffered, so have the newspapers, for which they were usually the biggest advertisers. Specialized shops have found more efficient ways to reach the customers they are looking for, from targeted catalogue marketing to infomercials on cable TV.

The decline of the retailers has been hardest on newspapers, but the magazine and broadcast businesses have been caught in a similar squeeze. Most magazines live or die on advertising, rather than what they charge on the newsstand or to subscribers. Through the late 1960s, *Life, Look,* and the *Saturday Evening Post* delivered a broad middle-class readership that was attractive to companies advertising refrigerators, or station wagons, or carpeting, or Scotch. The magazines disappeared, some to return in shrunken form, because the audience they delivered was no longer so valuable. Teenagers were spending money on music, and magazines from *Rolling Stone* to *Sassy* were an easier way to reach them. The growing professional class was spending money, and *Architectural Digest* or *Gourmet* were easier ways to reach them. More "serious" magazines, like *Smithsonian* and *The Atlantic Monthly*, benefited from this same segmentation of the advertising market. Their readers had always been well educated, but while that once may have meant a college librarian in a small town, now it meant two-income households who would look at ads for Cunard cruises or Montblanc pens. The gains for all these targeted magazines came out of the hide of more broadly aimed publications, including newsmagazines and to some extent newspapers.

Life and *Look*, in particular, were undercut by technology. Their original success depended largely on the impact of the images they presented, through extraordinary photographs of a world that readers would otherwise have had no chance to see. While exceptional photographs retain a power that ever-moving televised images cannot match, the arrival of TV in the 1950s made the image-based newsmagazine pioneered by *Life* obsolete.

Newspapers and newsmagazines faced their own ongoing struggle to cope with the effects of broadcast technology. Each advance in timely broadcast reporting—evening newscasts starting in the 1950s, breaking-news coverage starting with the Kennedy assassination in the early 1960s, CNN saturation coverage starting in the 1980s—eliminated part of the previous function of the printed media. As early as the 1950s, newspapers and newsmagazines were struggling to determine what value they could offer to their readers, now that TV and radio were removing the value of simply reporting what happened the day before. Newspapers began providing more interpretive and analytical articles. Newsmagazines began struggling, as they struggle still, to find what role remained for them in an age of saturation TV coverage and more in-depth newspaper stories.

Even network news operations have felt the same pressure. With the coming of cable their market has been nibbled away—by CNN, by the Discovery Channel, by round-the-clock sports or talk or trials. The core audience that is left for nightly newscasts is suggested by what seem to be their most frequent advertisers: Geritol, Polident, Mylanta, Attends.

The long-term financial pressures on the news business have a subtle effect on reporters, by diminishing their sense that they are reaching a broad audience that cares about their work. Enfeebling doubts about whether the public even notices the difference between a good or bad reporting job have been encouraged by the rise of the so-called "new media"— especially the Limbaugh-style radio talk shows and the Internet "newsgroup" discussion forums that generate political discussion in disregard of what the mainstream press says. In 1993 the House of Representatives "check kiting" scandal was largely ignored by TV networks and the national newspapers, but it became a political issue because Rush Limbaugh and his counterparts in local markets discussed it so often. The idea that Vince Foster's death resulted not from suicide but a murder conspiracy was also sustained on talk radio.

But there is a far more direct connection between these business changes and journalists' behavior. Reporters have come to think of themselves as employees trapped in a "sunset industry." Like steel workers or machine toolmakers, many of them feel compelled to scramble and jealously protect their own financial interests, rather than having the luxury of worrying about their "responsibility" to the public.

Through the last two decades, locally owned papers across the country have been taken over by national chains. Family-owned papers in small towns can play favorites and push their enemies around. Chain ownership brings a different problem, which is a counting-house mentality determined to "downsize" newsrooms and cut expenses to satisfy quarterly earnings demands. The nation's largest chain, Gannett, with its nearly two dozen TV and radio stations, its ninety-plus newspapers, and its profits of $800 million in 1994 (up 17 percent from the previous year), is widely seen—and often resented—as a pioneer in this trend. It is significant that the four most widely admired newspapers in the country—the *New York Times,* the *Washington Post,* the *Los Angeles Times,* and the *Wall Street Journal*—have all been buffered in some way against the harshest quarterly-earnings pressure. Stock in all these papers is publicly held and traded, but in three cases the original family members control enough stock to affect the paper's plans. (These are the Sulzberger family for the *New York Times,* the Graham family for the *Washington Post,* and the Chandler family for the *Los Angeles Times.*) The *Wall Street Journal's* protection has been its niche market for financial industry readers and advertisers.

Yet the "downsizing" trends that have transformed American industry touch even these family-owned institutions. In 1995, the Times Mirror Company, parent of the *Los Angeles Times* (and *Newsday*), appointed as its chief executive Mark H. Willes, whom it brought in from General Mills. Willes, who had no experience whatsoever in the news business, said that the same techniques he had used in marketing foods would be useful in newspaper management. William Glaberson of the *New York Times* interviewed Willes soon after his appointment. Willes told him that newspapers must "refresh" their product offerings, much as General Mills had revamped its lines of food. Glaberson added: "Asked for examples of what he meant, he cited the successful marketing of cereals, Hamburger Helper and cake mixes." And it was important to cut costs too: "If you're not the low-cost producer," Willes said, "you're not going to have the kinds of margins you need to work with."

A few weeks later, Willes surprised the newspaper community by using another General Mills analogy to quite different effect. He wanted to rebuild the financial strength of the *Times*, he said, precisely so it could regain its traditional and largely-lost role as a vehicle that tied together the ethnic and economic subcultures that lived such separate lives in Southern California. In this case his analogy was based on Cheerios. General Mills had found that some low-income, Spanish-speaking customers choose Cheerios rather than store-brand generic cereals that cost less, because possession of "yellow box Cheerios" symbolized their inclusion in mainstream culture. By choosing genuine Cheerios, "they also become a part of what the real thing is part of: the bigger community." In keeping with this principle, Willes would close down the Spanish-language version of the *Times* and other targeted subeditions and work on making the "real" paper a stronger presence in the whole community.

Many reporters would have been heartened by that goal, but every analogy to Hamburger Helper and Cheerios went through newsrooms in a matter of minutes. Similar quotes, without the Hamburger Helper fillip, had gone through each of the network news operations after it went through a corporate takeover: CBS by Lawrence Tisch, NBC by General Electric, ABC by Capital Cities and later by Disney.

Of course news organizations need to adapt to serve their public, and of course they need to hold the line on cost. But the results are very similar to what happens when manufacturing employees cope with the constant threat of layoffs or when teachers are put on unpaid furloughs because the voters have rejected the latest bond issue for school financing. In these circumstances, even the most dedicated and principled professionals realize they must look out mainly for themselves, since no one else is watching out for them. Through the last decade, corporate officials and management experts have told employees that they must learn to be "flexible," so that they can "retool" and "repackage" themselves for the demands of an ever changing economy. Journalists have heard these speeches and have begun to realize that they apply not just to people working at IBM or Chrysler but to employees of CBS and the *Los Angeles Times* as well. They have responded to a changed environment as rational people inevitably will: by developing the survival skills necessary if they hope to earn a living in a troubled business. Reporters have always needed a survivor's instinct in pursuing the news. Increasingly they must be economic survivors as well; the result, as the next chapter discusses, is a subtle skewing of the news.

In their varied and often indirect ways, these changes in finance and culture and politics have undercut the authority, steadiness, and wholeness of the American media. The era of TV-celebrity journalism has offered correspondents greater rewards than ever before, but only if they forget what it means to be a "reporter." The ever-increasing "spin" of politics, and the ever-decreasing sense that the U.S. president or government really lead the world, tempt reporters to think that everything they witness is a game. Bottom-line pressure—for survival in newspapers, for increased ratings and profits in TV—has made editors more like managers, and has made reporters more conscious of increasing their flexibility and salability. These are sound concepts in most businesses but can put the wrong kind of pressure on schools, or military units, or news organizations. These changes matter to the American public because they have weakened the media's ability to tell us what we need to know.

Chapter 3

The Gravy Train

Any reporter born before 1965 did not go into journalism for the money. The money wasn't there. Salaries in journalism have risen substantially in the last generation, but even now, young people concerned mainly with attaining a steady, high income will not consider reporting. The law, medicine, big business, banking—these and similar pursuits require more formal preparation than journalism does but offer much higher average earnings.

The people who do choose journalism, then, have decided that it will compensate them in other ways: independence and variety; a chance to see the world; the satisfaction of being known and noticed, with your name in print and perhaps your face on the air; the opportunity to play a part in shaping public issues without having to go into politics. These and similar motives that have drawn people into journalism could not all be called "noble" but they have been largely nonmonetary.

But in the last generation the role of money has changed. Even as the industry as a whole has struggled, the best-paid media figures have done better than ever before. This helps account for the overripe, fin-de-siècle mood in the elite press corps, especially in Washington. Reporters hear constantly that their institution is troubled and that they are despised. Yet day by day the most powerful members of the press are surrounded by flatterers who compete for their attention and compliment their work. Their earnings go up, with few of the layoffs and none of the "wage stagnation" that has affected most of America, and they know they have the chance for dramatic windfall earnings if they can establish themselves on the lecture circuit. Like baseball stars pushing for big contracts even as the sport itself struggles, many media celebrities are tempted to make the most of the good times while they last.

Until about the mid-1960s, journalism was essentially a high working-class activity. In big cities the typical reporter would make about as much as the typical cop. Many reporters had not gone to college. "College boys" existed in isolated pockets in journalism, for particular reasons. *Time* magazine under Henry Luce had stockpiled Yale graduates and Rhodes scholars. Ben Bradlee, a Boston aristocrat and Harvard graduate, exemplified the glamorous foreign correspondent when he reported for *Newsweek* from Paris in the 1950s. The Bingham family in Louisville liked recruiting Ivy Leaguers for its papers. Walter Lippmann and John Reed of Harvard had gone into journalism early in the century, and Anthony Lewis, J. Anthony Lukas, David Halberstam, and others from Harvard did so in the decade after World War II. In making the choice for journalism, the college boys knew that their earnings would be nowhere close to what their classmates were making on Madison Avenue or with General Motors. Most of the people they worked with were not college boys.

"In the early times, we were not only describing the life of normal people, we were participating in it," Richard Harwood, a longtime correspondent for the *Washington Post*, said. Harwood had fought in the Pacific as a Marine in World War II and, after college on the GI Bill, started as a reporter for small papers in the South.

> Most of the reporters came from the lower middle class, which is where the readers and most of the subjects came from too. We were more or less on the same level with the people we dealt with. We lived in the same neighborhood. Reporters regarded themselves as working class.

Of the forty editors and writers on Harwood's first paper, in Nashville, perhaps half a dozen had even started college. The owners of these small papers definitely did not consider themselves part of the working class. They were among the richest and most powerful people in their communities, and as Harwood put it, "our function was to elect the publisher's candidates and push his issues. We organized rallies for the candidate, wrote speeches, that kind of thing." The circumstances of their lives, including the demands of the papers' bosses, gave many reporters an instinctive pro-little guy outlook. *PM,* a leftist newspaper with great influence in New York in the 1940s, had a motto that most reporters of the era would have approved as a professional creed: "We're against people who push other people around." The typical reporter of that time would have loved to think of himself as Humphrey Bogart's "Rick," in *Casablanca*—hard-boiled, tough-seeming, but surprisingly brave and idealistic when bullies threw their weight around.

By the 1990s, "crusading" journalists on TV newsmagazine shows might also say they were standing up for the little guy. But viewers would sense something phoney in this pose. Reporters had moved into the class of Americans who can do the pushing.

Starting in the mid-1960s, it became less and less accurate to consider reporters the upper end of the working class. With the rise of TV, every branch of journalism knew that its function had to change. Newspapers could not get by simply by telling what had happened the day before. They had to add something extra—expertise, analysis, colorful writing—and reporters who had been trained in science, Russian, economics, legal history, became more valuable.

Although evening newspapers were failing and more cities became one-paper towns, the newspapers that remained grew rich during the long American boom of the 1950s and 1960s. Better-educated people became reporters; their salaries went up; even better-educated people applied. If, during Richard Harwood's early days in Nashville, reporters had living standards slightly higher than those of their neighbors the factory workers, by the 1980s reporters in big cities had living standards slightly lower than those of their neighbors the lawyers and corporate middle managers. It became an oddity to find a reporter or editor who had not gone to college. (Peter Jennings and David Brinkley of ABC are the only current famous examples.) At big newspapers, it became unusual to find editors and star writers who were not from very prestigious colleges. Before Leonard Downie was chosen to succeed Ben Bradlee as executive editor of the *Washington Post* in the early 1990s, he was known to catty Ivy Leaguers in the *Post* newsroom as "Land Grant Len," because he had graduated from Ohio State.

The status revolution that has transformed parts of journalism has not changed all of it. At small newspapers and broadcast stations reporters are paid modestly and in no sense live above the people they are writing about. But a sizable group of people—thousands—have salaries near $100,000 and above. These are the reporters, editors, columnists, and other journalists connected to broadcast networks, big newspapers, and national magazines. And a significant group—

scores, perhaps hundreds, nearly all with connections to TV—have incomes of several hundred thousand dollars and above.

It is hard to generalize about an occupation that contains both Diane Sawyer, who is paid $7 million per year by ABC, and the reporter in Wichita who earns $24,000 (which is less than Sawyer gets per working day). The people at the top of the income scale are clearly not "typical" of today's journalism, but they are "representative" of it, since they set the standard others envy and aspire to, and since they dominate the face that journalism presents to the public. Despite the majority of reporters who are underpaid, the business as a whole has carried out a successful social climb since World War II. This colors the way they live their daily lives and the issues they choose to stress.

When Bill and Hillary Clinton attended their last "Renaissance Weekend" gathering on Hilton Head before Clinton's inauguration, scores of the guests who mingled with them there were national-level journalists. The Clintons were deciding at the time whether they should send their daughter Chelsea to public schools, as they had done in Little Rock, or to Sidwell Friends, a private school in Washington where tuition costs more than $10,000 per year. In covering this decision—which the Clintons eventually made in favor of Sidwell—the national press corps displayed the instinct of the urban professional elite, which believes that "everyone" sends their kids to private school, rather than that of most of America, where "nearly everyone" still goes to public school.

"It is not entirely surprising," Jacob Weisberg wrote of the Sidwell affair in the *New Republic,* "that the Clintons' choice was avidly endorsed by various TV journalists whose own kids go to or went to Sidwell: Mark Shields, Jim Lehrer, Judy Woodruff and her husband, Al Hunt (who dismissed the flap over Chelsea's schooling, saying the Clintons' deci-

sion was 'simply a private matter')." Howard Fineman, a political correspondent for *Newsweek,* went further than approving the decision after it was made. He and his wife, a
lawyer-lobbyist named Amy Nathan, were guests at Renaissance Weekend. There, the two of them told the Clintons
how happy their own child, who had just started kinder-
garten, had been at Sidwell and urged it on them as the right
choice for Chelsea.

"Was I using the opportunity of being at Renaissance
Weekend to try to do something for Sidwell?" Fineman later
asked. "Yes, I plead guilty to doing that. But I don't think it
compromised me journalistically."

Lobbying a new president about a highly symbolic decision, which your publication may have to comment on,
and which will affect your personal prestige ("The First
Family chose my school!")—to do this is to beg for trouble.
But the instincts of modern journalists told him it was OK.
Experience in the modern Washington press corps taught
him that, by social standing and by income, he belonged on
the inside, giving personal advice to a president, rather than
on the outside, observing and analyzing the decision.

"Most journalists, of course, don't like to think of
themselves as *anybody's* advocate," Jonathan Cohn wrote in
the *American Prospect* in 1995. "But that's most likely because advocacy of elite interests comes so easily that it
scarcely seems like bias at all."

A few months after Renaissance Weekend, Bill Clinton
was involved in negotiations to create his new "Americorps,"
a system that would let young people earn money for college
through several years of national-service work. After endless
budgetary calculations (described by Steven Waldman, of
Newsweek, in his 1994 book *The Bill*), the administration determined that Americorps could offer college benefits worth
up to $10,000 per year. To most Americans that is a lot of
money, especially for students who are juggling loans and

jobs to cover tuition at night school or community college. Waldman says that when Clinton described this plan to a college-aged crowd in New Jersey in 1993, the students erupted in applause. The reporters who had come along from Washington, however, were not impressed. Waldman recounted this conversation from the plane flight back home:

> "Ten thousand dollars?" one reporter said snidely about
> the annual scholarship. "What's that gonna buy you?"
>   His buddy agreed. "Yeah, I mean it costs four
> thousand to send your kid to nursery school."

The plan was treated as an insignificant gesture by most of the national press corps, and Clinton's speech was a tiny blip in that week's news. Reporters instinctively viewed the proposal from the standpoint of families planning to spend $4,000 a year on kindergarten, and $25,000 a year on college, rather than that of the majority of Americans for whom $10,000 would make a big difference.

The press displayed a similar, instinctive sympathy with the interests of the educated elite during the debates over passage of the NAFTA and GATT trade treaties in 1993 and 1994. (NAFTA, the North American Free Trade Agreement, was being expanded to include Mexico. GATT, the General Agreement on Tariffs and Trade, was being extended so as to create a World Trade Organization that would resolve trade disputes.) During these debates most of the press chose the "college-boy" side of the argument—apparently without realizing that it was choosing sides.

According to principles taught in introductory-level economics courses, steps that expand world trade—as NAFTA and GATT would do—are always good. As a practical reality, however, these changes are either beneficial or harmful for individuals, depending on how well educated they are. If you are a TV broadcaster or an editorial writer (or a doctor or a lawyer or an inventor), freer trade is nearly all to the good. You can more easily sell the products of your intellectual labor to a world market; at the same time, you can take advantage of lower-priced food, clothes, and machines from overseas.

But not everyone benefits equally from freer trade. As even Econ 101 students have heard, treaties like GATT and NAFTA inevitably create "dislocations"—the lost jobs and uprooted families for those people who are threatened by lower-cost foreign manufacturing competition. These drawbacks probably were not, on balance, a reason to reject either treaty. The long sweep of American economic history suggests that eventually the gains will probably outweigh the losses. But most media coverage of GATT and NAFTA coverage made it sound as if the losses would be nonexistent—as indeed they would be in the world that most big-time reporters saw each day.

After the Republicans took control of the House of Representatives in 1994, thousands of Democratic Capitol Hill employees who thought they had lifetime jobs were suddenly out on the street. Washington journalists knew these people personally—they were neighbors, college classmates, friends from the PTA. Many were married to journalists. From the country's point of view their loss of jobs was perfectly natural. The jobs had come through political patronage, and now the patrons were gone. Yet the Washington press covered the plight of these out-of-work staffers with a care for the human nuance—the effect on the children, the devastation of waking up one morning without a job—that it almost never showed when describing the casualties of corporate "downsizing" or "America's inevitable shift from manufacturing to service-sector jobs."

"It is a major problem that journalists have come to identify with the rich or upper middle class rather than with the poor," Charles Peters, editor of the *Washington Monthly,*

has said. "It has a tremendous effect on what they're interested in reporting. Because they are identifying up, their
first thought is how the situation would look from the top
rather than how it would look from the bottom."

Peters has pointed to the way three kinds of taxes are
covered: inheritance taxes, payroll taxes, and the different
rate brackets for income taxes. From the bottom of society,
the tax you hate most is the payroll tax. The first dollar you
earn has fifteen cents taken out for Social Security and
Medicare—even if you make so little money that you pay no
income tax at all. Payroll taxes discourage you from working, and they discourage an employer from hiring you, since
his tax burden goes up with each new hand he takes on.
You'd rather slash the payroll taxes—and make up the difference from inheritance taxes and higher tax rates for people
who make as much money in a week as you do all year.

From the top of society the situation obviously looks
different. Payroll taxes are not so big a problem. Sooner or
later during the year—sometime in the summer, if you're
making over $100,000; sometime in the fall, if you're mak-
ing around $80,000—the annoying Social Security bite
stops being taken out of your paycheck. It will start again
the following January, but for better-paid people it's not
there all year round—as it is for most Americans. Higher income tax brackets or inheritance tax rates, on the other hand,
hit higher-income people directly.

Economists can argue both sides of the tax issues. The
payroll tax is regressive and discourages the creation of jobs,
while higher tax rates in upper brackets distort economic behavior by tempting people to make decisions so as to mini-
mize taxes, rather than on normal business grounds. On tax
issues, as with GATT and NAFTA, elite national reporters
end up listening to one set of economic arguments much
more carefully than to others, in part because their experi-

ence makes the predicament of well-off people far more vivid to them than the plight of those working at minimum wage.

Peters says that he had tried for many years to get reporters to look into these tax questions, with increasing difficulty. "The meritocratic class has shifted its values to 'identify up,'" he has contended. Peters grew up in Charleston, West Virginia, during the Depression. Although his father was a lawyer and therefore less hard-pressed than many neighbors, "everyone could still identify with the people back on the farm." Now, he says, "the shift has gone so far that it affects even the young."

The status revolution in big-time journalism has given many reporters a strong if unconscious bias in favor of "haves" rather than "have nots." The consequences of this economic shift are in theory correctable. A journalist who recognized that his own economic, social, and educational background might skew his observations could work to avoid being trapped by it, for example, by deliberately exploring, through his reporting, conditions of life he was not familiar with.

But another part of the shift has far more ominous consequences. It involves an aspect of the status revolution that has created the clearest possible conflict between what is good for the individual journalist and what is good for the public that relies on the journalist's work.

The Era of Talking Heads

The episodes that get people and institutions in trouble are not always objectively the most important. The $600 toilet seat was not the heart of the Pentagon's budgeting problems in the 1980s. The "House Bank Scandal," in which congressmen were allowed to overdraw their accounts, had no direct connection to federal budget problems. Marie Antoinette did not cause the French Revolution by saying "Let them eat cake." And journalists who earn more in a day, by giving a speech, than the average American family earns in a year are not what's most wrong with today's press.

They are, however, vivid symbols of larger attitudes that the public dislikes in the media. Like other symbols of excess, from Marie Antoinette to the toilet seat, today's journalistic "buckrakers" have the potential to undermine themselves and their institution by weakening such trust as the public now has in them. The media establishment may soon wish that it had corrected the problem while it could.

The growth of large-scale, for-pay speaking is directly connected to a seemingly separate phenomenon: the spread of TV talk shows modeled on *The McLaughlin Group.* The two trends—more journalists on the lecture circuit, and more journalists on TV—cannot be understood apart from each other. The lecture circuit matters because it is the way for journalists to make real money, and the talk shows matter because they are the way to get lecture dates. Outside of Washington, the talk shows may be viewed as mere oddities. Even in Washington, it is fashionable to act as if they are a joke. This bemused stance is a fraud. If most journalists really thought the shows were laughable, they would be reluctant to appear. Most of Washington is anything but reluctant, because everyone understands the stakes in being on TV.

THE MODERN BOOM IN THE LECTURE BUSINESS. As long as audiences have gathered to be entertained by speakers, prominent writers—Ralph Waldo Emerson, Charles Dickens, Mark Twain—have done part of the work of entertaining them. Although some writers have a horror of public speaking and view written and oral expression as completely separate realms, others view the podium as a natural extension of the writer's desk. In each case they are telling a story, trying their best to reach an audience, expressing themselves in a slightly different style of prose. Since at least the time of Mark Twain, lecturing has been an important way for writers to leverage their name recognition into extra money; after all, a reader who has paid $10 for a book might decide to pay $20 to meet the author in person. In Twain's day, the lectures were run on a purely market basis. The speaker would come into town and pay to rent a hall. Then he would sell tickets, and the more people he could attract, the more money he would take home. (This is in contrast to today's protected-market system, in which celebrity speakers are guaranteed fees for their appearance, rather than taking their chances with ticket sales.)

Since the time of the Chautauqua circuit in the late nineteenth century, people whose principal job was lecturing could make comfortable incomes. The best-known illustrations these days would be "motivational speakers" like Zig Ziglar, little known to the general public but famous in business-convention circles, or prominent figures who have just stepped off the public stage, from Joe Montana to George Bush. Early in the Whitewater "scandal," when Bill and Hillary Clinton were scrambling to cover their legal bills, one lecture agent was quoted in the *Washington Post* as saying that the president didn't really have to worry, since after leaving office he would have twenty-five years of lecture dates ahead of him.

The market for those who lectured as a sideline to their main work of writing began to boom in the 1970s. In the mid-1980s, a lecture agent named Joe Cosby, head of an agency that represented the columnist and ABC-TV commentator George Will and members of the talk show *The McLaughlin Group,* explained the dynamics behind the growth. "Let's use fictional numbers," he said:

If there were 100 organizations that put on programs using celebrity speakers in 1970, in 1975 there were 200 and now [1985] there are 500. And if the programs in 1970 used one speaker, now they use three, so you have two different kinds of math working here. In 1970, the National Boilermakers' Association might have gone to Las Vegas for their convention, and the *pièce de résistance* was a young lady jumping out of a cake. They decided to upgrade it a tad, or maybe their wives started coming along. They wanted more interesting programs. That's what's made the whole business expand.

In the decade since then, the business has grown substantially. More and more professional groups have scheduled junkets in Florida, the Caribbean, Hawaii, Napa Valley—and they need lecturers and "educational content" to justify the tax-deductability of the excursions. "The whole industry used to be more narrowly focused," Steve Hofman, a "policy communications" specialist who worked in the government for more than a decade, said in 1995. "In the past you wouldn't see too many colleges and universities paying major speaker-fees. Now a lot of them do. You are seeing trade associations doing it more than ever before." Part of the reason the market for journalist-speakers has expanded, Hofman pointed out, is that congressional-ethics reforms since 1990 have made it illegal for congressmen to accept speaking fees from interest groups. He said:

> You've still got programs to put on and you still need prominent people. But in the past you used to be able to get them on the cheap, if you used Congressmen. You used to be able to get Rosty for two K [Representative Dan Rostenkowski, longtime chairman of the House Ways and Means Committee, for $2,000]. Now

you're paying fifteen K for a journalist who's got no official power.

The money to sustain the speaking fees comes from a
variety of sources. Some organizations book famous speakers
for their large annual conventions, so the cost can be amor-
tized over a crowd of several thousand attending a dinner or
lunch. (By the mid-1980s, as Jacob Weisberg pointed out in
the *New Republic,* such relatively obscure trade organizations
as the National Association of Chain Drugstores had already
budgeted $200,000 per year for speakers at large events.)
Groups may book a famous speaker precisely in hopes of attracting a large crowd to a convention or fund-raising meeting. In one well-publicized recent case, described by Alicia
Shepard in the *American Journalism Review,* the Junior League
of South Florida booked ABC's Cokie Roberts as the star
speaker for a fund-raising event. But since the $35,000 she
charged them for a one-day trip would have eaten up the
funds they hoped to raise for charitable projects, the Junior
League turned to a corporate sponsor, the umbrella organization for local Toyota dealers, to pay Roberts's fee.
    Sometimes corporate officials will invite prominent
speakers for small gatherings of important clients. "Companies are constantly trying to connect with what they think of
as high-level people, so they can demonstrate to their customers and their employees and themselves that they are in
the know," one man who has helped arrange such events
says:

> If a CEO says, "Let's do a dinner for our board and the
> CEOs of our major customers, and let's invite a high-
> level person like a Jennings or George Will," for that
> kind of an event, thirty, forty, fifty thousand out of
> budget for a Fortune 500 company, it's a drop in the
> bucket. It demonstrates to their big customers that

they are a major player. They spend more to test-market one commercial.

THE NEED FOR STARS FROM TV. "Do they want these people because of their skills or what they've accomplished?" the booking agent Joe Cosby asked an interviewer rhetorically in the mid-1980s. "Not really. It's because they're on TV *a lot, a lot, a lot.*" "We are booked as entertainers," Jeff Greenfield of ABC has said. "They believe there is some value to holding an audience's attention for some time or enlivening a panel." "We know what we are being paid for," Ted Koppel said in 1995. "We are being paid to fill seats. By and large we are being paid the same way a guitar player or singer or comedian is paid. It is name value."

For the journalists with the very greatest name value on TV, demand for speaking engagements far outstrips the supply of available time. Ted Koppel says that he was on the for-pay speech circuit for roughly twenty years. After he returned from a tour as a correspondent in Vietnam, in the mid-1960s, he began taking engagements at around $500 each; by the mid-1980s, because of his eminence as host of *Nightline,* the stakes had gone much higher. "Because I was only interested in doing six or eight a year, and I got many more offers, I used the capitalist system to calibrate that," he said. "I told my lecture agent to keep cranking the price up until we reached the point at which I only got six or eight offers at that price." Finally Koppel determined what that price was; it was $50,000 per speech. The sum was so large that, as we will see, it led Koppel to reconsider whether he should be giving paid speeches at all.

Because there are only a few figures as well known as Koppel and because the number of speeches they can give is finite, the market for lecture fees has been distorted over the last decade much the way that salaries for basketball or baseball players have been. Fees for those at the very top of their field—Koppel at $50,000 a speech, Cal Ripken at $6 million a season, Michael Jordan at many millions for an endorsement campaign—have skyrocketed, but for more or less market-driven reasons. The biggest stars can draw the biggest crowds and cover the fees they are paid. Yet once they have set a standard, they pull up the price for lesser figures. In Ripken's lee, a .220 hitter gets a $4 million contract. And in Koppel's lee, a medium-well-known journalist figure gets $15,000 per speech.

"There are organizations that would really like a George Bush or a Margaret Thatcher, but they can't get them," the consultant Steven Hofman explained.

> These organizations are driven to the second and third and fourth tier of people, but because the people at the top have bid up the rates enormously, it bids up the rates for everybody else. You take somebody who is now commanding $30,000—without the top of the pyramid being at $60,000 or 70,000, they would have commanded maybe $10,000. But all the bureaus I know say the business still is booming.

This brings us back to the TV shows. An awareness of the possibilities of the lecture boom began setting in among national journalists, especially those based in Washington, by the late 1970s. The career of James J. Kilpatrick was an instructive early example.

Through the 1950s, as chief editorial writer for the *Richmond News Leader,* Kilpatrick relentlessly denounced school integration and the "evils of race-mixing" that it would bring. He urged the strategy that became known as "massive resistance," in which southern states would close public schools rather than knuckle under to desegregation orders from the U.S. Supreme Court. (Decades later Kilpatrick, like former Alabama governor George Wallace, said that he regretted having opposed integration.)

By the early 1970s, Kilpatrick was writing a nationally syndicated column called *Conservative View* and had developed a lucrative side career as a lecturer to corporate audiences. The secret of his lecture business, however, was less his writing than that he had become well known through TV. He was a regular panelist on one of Washington's few talk shows of the era, *Agronsky and Company*, and on *60 Minutes* he was matched in "Point-Counterpoint" exchanges with the writer Shana Alexander. His sessions with Alexander had a staged-seeming excess. They became so familiar and so histrionic that they were parodied on *Saturday Night Live*, with Dan Ackroyd (as Kilpatrick) saying to Jane Curtin (as Alexander), "Jane, you ignorant slut . . . ." This notoriety proved only to increase demand for Kilpatrick on the lecture circuit. Audiences might agree or disagree with him, but they all knew who he was.

The two writers whose success on the lecture circuit next attracted attention were William F. Buckley and George F. Will.

It may or may not have been coincidence that both of them were, like Kilpatrick, conservative. It clearly was not a coincidence that both were on TV. In addition to his work as godfather of modern conservatism as editor of *National Review*, Buckley had become known nationwide as the host of his talk show *Firing Line*. George Will, who burst onto the scene during the Watergate years as a young, clear-writing conservative columnist willing to criticize Richard Nixon, had obtained a chair on *Agronsky and Company*. With his bow ties and thick glasses and neatly parted hair, he had a nerdish glamour, rather like a lighter-haired and better-spoken Clark Kent. Like Buckley he made himself a memorable figure through TV, and because of his obvious eloquence was in demand on the lecture circuit.

Henry Fairlie, an expatriate British writer who coined the term "the Establishment," said that as early as 1975 Will had deduced the fundamental logic of modern journalistic careers. "He said that his column was important to him because it got him on TV. And the Agronsky show was important because it got him on the lecture circuit. He told me that I should be doing the same thing, because if you chose your audiences right you could give the same speech every time."

Because journalism is not a profession and has no formal rules, it is made and continually remade by individual examples of new routes to success. John Gunther in the 1930s and after, Ernie Pyle in the 1940s, Theodore White in the 1950s, correspondents of war and upheaval in the 1960s as varied as David Halberstam, Tom Wolfe, J. Anthony Lukas, Norman Mailer, Nicholas von Hoffman, and Hunter S. Thompson—each of these people affected other writers by demonstrating new ways of telling the story and presenting the truth. Bob Woodward and Carl Bernstein had the greatest influence on political journalism in the mid-1970s. By the end of the decade George Will arguably did, through his demonstration of new ways to construct a journalistic career. It was a career that was based in writing—journalists who went on TV were reluctant to give up the newspaper or magazine base that conveyed a sense of seriousness—but that was magnified by TV.

Through the late 1970s, very few berths were available for those who hoped to follow Will's example. Political-talk TV came in three forms. On Sunday morning were the respectful Q-and-A shows: *Meet the Press, Issues and Answers,* and *Face the Nation.* On Friday night, on public broadcasting, was *Washington Week in Review.* And on Saturday evening, in Washington and a few other newshound markets, came *Agronsky and Company.* That was about it.

This talk show industry was small, and it had very little room for on-air pundits. The reporters who appeared on the

Sunday morning shows really were reporters, respectfully
seeking answers from the secretary of labor about the unemployment rate. The four panelists on *Washington Week in Review* did not offer opinions on every subject under the sun
but reported what had happened on each of their beats—
Congress, the State Department, the White House, and so
on. Only on *Agronsky and Company* did Washington veterans
like Hugh Sidey and Carl Rowan talk about "the mood of
the capital" or "the president's week," but they harrumph-
ingly traded views, in the fashion of codgers at the Club,
rather than mixing it up with the mannered, pro-wrestling
style combativeness of today's talk shows. The Agronsky
show was also powerfully influenced by the late Peter Lisagor, of the *Chicago Sun-Times*. Lisagor, a regular panelist on
the show, had a gentle but relentless wit, with which he constantly made fun of the whole concept of journalists sitting
around pontificating.

TALK SHOWS EXPAND TO FILL THE NEED. In 1980
everything changed, and it changed because of John McLaughlin, creator of *The McLaughlin Group*. Well into his show's
second decade, McLaughlin may seem a buffoonish character
outside Washington, fit for satire on *Saturday Night Live*. His
mocking names for his panelists—"MorTOHNN" Kondracke and the rest—and his self-parodying shouts of
"WRONG!" suggest that everything he does is an outrageous act, in the fashion of PeeWee Herman or Tiny Tim.
Whether or not McLaughlin's mannerisms are cultivated to
build brand identification, his effect on political journalism
is hard to overstate. He created a new industry, one that
matched the demand for lecture speakers with a supply of
"personalities" from TV.

Christopher Wren, the great architect, is buried in St.
Paul's Cathedral in London, which he designed. An epitaph
in the cathedral says, *si monumentum requiris, circumspice*—"if

you seek his monument, look around you"—at the cathedral he planned and the architecture of London that he influenced. If you seek John McLaughlin's monument, *circumspice* at talk TV. Where once there were only the staid-seeming Agronsky and *Washington Week* talk shows, now there is a political talk industry. Saturday and Sunday editions of *The Capital Gang,* on which a panel of journalists trade banter with each other and often with an invited political guest. *Crossfire* five evenings a week, with every issue forced into a stark, polarized pro-versus-con showdown. *Weekend Crossfire* to boot. Evans and Novak in various incarnations. David Gergen and Mark Shields as matched pundits on *The Mac-Neil/Lehrer NewsHour,* succeeded now by Shields and Paul Gigot. *Reliable Sources. Inside Politics. Off the Record.* Weekend wrap-up talk programs. Lawyers debating the Simpson trial. Dee Dee Myers and Mary Matalin on CNBC. *America's Talking* on late-night TV. The expansion of cable channels created a demand for programming, and the least expensive time-filler of all is a panel talk show. The Sunday morning shows themselves have become miniature monuments to McLaughlin, abandoning the straight Q-and-A format to give us pundits often flinging views at one another. The differences are thinning fast between John McLaughlin's spawn and Phil Donahue's—that is, between the weekend talk shows about politics and the weekday *Jenny Jones-Jerry Springer* programs. One features a cast of regulars arguing about Newt Gingrich and Hillary Clinton and the other features a changing cast of nobodies arguing about diets and sex.

By the standards of prime-time network TV or even the daytime talk shows, political-chat shows draw tiny audiences. But they are cheap to produce (panelists are paid a few hundred dollars per session), they count toward a network's quota of "public service" broadcasts, and they are under tremendous supply-side pressure from journalists who want to be on.

Why do they want to appear, when so many reporters make fun of the shows? At least initially, the reason for making this change is not anything as blunt as the hope of big lecture fees. The most immediate payoff is the simple thrill of being noticed and known. Political-journalistic Washington functions much like a big high school, with cliques of the popular kids, the nerds, the rebels, the left-outs, and so on. To be on TV is to become very quickly a cool kid. Friends call to say they've seen you. People recognize you in stores. Whether people agree or disagree with what you said (or whether they even remember), they treat you as "realer" and bigger than you were before.

TV reaches an audience in a way that print simply cannot. Everyone who has been on a TV show, whether C-SPAN or *Ricki Lake* or *Jeopardy,* hears from friends and relatives for weeks afterward, "I saw you on TV!" Those who take the next step up, toward regular berths on a show, have that extra, sizzling experience of seeing strangers' heads flip back, for a second look ("Is it really him?") as they walk into restaurants or through airport corridors. In each case the recognition is almost totally judgment-free. People who operate in the world of print are used to hearing "I liked your story" (whether meant sincerely or not); but they also frequently hear, "I think you had it wrong." Print forces the reader's attention past your personality to whatever your article is trying to say. TV's effect is mainly to make you bigger than life. For each hundred acquaintances who will say, "I saw you on the show," only one will say, "I agree [or disagree] with what you said."

Washington life is organized around the "week"—the newsmagazines announce a theme for the week on Monday; in the *Washington Post*'s newsroom editors discuss what will be "Topic A" for the week's coverage; the story builds through the weekdays; then the week's performance is resolved and re-capped on the weekend talk shows and in the

"Outlook" and "News of the Week in Review" sections of the *Washington Post* and *New York Times,* respectively. To be on the talk shows is to have a role in the week. On Monday and Tuesday people tell you that they saw you over the weekend. You work on your stories and interviews through Thursday at lunchtime. On Thursday afternoon you get a call from the show's producers telling you what the topics will be for the show's taping the next day. You check the "Nexis" files—a vast computerized database of newspaper and magazine articles and broadcast transcripts from around the world—on Thursday night for subjects you don't know about, and on Friday morning you work up one-liners, predictions, and comebacks to use on the show. The taping for Saturday-night shows is late on Friday, and when it is over the producers always say, "Great show! Great job, everyone!" On Saturday you meet people for dinner minutes after they finished watching you on TV.

"When I left Washington in 1982, one of the reasons I was happiest to get away involved TV." So says Peter Osnos, at the time a reporter for the *Washington Post,* now an editor at Random House. "If I had been on *Washington Week in Review,* people for the next three days would be pulling at their forelocks and telling me how great I was, because I had spent a few minutes bloviating on TV."

For many people this magnification of personality is enjoyable in itself. (I understand this sensation, having appeared on a variety of programs.) If there were no other reward whatsoever associated with TV appearances, people would still fight for the chance. But for many reporters covering big institutional beats, TV prominence also has a practical advantage. When you call to make an appointment, the secretary recognizes your name. The person you want to interview has an idea who you are.

In short, many people would love being on the talk shows even if no money were involved. But money is. The number of lecture bookings and the size of lecture fees vary directly with the number of hours you have spent on TV.

"I have seen it time and again," Steven Hofman, the Washington-based communications consultant, said:

> I deal with people who have had high profiles through TV. Every time they vanish from the tube for a period of time, the requests for their speaking and lectures drop off appreciably. Then they do a spate of TV appearances and they become more on the visible side of things and the requests for speeches come rolling in. The second someone is scheduled to be on TV, the speakers bureaus will send out marketing announcements to their clients. "Watch our person, who is on TV at this and that time—and you can have him Live!"

"It is a package," says Rem Reider, the editor of the *American Journalism Review.* "You say outrageous things to get attention on the shows so that you can become a regular, and once you become a regular you can get the speaking fees."

A network TV correspondent observed, "If you look at the system as it exists today, you've got a cycle. There is a group of people who write a little, are on TV a little, and are out speaking a lot. Each part of the cycle feeds the other. They're part of a fraternity or club, and they meet every four days at O'Hare, off to the Institute of Bootmakers or Investment Bankers LTD. There are people who will *kill* for two minutes on *Good Morning America,* because it brings in another raft of lecture dates."

"You can now aspire to be a political journalist in the hope that you can earn what a Washington lawyer earns," Jeff Greenfield of ABC said in an interview in the mid-1980s, when the speaking revolution was still under way. "I am the last person in the world to say that this is awful. But it *is* different. In the same way that people might have started out in federal agencies in expectation of becoming Washington lawyers, you can now start in Washington journalism and realistically aspire to become a commentator, columnist, TV personality, and lecturer and ascend comfortably into the six-figure range."

Comfortably indeed. In 1992, while he was working at *U.S. News & World Report* and appearing on *MacNeil/Lehrer,* David Gergen's aggregate income from speeches alone was $466,625, according to the financial statements he had to file when signing on as a White House advisor in 1993. In the mid-1980s, George Will's lecture agent said that Will charged $15,000 for a speech "but might do it for $7,500 if he doesn't have to leave town. They put a premium on not having to travel." By the 1990s the figures had more than doubled, and Will's annual earnings were estimated at well over $1 million per year. Sums of this size might not seem significant in New York or Los Angeles, where the money to be had from finance and entertainment, respectively, makes the gradation between "high" and "low" journalistic incomes seem trivial. But Washington, despite its concentrations of power, is not really a center of money; a TV journalist like Will in his heyday and Cokie Roberts, his successor as big-ticket speaker, now can be among the biggest earners in town.

DOES IT MATTER? "Being paid more than you're worth is the American dream," Michael Kinsley, of *Crossfire,* wrote in a *New Republic* article called "Confessions of a Buckraker" in 1995. "I see a day when we'll all be paid more than we're worth. Meanwhile, though, there's no requirement for journalists, alone among humanity, to deny themselves the occasional fortuitous tastes of this bliss."

Is this the right way to view the rise of the talk-TV-and-lecture business that has transformed the finances of political journalists? The people who are on the circuit have found ways to rationalize the choices they have made. Yet the very reasons they offer underscore the ways that this activity, while profitable in the short run for individuals, is damaging in the long run because it erodes their credibility and that of journalism as a whole.

One frequent, flip defense of "buckraking" by its practitioners is the contention that anyone who complains about it must just be envious. It is hard not to admire the logical elegance of this claim. Most people who have warned about the dangers of "buckraking" are other journalists. Either those journalists give paid speeches themselves, in which case they can be called hypocrites; or they don't give paid speeches, so that their complaints can be attributed to simple jealousy. Therefore, criticism of any sort can categorically be dismissed.

Yet it is also hard not to see that this argument is merely a distraction. Whether or not certain critics are "hypocritical" or "envious," the arguments about what "buckraking" does to journalism remain.

A more refined rationalization for the decision to go on the speech and talk-show circuit is that the travel and face-to-face interaction involved are "broadening." You see new corners of the country, you hear new things, you come back to Washington or New York with a new store of impressions about what people are saying "out there."

In principle broader exposure is always a plus, and in some circumstances—especially at universities but at any session where the journalist stays long enough for genuine give and take—the reporter can leave after a day or two knowing more than he did before he arrived. But the reality of the speaking circuit is that the higher powered and more lucrative it becomes, the more narrowing, rather than broadening, its effects are.

You are met at the airport. You go to the conference center and are sent to the holding room. You may have a reception or lunch with a group of local worthies. You give the speech and take questions—and as soon as you decently can, you're on your way to the airport again. You've seen a succession of not-very-different banquet halls and hotel rooms (if you can't avoid staying overnight) and airports, and you've talked with people who are mainly the local upper-crust and are all impressed with you. The old cliché about America being the same from coast to coast is obviously not true, as anyone who has spent time learning the realities and values of different regions understands. But the cliché can seem true if you're always flying over America, or are on your way to make lecture connections at O'Hare, or if what you see of Anchorage or St. Louis or Portland is the place where you give your speech.

The ultimate comment about the broadening effect of the lecture circuit came from John McLaughlin. Nearly ten years ago he was being interviewed about the talk show/lecture cycle that was then just past its infancy. The writer Ken Auletta had recently commented on the way that the celebrity-lecturer's life undermined the ability to observe, travel, and learn that a reporter relies on. "It confuses people about the role they're supposed to play," Auletta said.

> When you're treated like a celebrity, and people know your face, you become full of yourself. It robs you of the humility you need to do your job as a journalist, which is fundamentally based on asking other people questions. In New York you can hide, nobody recognizes you on the street, but in Washington everything feeds your self-importance. Once you are on these talk shows and assume that the world awaits your opinion, you get the idea that you're supposed to be answering questions, not asking them. You start thinking, Why should I go interview some thirty-year-old kid who thinks he can run a campaign for president?

When John McLaughlin was asked about the problem of people who became too prominent to work as reporters any more, he agreed. "The great danger is getting out of touch. That is why it is so important to go on the road. You get to talk to the person driving the car, you get to hear the whole range of views from the trade association."

The person driving the car! This is the broadening effect of celebrity travel! In a way it is unfair to pick on McLaughlin for this disclosure, since he had never pretended to be a reporter, and therefore his embrace of the talk show life represented no sacrifice of a preexisting journalistic career. (McLaughlin, ordained as a Jesuit, had worked as an assistant to President Nixon and then left the priesthood.) But he unself-consciously exposed what's wrong with the "travel is broadening" concept.

Of course there is a simpler way to make the point. If there were no speaking fee, would journalists consider the "broadening" experience worth it?

Some journalists add a further justification: In addition to being "broadening," the speaking engagements are also "good for the company." If John McLaughlin illustrates the self-deluding nature of the "broadening" argument, James Warren illustrates what is wrong with the "company" rationale.

Warren came to Washington early in 1994, as a young, free-thinking new bureau chief for the *Chicago Tribune.* For the first year and a half of his stay he wrote Sunday columns for the *Tribune* called "Weekly Watch," which lampooned the pomposity he saw around him. Reporters mingled with sources as social equals. They had gigantic egos, which clever politicians could exploit—"*Brilliant* column this morning, Bob. You really are the best! Now have I mentioned . . ." And they were shamelessly on the gravy train. In nearly every column Warren had an item called "Cokie

Watch," about the latest big-ticket speaking engagement that Cokie Roberts or her husband, Steve, had lined up.

In the summer of 1995, Warren took on a new role: as a panelist on another pundit talk show. CNN, operating on the belief that there were not yet enough political-talk shows, decided in 1995 to start a new one, a Sunday-night edition of *The Capital Gang.* "We're going to do something a little different on this show," Wolf Blitzer of CNN had said when promoting the program (in an appearance on yet another talk show, *Equal Time,* with Mary Matalin). "We're going to pick some winners and losers. Give some thumbs up and thumbs down. Do what we should have done all along, which is cover politics as sports." Blitzer sounded as if he considered these to be fresh ideas.

This was the cast that James Warren had joined, as a regular. Soon after he began this engagement he was asked why he had joined the panel, when all of his previous writing had mocked exactly this sort of self-important buffoonery. Well, he said, it was good for the company. The *Tribune* was trying to make itself better known, and it really helped the newspaper to have his name on the screen.

This too is a standard defense, and like the others it contains some element of truth. The business staffs of publications are almost as attuned as the lecture agents to who is and who is not getting airtime. It becomes easier to sell ads, or at least get listened to, if people are reminded of your company's name. In Chicago itself, the *Tribune* is not exactly unknown, but somehow the corporate officials felt better thinking that people around the country and in the capital were seeing the paper's name.

Sometimes the management cares enough to push reporters to be more aggressive in getting on camera. In 1994, *Business Week*'s leadership decided that it had to try harder to get its Washington staff on TV. Yes, they were already on C-

SPAN and had the occasional CNN interview, but the real prize was the weekend pundit talk shows, such as *The Capital Gang*. The magazine hired a consultant to come in, take sample tapes of the reporters and editors in the Washington bureau, and give them advice about how they could "increase their Q rating" and come across better on TV.

"This is a pretty serious magazine," Paul Magnusson, of *Business Week,* said after the sessions. "People work here because they like dealing with issues seriously. But the guy who was coaching us kept telling us that we had to 'throw grenades.' He said that it doesn't matter really what you say so much as how you say it. You say something on TV and it immediately disappears into the ether. No one is going to remember what you say when you're on the talk show. What they'll remember is how you looked and your general bearing."

At *Business Week,* the plan didn't work. Magnusson and his colleagues refused to make their comments short and snappy enough to suit TV, and the instructor went away defeated. But at many other publications the pressure runs the other way. For their own reasons journalists leap at chances to be on the shows, and then use the "it's all for the company" line to explain a decision they think they're supposed to feel embarrassed about. The more time you spend on shows, the more you have gotten accustomed to the idea that you are an interesting person whose views others would naturally want to hear. And as you are moving through this shift of perceptions you use the "good for the company" rationale as an explanation to others, since it's awkward to talk about how your sense of self is being enlarged.

"Look, I know this has been better for me than for *Time,*" Margaret Carlson, a *Time* columnist who appears on *The Capital Gang* (original Saturday edition), has commented. She is more honest than most about a reality they all recognize.

DEGREES OF CORRUPTION. The bluntest way to criticize journalists on the lecture trail is to say, simply, that they are corrupt. Someday, in some form, they may have to write about the groups they are addressing. If they have taken big money from these groups, they can't give the reader as honest—or as honest-seeming—an assessment as if they had kept their distance. Ben Bradlee, legendary executive editor of the *Washington Post,* has put the case in just these terms:

> If the Insurance Institute of America, if there is such a thing, pays you $10,000 to make a speech, don't tell me you haven't been corrupted. You can say you haven't and you can say you will attack insurance issues in the same way, but you won't. You can't.

In the same vein, Alan Murray, the *Wall Street Journal*'s Washington bureau chief, has said, "You tell me what is the difference between somebody who works full time for the National Association of Realtors and somebody who takes $40,000 a year in speaking fees from realtor groups. It's not clear to me there's a big distinction."

The people who work the speech circuit reject these claims as being unnuanced. Of course, they say, they would never take money from a group they are covering directly. Moreover, most news organizations have rules prohibiting such out-and-out conflicts. These rules are not exactly airtight, since the most influential correspondents tend to have the least specifically defined "beats," allowing them to say that no particular engagement constitutes a direct conflict. During the debate on health-care reform, for instance, Lesley Stahl of CBS was paid a reported $20,000 to moderate a program for CIGNA, an insurance giant with an obvious stake in the outcome of the debate. Since Stahl covers many topics but is not specifically on the health beat, she could participate, whereas CBS's health correspondent could not have done so. By similar logic Cokie Roberts could accept $35,000 raised by Toyota dealers for a speech in Florida, delivered shortly before the big U.S.–Japan auto trade showdown. She would be commenting on the politics of the trade issue, but she was not on the trade beat. (Because of controversy over such engagements, by mid-1995 all three broadcast networks had imposed restrictions on their correspondents' ability to speak for pay to commercial or lobbying groups.) Early in 1995 the members of *The McLaughlin Group* conducted a paid mock-debate before the American Association of Retired Persons, which has a huge and obvious stake in the budget matters the group will discuss. In the fall of 1994, Bob Dole and Robert Rubin, who was at the time the head economic advisor to President Clinton, appeared jointly at an American Bankers Association convention in New York, where for twenty minutes they answered questions posed by Tim Russert, moderator of *Meet the Press.* For this appearance, before one of the strongest financial lobbying groups in the nation, neither Dole nor Rubin received any compensation. If they had, they would have violated ethics rules. The ABA officials told a reporter they paid Russert about $20,000, but Russert later said that his fee was "nowhere close" to that amount. (Russert also pointed out that *Meet the Press,* unlike *The McLaughlin Group* and many other talk shows, does not conduct for-profit road versions before commercial groups. He appeared before the bankers in his own capacity, not in a mock *Meet the Press* format.)

This sort of spectacle—journalists receiving pay at events where politicians must appear for free—has become a regular occurrence in Washington. It could be argued that Dole, Rubin, and other governmental figures appearing before such an audience were receiving a kind of deferred compensation. A politician like Dole might hope to come back to this group for support and donations in future races. A presidential advisor like Rubin could make the case for his administration's policies to this influential audience. Even so, the rewards the politicians received are a natural extension of their normal work—that of building support for candidates and plans. For the journalists, by contrast, the appearances are individually rewarding but collectively damaging, since they reinforce the idea that journalists are really just performers, who will put on a show for a price.

Even with interactions of this sort, involving huge sums of money from groups with political agendas, celebrity-journalist speakers say there is no danger of the corruption Ben Bradlee warned against. Jeff Greenfield, of ABC, says that one seeming example of journalistic hypocrisy actually proves how little danger there is. Early in 1994, ABC's *Prime Time Live*, co-hosted by Sam Donaldson, ran a feature on an insurance-lobbying association which took congressmen on junkets to resorts. One week later the show had to run a brief disclaimer, saying that Donaldson himself had spoken, for pay, to the same group the previous year. (His fee, which was not announced on the show, was $30,000.)

"You can look at this as hypocrisy," Jeff Greenfield said of the Donaldson episode. "Or you say it shows that he took the money and then the show beat the crap out of them anyway." That is, even if the engagements were intended to buy sympathetic coverage—which Greenfield says they aren't—they don't succeed. Never, Greenfield says, has a group to which he's spoken come to him later with any hint of a request for favorable coverage. And if they did?

> I concede to you fully that a lot of people would never believe it, but when people say to me "I saw you speak at X," the odds are that I don't remember speaking at X.

"No group I've spoken to has ever made the slightest effort to ply me with its policy agenda," Michael Kinsley wrote in "Confessions of a Buckraker." "This really seems to

be the furthest thing from anyone's mind (unless these people are a lot more nefarious and subtle than I give them
credit for). So what are they buying? They're buying entertainment, insight (they hope), propinquity to someone who's
on TV." Almost everyone who has appeared before commercial groups repeats the same assurance—that no one has
asked them for favors, and if someone had, the journalist
would not dream of complying.

One response to this assertion is to say that the transac-
tion often looks different from the buyer's end. "I am sure
that many interest groups never even dream of influence," a
man who has booked speeches said. "On the other hand,
these are strategic decisions."

> You're not necessarily getting something immediate,
> but you are establishing a *relationship.*
>
> Let me give you a hypothetical case that may not
> sound so hypothetical. If you have had a big-time jour-
> nalist to your annual meeting, you've had drinks, din-
> ner with him and the spouse, it's not that the journalist
> is going to do something for you. But I guarantee you
> that every person who has been part of that deal now
> thinks, and probably with justification, that the jour-
> nalist is not going to do something *to* them. You can't
> call that journalist up and say, Hey, do a puff piece
> about us. But it is more likely that you can call up the
> journalist and say, You know those rumors that are
> going around? Well, you know me, and I can tell you
> it's a bunch of junk.
>
> The real question is, would these executives and
> lobbyists have the occasion to relate to the journalists
> if they didn't spend the money? The answer is No.

Journalist-speakers who go to big events can tell themselves that they will guard zealously against such tempta-

tions—after all, Sam Donaldson did do something *to* the health insurance industry after they paid him. But even the most hard-boiled correspondents have their human side and are likely to sympathize with people they have seen face to face. At about the time Ronald Reagan became president, Charles Peters, of the *Washington Monthly,* made a speech (for free) to a group of young people considering careers in journalism. Michael Kinsley, who was then editor of the *New Republic* but was not yet well known as a TV figure, appeared with Peters. During the question period, a woman in the crowd asked Peters what preparation he would recommend for students who hoped to be writers. Peters launched into a tirade about the importance of studying history, literature, government, science, or *anything* other than journalism. It was easy to learn the craft of journalism on the job, but it was very hard to make up for the lost general education that college years should represent.

"How could you have done that to the poor woman?" Kinsley asked Peters when the session was over. Kinsley knew, as Peters apparently did not, that she was a prominent official at a journalism school. Didn't Peters feel bad for dismissing her whole life's work? Peters found the episode charming, in a way—it showed that even commentators as acerbic as Kinsley could care about the feelings of those they met. But in a larger sense that natural human reaction showed the danger of spending time on a lecture circuit populated mainly by corporate officials. No matter how steely your resolve, no matter how firm your commitment to remain unswayed by the interaction, if you have normal human sympathies you'll be more reluctant to offend people with whom you have spent a pleasant day than ones you have never met.

INESCAPABLE APPEARANCES. "Buckraking" speakers may tell themselves that their behavior is in no way affected

by this new source of income. For some of them that may actually be true. But they cannot undo the way this practice
changes the public's view of prominent journalists and of
journalism as a whole.

The groups that sponsor big-fee events have an altered
sense of the journalists who accept their invitations. Steve
Hofman, who has worked in politics and helped arrange
speeches, made the point with particular eloquence. "There
is a factor that's hard to explain but counts for a lot," he said.
"When you have a journalist who is commanding major dollar fees, it says to the people who are paying them, *they are all
part of the same club.* When the American people look at what
goes on in governance and leadership institutions, and they
think it has nothing to do with their real lives, it is this kind
of thing that they hear about and say, 'Well, they all take
care of themselves.'"

Brian Lamb, founder of C-SPAN and its most recognizable on-air host, has declined on principle to give speeches
for pay. The practice, he said, "sends out one of those messages that's been sent out of this town for the last twenty
years: Everybody does everything for money." (Lamb also
makes a point of not saying his own name on C-SPAN
broadcasts he is hosting, in contrast to typical TV figures
who act as if their own identity is the most important information they have to impart.)

"I call it white-collar crime," Tom Brokaw, of NBC, has
said. "That's just what I think it is."

When Ted Koppel realized, in the late 1980s, that the
market-clearing price for his speeches had reached $50,000,
he did something unusual: he stopped speaking for pay. No
matter how incorruptible he might feel inside, he thought
that the situation would look corrupt to members of the
general public who found out about it, as they inevitably
would. When his agent kept bidding up the price to weed
out offers, Koppel says:

One day we reached this price that was so astronomi-
cally high that I went home and talked to my wife
about it. I said that nobody out there who makes a normal salary is going to hear that amount, and realize
that it was paid for a day's work—to put it gener-
ously—and believe that there wasn't something else
that was being purchased for that price, beyond my
time for a day. It wasn't true that that had ever happened, I am unaware of ever having given anyone anything other than an hour's good information and
entertainment, or the willingness to meet people and
greet them at a cocktail party. But the sums are so
large that they exceed now the earning power of most
people for a year or sometimes two years, or more. Particularly since I am extremely well paid by ABC, I felt
that it was easy for me, at least, to make the decision
and say, Why run that risk of losing whatever credibility I have for the sake of something we don't need?

Several other prominent media figures, including Tom
Brokaw of NBC, Dan Rather of CBS, and Peter Jennings of
ABC, have either abandoned speaking for pay or have set up
charitable foundations to which they donate their speaking
fees.

Because these network stars are so well paid to begin
with, their decision to forgo speaking income may seem
something less than saintlike. Koppel's salary from ABC is
reported to be $6 million per year, and Brokaw, with re-
ported annual earnings of some $2 million, is the most mod-
estly paid of the other anchors. For Koppel, a $50,000
honorarium works out to the equivalent of two days' normal
pay. But at any income level extra money is attractive. The
anchors turned it down because they realized it had a cost: it
would cement the impression that the country's best-known
journalists were in business *mainly* to maximize their in-

comes. Bond traders can operate with this goal. Indeed, their desire to maximize earnings is what makes financial markets work. But if soldiers, or teachers, or politicians—or reporters—leave the impression that they care more about making money than about any other goal, they—and their business—will be considered corrupt, even if they earn the money "honestly."

Each of these troubled institutions—the military, education, politics—has a symbol of its excesses. In the mid-1990s the symbol of speech-circuit excess has become Cokie Roberts, of ABC and NPR. Like many such symbols she is in a sense blameless. She played by rules that were called into question just as she was moving to the front of the pack. She is a gifted and witty speaker, who gives more value for lecture-fee dollar than many other speakers. She is also well schooled in the nuances of Capitol Hill politics, having been raised in that very culture. Her father was Hale Boggs, long-time Democratic congressman from Louisiana. Her mother is Lindy Boggs, who was elected to Hale's seat after he was killed in an airplane crash in Alaska. Her brother, Tommy Boggs, is one of the most powerful and well-connected lobbyists in the country, who was a major figure in beating back the Clinton administration's health-reform plan. She lives in the house in Bethesda, a suburb of Washington, where she was raised.

Through the 1970s, Steve Roberts was the better known and more glamorous member of the couple, as a young, star correspondent for the *New York Times* both overseas (notably in Greece) and in Washington. Cokie began working for National Public Radio and was, with Linda Wertheimer and Nina Totenberg, part of its first wave of remarkable women correspondents.

In the late 1980s, Steve Roberts left the *Times* for *U.S. News* mainly because the *Times* would not let him appear on TV as much as he wanted. The *Times*'s policy forbids staff members to be regular panelists on TV shows. When Joseph Lelyveld, the *Times's* executive editor, was asked whether this policy had cost the paper any employees, he said: "One. Steve Roberts, who wanted a regular spot on *Washington Week in Review.*" Cokie Roberts, at this time, had impressed Roone Arledge, the master of news and sports at ABC, and he began adding her to the network's mainly male lineup as a panelist on David Brinkley's show and occasionally on *Nightline.* Meanwhile she loyally maintained her connection to National Public Radio, which paid a relatively low salary but had given her her start.

By the time of the 1988 convention, Cokie Roberts was poised for blast-off as a star, much as George Will had been fifteen years before. Steve was appearing frequently on Washington talk shows. By the early 1990s they were the most bookable couple on the speech circuit except perhaps for the Doles (and Bob, of course, could not take any money).

As an illustration of Cokie Roberts's prominence: in May 1995, the "Silicon Valley Business and Leadership Conference," underwritten by Tandem Computers and Silicon Graphics computer systems, sent out flyers for a conference featuring "The Most Exciting and Influential Leaders of Our Time." Two former presidents, Ford and Bush, were on the list. One former chairman of the Joint Chiefs of Staff, Colin Powell. One former governor, Mario Cuomo. And one influential figure whose leadership was manifested in being a TV and radio correspondent, Cokie Roberts.

The Robertses enjoyed this success just as the success began to be scrutinized. In the relentless drip-drip of his "Cokie Watch" items, James Warren of the *Chicago Tribune* (and later of *The Capital Gang*) chronicled the amazingly lucrative engagements they were accepting to appear before commercial audiences—for instance, $45,000 for a joint speech by Steve and Cokie Roberts, addressing potential clients of a banking group in Chicago in 1994.

Early in 1995, the Philip Morris corporation invited its executives to a golf tournament and conference in Palm Beach, Florida. The printed schedule showed that the program for one breakfast session would be "Change in Washington: A Media Perspective with Cokie and Steve Roberts." There were many reasons to consider this a wildly inappropriate engagement for journalists to accept. The sponsor was a tobacco company, whose products were sure to be the subject of ongoing political debate. Journalists who might well report on those debates were accepting an enormous fee. Neither of the Robertses would discuss the details publicly, but lecture agents estimated that they received at least $30,000. In response to complaints about similar engagements by Cokie Roberts, Jeff Greenfield, Brit Hume, and other ABC figures, the network's senior vice president, Richard Wald, had laid down rules greatly restricting speeches by correspondents to groups that might lobby the Congress, as Philip Morris does. Those rules took effect just two months before the Philip Morris engagement. (*Time* magazine and CBS News put a similar policy into effect in 1995, and NBC was preparing one late in 1995. The *Washington Post* and the *Wall Street Journal* had for years forbidden reporters to accept speaking fees from corporations, lobbying groups, or even governmental organizations.) To make matters even more awkward, at the time of the Philip Morris event ABC was fighting off a gigantic, ten-billion-dollar libel claim by Philip Morris and R. J. Reynolds, which objected to a report on ABC's *Day One* that the companies had "spiked" their cigarettes with extra nicotine to make them more addictive. (In late August 1995 the tobacco companies dropped their claim after ABC apologized for the report and agreed to pay the companies' legal expenses, totaling $3 million.)

In short, there were plenty of reasons not to go. Indeed, although both Robertses were listed as speakers on the program, Cokie Roberts (according to the event's organizers) bowed out at the last moment, saying that she was sick. Steve Roberts went by himself—and, according to Philip Morris spokesmen, did a wonderful job. His gain, and that of the audience, was journalism's loss.

"Journalism, or reporting, whatever you want to call it, is diminished at its roots by money, by the quest for money," Jim Wooten, a former correspondent for the *New York Times* who is now a senior correspondent for ABC News, said in 1995. "The availability of money now, in the quantities journalists are earning from lectures, from TV, from columns—that availability may represent proper capitalism, but in its essence it is corrupting. It becomes the *raison d'être* of one's life. Reporters should not do things mainly for money. And many of them do, as I sometimes have."

As her speaking engagements became the subject of press scrutiny after 1993, Cokie Roberts refused to respond to any press inquiries about the sums involved or the potential conflicts of interest, contending through a spokesman that "it's not something that in any way, shape, or form should be discussed in public." (Steve Roberts was in principle willing to answer questions, but did not respond to questions about the engagements mentioned here.) While their level of earnings was unusual, the Robertses' reluctance to discuss the matter was typical of the "buckraker" community, which has dug in its heels about suggestions that prominent journalists should disclose sources of their income from special interest groups, much as politicians are required to do. The basis of the argument for disclosure is not that a pundit's power is identical to a politician's. Rather, it is that both groups operate in the public eye, rely on public trust, and deeply affect public opinion and public life. Both therefore need to make extra efforts at disclosure because of the consequences when the public suspects the worst of them.

TURNING A CALLING INTO A SIDESHOW. Even if practiced perfectly, journalism will leave some resentment and bruised feelings in its wake. The justification journalists can offer for the harm they inevitably inflict is to show, through their actions, their understanding that what they do matters, and that it should be done with care.

This is why the most depressing aspect of the new talking pundit industry may be the argument made by many practitioners that the whole thing is just a game, which no one should take too seriously. Michael Kinsley said that his paid speaking engagements are usually mock debates, in which he takes the liberal side. "Since the audiences are generally composed of affluent businessmen, my role is like that of the team that gets to lose to the Harlem Globetrotters." This would be the Washington Generals, whose members knew they were just putting on a show. Kinsley is by most accounts the most talented policy writer of his generation, so his participation at these events is as if Michael Jordan moonlighted with the Washington Generals. "But I do it," Kinsley wrote, "because it pays well, because it's fun to fly around the country and stay in hotels, and because even a politically unsympathetic audience can provide a cheap ego boost."

"This is not writing, this is not thought," Morton Kondracke, of the McLaughlin show, told Mark Jurkowitz of the *Boston Globe* in 1995. He was describing the talk show activity to which he has devoted a major part of his time for fifteen years. "You should not take it 100 percent seriously. Anybody who does is a fool." Fred Barnes, also of the McLaughlin show, offers a similar "we're just fooling around" dismissal of any real complaint about the show. "People generally don't take *The McLaughlin Group* that seriously," Barnes told Howard Kurtz of the *Washington Post*:

> Does *The McLaughlin Group* use gimmicks? Sure. They work on TV. Do we try to appear to know more than

we do? Yep. I guess that's a little phony, but I can live
with it.

Barnes can, but it's not clear that journalism as a whole
can live with the talk show/lecture circus quite so comfortably. *The McLaughlin Group* often takes its act on the road,
gimmicks and all, for fees of $20,000 per appearance. *Cross-
fire* goes for paid jaunts on the road. So do panelists from *The
Capital Gang.* Contracts for these appearances contain a routine clause specifying that the performance may *not* be taped
or opened to cameras, such as those for C-SPAN. This provision allows speakers to recycle their material, especially
those who stitch together anecdotes about "the mood in
Washington today." It also adds to the speaker's impression
that the sessions aren't really serious. He won't be held to account for what he says, so the normal standards don't apply.

Yet the fact that Barnes and others find reassuring—
that no one takes the shows seriously—is precisely what's
wrong with them, because they jeopardize the credibility of
everything that journalists do. "I think one of the really destructive developments in Washington in the last fifteen
years has been the rise in these reporter talk shows," Tom
Brokaw has said. "Reporters used to cover policy—not cover
each other and spend all of their time yelling at each other
and making philistine judgments about what happened the
week before. It's not enlightening. It makes me cringe."

When talk shows go on the road for performances
whose hostility and disagreement are staged for entertainment value, when reporters pick up thousands of dollars appearing before interest groups and sharing tidbits of what
they have heard, when all the participants then dash off for
the next plane, caring about none of it except the money—
when these things happen, they send a message. The message is: We don't respect what we're doing. Why should
anyone else? Journalists and the act of journalism are cheap-

ened—for the short-term profit of the troupers on the road. "We are booked as entertainers," Jeff Greenfield had said— and through such bookings mere "entertainers" is what journalists become.

THE COST OF LIFE AS A TALKING HEAD. Where does the food chain begin? How does one end up getting a seat on the TV shows? The literal-minded answer is that you get invited by John McLaughlin or the CNN producers lining up each installment of *Crossfire* or *The Capital Gang.* This is one reason McLaughlin is such a beloved and warmly greeted figure at Washington social gatherings.

The larger answer, which involves biological processes of adaptation, is that you shape your behavior in a way that suits the changed journalistic environment of the 1990s. Like the first limbed fish who struggled their way out of the sea to set up life on land, the most ambitious political journalists of the 1990s struggle their way to a new life that involves talk shows. The similarity in both cases is that the site for beginning this new life is a bog of mud. The features that let the fish live on land—lungs not gills, legs not fins—were at direct odds with what it took to survive in the old environment. And the traits that are rewarded, through processes of selection, in the talk show age are at direct odds with what "reporters" have traditionally done.

One of the traits that make people more successful on talk shows, but less useful as journalists, is predictability. Structurally, TV talk shows are sitcoms. People tune them in to see familiar faces displaying familiar personality traits, as they encounter mildly unfamiliar circumstances. So it was with *Leave It to Beaver,* and so it is with *This Week with David Brinkley.* It is because we know that George Will is starchy and that Sam Donaldson gets his goat that we want to see how they'll handle whatever they disagree about in this week's news. It is because we know that John McLaughlin is a blowhard that we enjoy his posturing, exactly as we did with blowhards like Fred Flintstone and Ted Baxter. For any of these figures to get out of character destroys the premise of the show. If Bart Simpson became sweet-tempered or Homer Simpson became smart, *The Simpsons* would fall apart—as *The Capital Gang* would if Robert Novak stopped attacking and interrupting all the other panelists. Debate shows like *Crossfire* are set up in an even more rigidly predictable way, with one host structurally forced to take the liberal side of any issue and the other host the conservative. As a novelty, the two *Crossfire* hosts will sometimes take the same side, against two guests who oppose them both. But a departure from steady left/right predictability would erode the basis of the show.

Such typecasting is down to a science when it comes to producing TV shows—but it is exactly contrary to the way a reporter should think. People bring their own relatively constant personalities and their own accumulated biases to each subject they approach, but the entire point of reporting is to allow yourself to be influenced by new material you see. Politics as a whole also suffers when interest groups and legislators lock themselves into predictable positions, like guests on a talk show. If each issue that comes up—gun control, North Korea, prayer in schools—is hammered into a *Crossfire*-like pattern of preexisting disputes, the issues themselves become less interesting than they might be, and much less likely to be resolved.

In addition to predictability, the talk show world cultivates an ethic of polarization and overstatement. The secret of success on TV is to be noticed. Being noticed depends much more on your demeanor—snappiness, body language—than on the literal content of the words you emit. When Paul Magnusson of *Business Week* was being coached for success on talk shows, his instructor spelled out the realities for Magnusson and his colleagues:

The guy who was coaching us kept saying the same thing over and over to different people. He'd interview us on the screen and then play back the tape. He'd say, "When I asked you this question, you gave me a long answer! You should give me a much shorter answer! If I ask you whether the budget deficit is a good thing or a bad thing, you should not say, 'Well, it stimulates the economy but it passes on a burden.' You have to say, 'It's a great idea!' Or, 'It's a terrible idea!' It doesn't matter which."

The coach had the better idea of what TV wanted. Magnusson, who resisted, had a better idea of what a reporter should do. During tapings of *Crossfire,* producers are shouting constantly in the earphones of the hosts, "Cut him off!" "Interrupt!" This makes for lively talk TV. But the culture of artificial polarization and overstatement spills over into the rest of journalism. Ambitious reporters know that these traits are rewarded.

Another part of the talk show mix is *competitive glibness.* Each morning fax machines around Washington disgorge their copy of *Hotline,* an extremely influential digest of the latest political news. The Monday issue contains a digest of the hottest, cleverest TV sound bites from the previous weekend's shows. "Journalists all over Washington are checking out *Hotline* on Monday to see if their quote made it," Fred Wertheimer, who was president of Common Cause from 1981 through the spring of 1995, said shortly after he stepped down from that position, "It becomes natural to spend your time working on quotable quotes."

This may sound similar to the normally writerly work of polishing your prose, but it is fundamentally different from reporting. Reporting means going out and collecting new material, the very existence of which you may not have suspected before you went to look. Sound-biting means working through material that everyone else is aware of, until you can come up with a brief formulation that is cleverer than anyone else's. Why does it have to be material with which everyone else is already familiar? Because otherwise they won't recognize the elegance of your sound bite. A winning sound bite from June 1995 was this view of Newt Gingrich: "He's not terribly eager to serve as Speaker of the House under President Dole." Understanding the joke requires knowing about the jealousies between the men, the status of Dole's presidential campaign, and so on. Putting things this crisply is a skill—but it is a salon skill, not reportage.

One of a reporter's most important functions is assessment—finding out and understanding what has already happened. The talk shows instead stress prediction—what might conceivably happen when the next election rolls around. Often a clear enough understanding of what happened yesterday may indicate what is likely tomorrow, but the difference between these two activities, assessment and prediction, is always clear in the reporter's mind. He can, within the limits of his abilities and his craft, come close to the truth about past events. He can at best offer his informed speculation about future trends.

On talk shows the difference between assessment and prediction may still be recognized. But as with the old joke definition of an editor as "someone who separates the wheat from the chaff—and prints the chaff," the purpose of the distinction on talk shows is to separate assessment from prediction—and emphasize the predictions. With the barest possible pause to note the events of the previous week, the talk turns quickly to what these events mean for future power struggles, future votes in Congress, future candidates for the presidency.

In this field as in so many others, John McLaughlin was a surprisingly influential pioneer. He institutionalized the "predictions" segment of his show, in which each of his panelists would make either a joking or a serious prediction. It would be unsporting to go back and demonstrate, from the transcripts, that huge numbers of the predictions have been laughably wrong. It would be unfair, for example, to point out that the political experts on the show strongly believed that Henry Foster would be confirmed as surgeon general, that Bill Clinton would get a health-care bill enacted, that the Democrats would retain control of the House of Representatives in 1994. It would be unfair to criticize these lapses because no one is very good in predicting political events. It is fair to say, however, that the shows have shifted emphasis away from what journalists can do and should, to what they shouldn't and can't.

David Letterman's "Top Ten List" rests on the joke format of shoehorning every possible subject into the same ten-point structure. This is comedy, and it works. John McLaughlin (again!) changed political discussion by shoehorning every public issue into a "scale of 1 to 10" ranking, or an even simpler choice between Thumbs Up and Thumbs Down. The practice of boiling all judgment of politics into "good weeks" or "bad weeks" has the same effect.

Reporters have to do something like this function—but only something like it. They need to indicate proportions but not to fit everything onto a two-dimensional scale. On a scale of 1 to 10, how's the technology business? Thumbs Up or Thumbs Down on the importance of religion? "Had [McLaughlin's] show been around during the Second World War, his closing question would have been 'Who had a better week, Hitler or Stalin? I ask you first, Walter (the Lip Man) Lippmann.'" (This is James Wolcott in the *New Yorker*.)

One-to-ten judgment was not common in politics before the McLaughlin era; now it is commonplace. The sincerest testimony to its effects may be the "Conventional

Wisdom Watch" column in *Newsweek*. This feature, de-signed by Jonathan Alter and Mickey Kaus, was meant as a wicked parody of the ever flip-flopping conventional wis-dom, making fun of people for saying Thumbs Up about is-sues they had ridiculed with Thumbs Down the week before. The mocking intention is still there; but most of its readers miss out on the joke and take this as another indica-tion of who is up and down each week.

Reporters know about some things but not all things. They are confident about areas they have explored, precisely because they have explored them. They are reluctant to de-liver tirades on other subjects because they have some dim awareness of what they might not know.

Washington Week in Review was established to work on this premise. Panelists talked about fields they understood, as reporters, and were restrained about everything else.

The other talk shows, and increasingly *Washington Week* itself, have dropped that quaint concept of limited spheres of knowledge. There will be four or five issues on the table, drawn from the most newsworthy events of the week. All the guests are supposed to be equally "interesting" participants, which means they are each supposed to weigh in on each issue as it comes up. The UN's mission in Bosnia. The relia-bility of DNA testing, as used in the Simpson trial. The ef-fect of cuts in capital-gains taxes. What is brewing in the Russian leadership. The legal ramifications of the latest affir-mative action ruling. Whether some new virus is about to spring out of central Africa.

There may be reporters who have deep enough, broad enough experience to have expert views in all these fields. If such people exist, they are rare. What is clear is that the typ-ical panelist on a talk show has a grasp on at most one or two of the issues that come up each week. But to stay on the show, all of them must be "interesting" on all five subjects. What can they do?

Most choose from two approaches. They can bluff their way through it, sounding extra confident to mask the fact that they are working from the one rushed conversation they had that morning with the normal beat reporter who covers the Philippines or Lebanon or the FDA. This leads, for example, to forceful-sounding declamations about trends in Japanese politics by pundits who could not name three politicians in Japan.

Margaret Carlson of *Time,* a regular on *The Capital Gang* program, was quoted in the *Washington Post* as saying that she had a simple rule for success on TV: "The less you know about something, the better off you are." She added:

> What's good TV and what's thoughtful analysis are different. That's been conceded by most producers and bookers. They're not looking for the most learned person; they're looking for the person who can sound learned without confusing the matter with too much knowledge. I'm one of the people without too much knowledge. I'm perfect!

This quote expressed with admirable candor a reality that few people on talk shows acknowledged but many knew to be true. TV journalism has always depended on people who could make simplified points in a bright and peppy way, and the talk shows are a transmission belt bringing the values of TV into the world of print.

The classic illustration of the shows' rush to judgment, unencumbered by fact, was reported by Tom Rosenstiel, who worked for the *Los Angeles Times* during the Gulf War (and later went to *Newsweek).* In March 1993, less than two months into his term, Bill Clinton had to decide whether to order retaliatory raids against Iraq, to convince Saddam Hussein that the United States was serious about the "no fly" zones. As the raids were beginning, but before their results were at all clear, the president's national security advisor, Anthony Lake, and his deputy chief of staff, Mark Gearan, sat in the White House and turned on the TV. There they heard members of CNN's *The Capital Gang* offer Thumbs Up, Thumbs Down judgment on the political wisdom of the attack—whose results no one knew at that point. "We didn't know if those bombs had landed in Boston or Baghdad," Gearan said.

The other strategy for being "interesting" despite being ignorant is to reduce all questions to the one subject on which most Washington journalists are expert, which is the politics of the issue. Instead of talking about Bosnia, you can talk about whether Bob Dole will criticize Bill Clinton over Bosnia. Instead of talking about the real situation of Medicare, you can talk about whether the Republicans have gone too far in scaring old people about Medicare.

LIVING FOR THE SHOW. In theory, a reporter organizes his life around the subjects he has to explore. His schedule can be unpredictable day by day, because reporting can't always be confined to nine to five. It can be unpredictable week by week, since events change and you can't be bound by the long-scheduled board meeting or seminar discussion or lecture date. It can mean long spells on the road.

In this way, too, the reporter's life is at odds with that of the talk show aspirant. The shows will, after all, need to be taped every Friday or Saturday. If you're a regular, it goes without saying that you must be around. If you're hoping for a guest seat, you have to live your life in a way that makes you available.

"People don't talk about it openly," said Walter Shapiro, who has covered politics for *Time* and *Newsweek* and now *Esquire*. "But you can see people in the second tier, the ones who are candidates for the show but not regulars, thinking about how to write an essay or make a point in a way that would get them on the Brinkley show that Sunday. No one with a regular TV slot can go off and do a four-month reporting project. They can hardly afford to get out of sight of the Beltway."

"The people in this situation are the role models," Shapiro said. "And you see *all* the little compromises that these people and the ones who want to be like them have to make in order to maintain what they've got. There are times when I strongly suspect that someone is taking an approach or pushing an angle because it is more likely to get him on TV."

Everyone who works in the same news bureau with a talk show regular has a tale of the panelist scrambling through the office on Friday to do a crash study about Bosnia or immigration and work up some predictions and *bons mots.* Through the office partition colleagues hear the aspiring panelist say on the telephone, "You know, I'm only five minutes from your studio!" or hear them trying to sound bright and snappy during the "pre-interviews" that producers conduct while trying to determine which journalists to invite onto the panel each week.

"Eventually it becomes the driving force in your life," James Wooten said. "How you make decisions. What you write about. Where you go. Your schedule becomes a religious document—sorry, I can't do that, I'm in Minneapolis that day."

"The endless traveling and talking becomes a real distraction," Leonard Downie, Jr., executive editor of the *Washington Post,* has said. "I can think of a number of journalists, even including opinion journalists, whose TV appearances have become so extensive, and for whom it's so easy just to give opinions off the top of their heads, that it really has eroded what they do in print. They're no longer as good in print as they would have been if they didn't have this distraction and couldn't get all this money for saying the first thing that comes into their head without having to think hard."

Journalists who operate in this environment start to think of themselves as small businessmen, doing everything possible to exploit new markets and maximize their returns. The increasing bottom-line orientation of the publishing and broadcasting industries has pushed many journalists in this direction; the culture of "buckraking" pulls them the same way. The Roberts household, again, illustrates the pattern. Steven Roberts is a columnist for *U.S. News & World Report,* a regular on several talk shows, and a frequent speaker. Cokie Roberts works for NPR and ABC in addition to her speaking engagements. Yet in 1994 the two of them decided to explore a new market, with a jointly produced column. The promotional flyer from United Feature Syndicate, the column's distributor, described it this way:

> "People often ask us what it's like around our house at dinnertime," says Steve Roberts. "What do we talk about? Do we ever disagree?"

The column proposed to answer these questions, with "a down-to-earth discussion of today's issues from the Robertses' perspective as journalists, Washington insiders and also parents and working professionals."

> This column is a personal conversation with readers on topics including: kids in Chicago; altar girls; the balanced budget amendment; is the Republican party out of touch?; and the real Generation X.
>
> Cokie and Steve Roberts occasionally write about deeply personal topics, such as the balance of power in their relationship and the stress involved within a family. They even occasionally disagree in print. Whatever the issue, Cokie and Steve Roberts get right to the

heart of it to uncover what's really important to your readers.

THE BOX-SEAT VIEW. A reporter's purpose, and his privilege, is to view society from as many levels as possible. Among his goals is to let readers see more than they could with their own eyes.

The talk show pundit sees much less. There is no way to improve on James Wolcott's description of the phenomenon. *The Capital Gang* and similar shows, he said, present

> their regulars' own luxury-skybox view of American politics and society. . . . Assurance fluffs up their every pronouncement, because they have permanent thrones. There are no term limits on pundits. The breezy disdain they display for Bill Clinton is akin to the condescension that country club members have for the golf pro. Not having to answer to angry constituents, they make everything sound easy. They dispatch imaginary troops overseas as if snapping their fingers for a taxi. Welfare cuts? No problem. Slash government payrolls? Make it so. While they assail elected officials for pandering to special interests, their own speakers' fees are skyrocketing and those who call their ethics into question are dismissed by Novak as "little weenies" who are "jealous." (The dying words of a hack: "I did it for the honorarium.")

The Payoff

Only a tiny minority of journalists, nearly all based either in Washington or New York, can turn themselves into pundit profit centers in such a spectacular way. But the effect of their example is much greater than most people outside the business would imagine. In cities across the country, TV and radio counterparts to the national pundit talk shows have sprung up. They do not lead to speaking engagements in the same way that nationally broadcast shows do, but they further strengthen the idea that you have not really made it is as a journalist until you've won a seat on a TV show. When John Hersey was the envy of the reportorial world for the observations and controlled description in his book about the atomic bomb, *Hiroshima,* ambitious young people wanted to be known for their reporting and narration. When Theodore White was celebrated for *The Making of the President,* 1960, when Truman Capote was on the cover of all the major news magazines after publication of *In Cold Blood,* ambitious young people dreamed of finding their own ways to re-invent descriptive technique. War correspondents were celebrated in Vietnam; Woodward and Bernstein were celebrated because of Watergate; young people wanted to be like them.

Now TV pundits are the best-paid and best-known representatives of the journalist's craft. Their work makes it harder, rather than easier, to cope with the nation's problems, because of their relentless emphasis on discord, prediction, and political spin. And it undermines the entire process of journalism, by suggesting that it should be viewed as a sideshow, most successful when it draws gawkers into the tent.

"Journalists have always been disliked," Fred Wertheimer, the former president of Common Cause, said in 1995. "Dislike as a profession is not the problem. The danger is if you lose credibility. That is what is happening right now," Wertheimer added.

> If I look at it from the standpoint of a TV talk show producer, a "good journalist" is someone who has "energy." You hear this all the time, So and so "has energy," or doesn't have energy. It means someone who is

noisy, opinionated, conflictual—and there is little interest in whether you know what you are talking
about. If the arguments are clever it doesn't matter if
they are factual. You are looking for journalists who are
opinionated and who stick it to the other guy in a
clever way.

If I am an average Joe, what is a "journalist" to
me? It is somebody who shows up on TV a lot, yells
and shouts, gives me all his opinions, and makes sharp-
edged remarks. He is ideological and is attacking other
journalists.

If the people who do this are journalists, isn't it a
logical conclusion for me to believe that this is what
journalists are? That's all I see.

The whole punditry world on TV has done a very
serious job of eroding the concept of credible journalism in the public's mind.

Journalists will pay a price for this loss, but so will the
public. Journalism is not mere entertainment. It is the main
tool we have for keeping the world's events in perspective. It
is the main source of agreed-upon facts we can use in public
decisions. The excesses of journalism have been tolerated because no other institution can provide the benefits journalism can. Yet some of today's leading journalists find these
responsibilities too tedious or unprofitable to be worth their
while.

Chapter 4

Bad Attitude

Why do we need the news? It is tempting to say, We don't. The intrusion. The ups and downs. The relentless focus on what has gone wrong. Life would seem happier and indeed might go better without such a depressing background beat.

Yet there is some human hunger that even the most annoying news system feeds. If the annoying, elite press somehow vanished, and if all of us could, through the Internet or 500-channel TV, get exactly the information we wanted, we would still want some way to compare impressions, to put things in perspective, to ask other people, "What do you make of this?"

Journalism, that is, exists for reasons other than satisfying the desire of publishing companies and broadcast networks to make money, or the desire of reporters to find out the real story, or the desire of celebrity journalists to become famous and cash in. Its real purpose is to satisfy the general desire for information to have meaning. People want to know the details, but they also want to see what the details add up to. Journalism exists to answer questions like, "What is really going on?" and "Why is this happening?"

What the Media Should Do for Us

What we read in the papers and see or hear on TV and radio should provide context that gives meaning to information. Here are the elements essential to establishing context:

PERSPECTIVE. Half the battle in daily life is telling the differences between things that really matter and those that are distracting for the moment but will soon go away. Management consultant Stephen Covey, author of the book *The Seven Habits of Highly Effective People,* has made a fortune largely by emphasizing the difference between "important" tasks (saving for retirement, studying for a CPA exam a year from now) and merely "urgent" ones (preparing a memo for a meeting that starts in fifteen minutes).

Newspapers have an amazingly nuanced set of signals for conveying both the importance and the urgency of an event. Whether an article is on the front page, how big the headline type is, how often the subject appears in the paper—these and other signs convey perspective to the reader in an instantly understood code.

TV news, which might seem to offer more possibilities for shading importance, actually offers fewer. TV can of course handle fast-breaking news and offer wall-to-wall coverage of emergency events, as it first did with the assassination of John F. Kennedy and as CNN now does with each new emergency (for instance, its "Terror in the Heartland" coverage of the bombing in Oklahoma City in 1995). But in day-to-day coverage, events tend to run together on TV more than they do in print, since the main variation among the stories is how many seconds of airtime each gets. In broadcast you don't have the opportunity to scan the headlines and flip to the next page. Radio news has largely degenerated to the headlines-on-the-hour format prevalent at most AM and FM stations. The great exception in radio broadcasting is National Public Radio's news operation. With its two-hour *Morning Edition* program each morning and the two-hour *All Things Considered* each afternoon, it has much greater latitude to indicate the importance of stories by the amount of time it devotes to them.

What is important is different from what is urgent. What is important is often not what's new. What is important is often crowded out by what is most novel or attention-getting that day—Lorena Bobbitt, the latest flood or earthquake, a scandal involving a movie star. During the early summer of 1994, when the American press was giving big-story treatment to the nuclear bomb that the North Korean government may—or may not—have manufactured, it made possession of those one or two bombs seem an intolerable threat to world peace. Perhaps it was, but if so, there should have been a thousand times more concern about the thousands of warheads floating around in the remnants of the former Soviet empire. Nearly all are controlled by the military, but some are apparently in the hands of the gangsters who have become the new power of the old Soviet territories. Yet because the existence of those warheads was old news, attention was focused instead on the rumored Korean bomb.

For the national press, scandals have become the main obstacle to keeping news in perspective. Real and alleged scandals, involving figures from Bill Clinton to Michael Jackson, have come to serve as a distraction machine, systematically diverting attention to a spectacle whenever the political system threatens to deal with an important but dull-seeming question affecting the way people actually live.

In 1994, the country's leading newspapers published more than twice as many stories about the Whitewater case as about the Clinton health-care proposals. Whether they supported or opposed the Clinton plan, most editors would have agreed that what happened to that plan mattered far more to the country than did Whitewater. Taken at its worst interpretation, Whitewater involved the claim that a shady savings-and-loan operator had cut the Clinton family in on a land deal in exchange for lenient regulation of his S & L. Yet the mechanics of the news business led these editors to give more time and space to the scandal than to the plan. When the first hint of a scandal breaks, reporters and editors know there is far less risk in over-covering it than in playing it down. If they hype a "scandal" that later proves to be no big deal—like the alleged connection between Libyan paymasters and President Carter's brother Billy, in 1979—the reporters and editors themselves have lost very little. But if they overlook the early indications of what later turns into a bona fide scandal, they run the risk of going down in history as "the reporter who missed the next Watergate."

In the twenty-plus years since the Watergate hearings eclipsed virtually all other political activity in the news for several months, the journalistic establishment in Washington has been constantly primed for the excitement of another such blockbuster event. The Iran-Contra investigations, the confirmation fights over Robert Bork or Zoe Baird, the promise to "get to the bottom" of the Whitewater case through congressional hearings—each of these issues had some real importance, but they all produced an adrenaline surge that simply can't be matched by the mundane efforts to cut taxes or reform government that politicians are supposedly elected to carry out. More and more journalists accept the view that government can't solve all of the nation's problems and that "decentralization" and flexibility are keys to success in the modern age. Nonetheless, the Washington-based press corps absolutely loves it when the nation's attention is centered on the capital, as it seems to be when some big scandal, confirmation fight, or suspense-filled hearing is underway. It's fine to do homage to the role of state government when running profiles of Newt Gingrich and his plans for breaking up over-concentrated federal power. But not even the conservatives in the Washington press corps are eager to be covering what happens in Sacramento or Harrisburg. Nor, for that matter, in Little Rock. One reason the Whitewater and cattle-trade "scandals" erupted after Bill Clinton became president is that national-level journalists had had no interest in them when they merely concerned a governor.

A convenient way to think about this side of journalistic culture is to imagine a seventh-grade science class in which kids are trapped and realize that they are finally going to *have* to learn the difference between metamorphic and sedimentary rocks. Then someone looks out the window and sees a fight on the playground or two dogs tangled up. The room comes alive, and by the time the teacher can get control the bell has rung.

In just the same way, a "running story" or incipient scandal can make it hard for anyone in the Washington branch of the press to concentrate on anything else. When a scandal is breaking, talk show figures wring their hands about the "agony" of Watergate or Iran-Contra; but the truth is that journalists are happier at such moments than at any other time. The country's attention is turned to Washington. People hang on disclosures of the latest "inside" news. Life is energizing and sweet for Washington journalists, even if the scandal of the moment is a big wheel-spinning exercise for the country as a whole.

The Iran-Contra allegations had more intrinsic meaning than most other recent scandals that have preoccupied the press and government, but even this case illustrates the difficulty of keeping issues in perspective. For most of a year, the exploits of Oliver North, Fawn Hall, Elliot Abrams, and Robert McFarlane occupied most of the attention of much of the press. During that same year, the federal government went another $200 billion into debt. The crack cocaine epidemic got under way. The savings and loan industry was about to suck incalculable sums from the national treasury. The United States spent nearly a billion dollars a day on the military, and added a billion dollars a week to its trade deficit with Japan. If all the citizens, politicians, journalists, and scholars in the country were working together, they might not have been able to solve any of those problems in a year. But by spending the year goggling at Oliver North, they guaranteed that they could avoid dealing with the issues that really threatened the country.

In short, during times of scandal our media abandons the pretense of maintaining perspective, and in times without scandal it hopes for a scandal to come. The financial press does the same thing waiting for the next big takeover deal. The foreign affairs press does so waiting for the next big international disaster. All of them are too busy looking for what is "urgent" to do the daily chore of telling us what is important, and why.

PLACEMENT IN TIME. Very few events come entirely out of the blue, even if headlines about them do. Not one American in a million could have found Chechnya on a map before fighting broke out between Chechns and the Russian army late in 1994. But from the Chechns' point of view, the roots of the dispute lay at least fifty years in the past. Before World War II, Josef Stalin rounded up most of the men in the Caucasus mountain region now called Chechnya and shipped them off to Siberia, fearful that they would collaborate with the Nazis. Those who eventually made it back found that most of their land had been appropriated. To grasp what happened in 1995, it was necessary to know what had happened in 1945.

Similarly, during the first two months of the Clinton

administration, pundits detected a number of "fatal" or "crucial" missteps that were sure to destroy the administration. Less than two weeks after the new president was sworn in, Sam Donaldson of ABC said on a weekend talk show, "This week we can talk about, 'Is the presidency over?'" and R. W. Apple of the *New York Times* wrote that the administration "desperately" needed to recover from its "politically devastating failure" in the Zoe Baird case. Yet the history of the past dozen administrations, which most of the pundits had witnessed themselves, indicated that whatever turned out to be best, worst, and most significant about each president's performance rarely happened during the first year of his term.

News coverage should ideally do what was not done in coverage of the Chechn upheavals or of Bill Clinton's early struggles: help us place events in time, pointing out what is different from past episodes, what is the same, what is changeable and unchangeable at this point in history. It would show us the background of events, which otherwise seem to come from nowhere, and it would indicate the likely consequences tomorrow of choices that we make today.

Sometimes coverage does rise to the challenge and show us the background of issues and their future implications. For instance, when the Republican Congress was proposing a dramatic roll-back of environmental regulations early in 1995, an ABC-TV news team went to the Pacific Northwest to see the aftereffects of the "spotted owl" controversy of the early 1990s. Because of environmental regulations protecting the owl's habitat in Oregon and Washington, logging in those states had been restricted and some logging jobs had been lost. But the reporters found that this shock to the existing job base had forced Oregon, in particular, to rethink its economic future, with the result that it was moving toward a far more diversified and promising mix of businesses. This report did not prove that the regulations were wise, but it did indicate what some of their long-term effects might be.

This is not how our press usually behaves. "I think of today's reporters as 'stenographers with amnesia,'" one of President Clinton's media assistants said in June 1993. "You really see this in the extreme up-and-down cycles of opinion in the press, with no reference to what they were saying the day before. In February, the communications staff—George Stephanopoulos and Mark Gearan—were 'geniuses' with 'youthful vigor.' Now these same people are callow, arrogant, inefficient, and the source of all that's wrong."

Too often the up-and-down tendencies of the mainstream media pluck many events wholly out of their timeline. They appear without explanation and disappear without resolution.

At the end of 1994, American readers suddenly learned about a crisis in Mexico. Guerrilla armies were prowling through the southern state of Chiapas. These armies were acting in the name of poor, mainly Indian farmers and against the U.S.-trained technocrats in Mexico City who had enacted a series of economic "reforms" that, while arguably good for the country as a whole, had squeezed many Indian farmers off the land. All of these issues had been in gestation for a long time. The plight of Indians in Mexico was not just decades but centuries old. The economic policy changes, whose capstone was the NAFTA agreement with Canada and the United States, had been under way since the late 1980s and had been hotly debated in Mexico throughout that time. But news of this dissent made its way into U.S. consciousness only when fighting began—to vanish again as the rebels were contained.

In the course of a year a parade of miserable people flashes briefly across the television screens. First we have the suffering Rwandans, then the suffering Bengalis in a flood, then the suffering people of Gorazde or Sarajevo, then the suffering Haitians and suffering Cubans penned up in Guantánamo, then the suffering people of Zaire perishing from the Ebola virus, then the suffering Sarajevans once again.

The suffering of each group is noteworthy, but on TV they become stock players in a drama whose real stars are the familiar disaster-correspondents. Christiane Amanpour of CNN is in one nightmare zone after another. This week's crop of victims fills out the set behind her as she describes their misery. Then they disappear and the next group takes their place. It is to Amanpour's credit as a reporter and a human being that she keeps going to witness these scenes. (Mike Wallace asked Amanpour, during a *60 Minutes* segment about her career, whether she had considered "moving up to the big leagues"—network news and perhaps even an anchor slot. Amanpour retorted that she already was in the big leagues, because she was able actually to see stories as they unfolded.) Yet regardless of her personal qualities, most of these tragedies show up on CNN with as little history and as little follow-up as the victims of a tornado or car wreck.

Larry Martz, a veteran reporter for *Newsweek*, pointed out in 1995 that most U.S. news operations had, because of cost pressure, shrunk their overseas reportorial staff. He said,

> Our remaining correspondents fly from earthquake to famine, from insurrection to massacre. They land running, as we were all taught to do, and they provide surprisingly good coverage of whatever is immediately going on . . . [But] we miss anticipation, thought, and meaning. Our global coverage has become a comic book: ZAP! POW! BANG-BANG!

So too has our local news coverage, in which tonight's victims of a drug bust or a drive-by shooting appear with no history, and are replaced tomorrow.

SIMILARITIES AND DIFFERENCES. Many events are important precisely because they fit a pattern. They have a meaning together that no one of them has on its own. The structural problems of Latin American economies have certain deep similarities—big landholding estates, a tradition of corruption in public service, huge gaps between rich and poor. Understanding the predicament of any one of the countries is easier with the others in view. The Chinese-dominated communities of Southeast Asia have certain similarities whether they are located in Taiwan, or Thailand, or Shanghai, or Singapore. The settled, old democracies of Western Europe have certain common problems dealing with unemployment and the costs of a welfare state.

An ability to see connections is what lets us form dots into patterns and separate signals from noise. Pattern recognition is one of a handful of areas in which the most powerful computers cannot compete with the least-talented human being. Any person can at a glance tell a truck from a jeep from a cow. Programming a computer to do so is an enormous challenge.

One reason this task is so hard is that pattern recognition means seeing differences as well as similarities. Brazil and Argentina are both "Latin economies," but Brazil has five times as much land and twenty times as many people. Taiwan and South Korea are both "little tigers" or "little dragons" in Asia, with export-based industries and high savings rates and highly disciplined students. Yet their politics, their economic structure, and their cultural backgrounds are so different that generalizations based on one experience may make no sense for the other. What are now the Czech and Slovak republics have so long been identified as a unit that most Americans still reflexively say "Czechoslovakia." But the experiences of each part of the country under communism were so different that now, in the post-communist era, they are heading in opposite directions. The Czech provinces had been rich before the communist era and became poorer during it. The Slovak story was the reverse. Now the Slovaks look wistfully back on the comparative wealth of the Brezhnev era while the Czechs view it as a blight to be overcome.

Because pattern recognition is so hard, no one can always be good at it. But this is one area in which American news coverage is improving. American readers have learned over the last decade that many countries in East Asia have similar economic systems; that many schools throughout this country face similar problems; that many U.S. presidents, regardless of party, face similar bureaucratic obstacles to getting their jobs done.

Granted, there are a thousand ways in which newspapers and TV could distinguish similarities and differences more skillfully. Half the news we read suggests that all "people of color" share an experience that is fundamentally similar, and also fundamentally different from that of all whites. The other half of the news dwells on the deep differences that separate African Americans from Asian Americans from Arab Americans from Latino Americans, as well as the many caste and cultural splits within each group. Half the news out of Japan suggests that it is an unfathomably exotic culture, where the students kill themselves if they fail their entrance exams and people work fanatically for the good of the state. The other half of the coverage suggests that Japan's government, businesses, and economies work by principles identical to those in America and therefore will respond to currency changes, election results, stock market trends, and so on, exactly as Western institutions would.

In these and other areas the press could do a better job of blending and synthesizing conflicting evidence. But if there is a place to declare victory or at least progress in media coverage, "pattern recognition" is it.

USEFULNESS. Journalists resist the idea of reports that are consciously "civic minded," since this calls up pictures of peppy, "feel good" stories that the city fathers like. But for journalism to matter it must be useful in one particular way. It must give people the sense that life is not just a sequence of random occurrences. That is how a cat or a horse sees the world. For a cat, everything happens by surprise and then ends without consequence. Useful information helps people understand what can be changed and what must be endured.

Useful information can be alarming—letting people know how much money is being wasted or what forms of cruelty or hatred are developing. It can be encouraging, about schools that are succeeding or problems that have resolved themselves. In either case it gives people the tools they need to feel in control of their circumstances rather than the reverse.

It may sound small-minded to say that the news should finally be "useful," but the truth is that people will not keep buying newspapers or watching network broadcasts unless the information expands their command over life in some way. Not all news has to be "news you can use," with recipes and investment tips and guides to fixing your car. But journalism, by definition, asks people to pay attention to things outside themselves, and that involvement will be worthwhile only if it helps people understand, cope with, and at times even control events that will affect them.

This, unfortunately, is the press's area of most grievous failure. The message of today's news coverage is often that the world cannot be understood, shaped, or controlled, but merely endured or held at arm's length. The foreign news is mainly a series of unexplained and unconnected disasters. Most of these flit in and out of the news so quickly that we learn mainly to ignore them, in full confidence that they will soon go away—Liberia, Zaire, Sudan. A handful of others become interesting in a narrow, narcissistic way, as tests of an American president's "resolve" and "will to act"—tyrants in Haiti, invaders in Kuwait, nuclear strategists in North Korea.

Americans seeing the outside world on TV could be forgiven for believing that all countries fall into two categories: those that are so messed up we shouldn't waste time thinking about them, and those that are messed up in a way that threatens our security or moral sensibility, so we should invade them, withdraw quickly, and forget about them again.

One inch beneath its surface, most domestic news carries a similar despairing message. The politicians may not all be crooks in an indictable sense, but they scheme endlessly for advantage and talk about abortion, foreign policy, and tax reform only as it serves their ends for gaining power. How do we know this? Because that is what the political news tells us day after day. Bill Clinton is supporting the B-2 bomber to win votes in California. Bob Dole is backing off his attacks on Medicare to keep the support of the AARP. After years of hearing such interpretations of political tactics, citizens are prepared to be disappointed by each new crop of incumbents.

Economic news is typically presented in a way that makes people feel that they are helpless in the face of large-scale trends and that they are always getting cheated by somebody. From 1991 through 1994, the price of gasoline in America fell to its lowest level ever, when adjusted for inflation. Gas at around $1.20 a gallon in the early 1990s was cheaper, in real terms, than gas at around 30 cents a gallon in the early 1960s. This decline received very little attention in the news. In 1995 the price moved up again, to a level that was still low in historic terms but 10 to 15 percent higher than the year before. The network news was all over this price increase. In the summer of 1995, *NBC Nightly News* ran a report that flashed shots of price listings at thirty-three gas stations across the country. At the time, the average U.S. price per gallon was $1.24. The report showed prices ranging up to $1.80, and 30 of the 33 prices it showed were above the national average for that week. A fatalistic, protect-what-I've-got mentality is increased by reports making people feel more beleaguered than they should.

Local TV news has for the last decade operated under marketing consultants who preach: "If it bleeds, it leads." The broadcasts invariably begin with the rape or car crash or shooting or fire of the day. Since even small towns may suffer at least one of these mishaps per day, every TV market can get the impression that life has turned into a *Blade Runner*-ish hell.

Journalists are taught the pat theory that since "news" means events out of the ordinary, all the nondisastrous things that happen each day are not their business to report. Within limits this is true—a shooting at a school is news, the absence of a shooting is not. But if an awareness of the parts of life that go right is not built into an enumeration of what is going wrong, the news becomes fundamentally useless, in that it teaches us all to despair. Since at least the time of Betty Friedan, advocacy groups of every sort have warned about the harm done by negative messages. Negative symbols can demean women. (*Hustler* magazine, unachievably thin models like Kate Moss.) They can demean racial minorities. (Aunt Jemima, Willie Horton, The Frito Bandito.) They can demean ethnic groups on the world stage (cartoon depictions of "sleazy" Arab oil tycoons, "cosmopolitan bankers," the "devious" Japanese). Sensitivity about such slights can go too far, but it is based on something real.

How much worse is the potential damage when the repeated slights involve *our whole society*—its connection to the world, its system of self-government, the communities in which its people live? We have a system of news that tells people constantly that the world is out of control, that they will always be governed by crooks, that their fellow citizens are about to kill them.

So why does the media fall so short so often? The answer lies with habits and attitudes that today's press has fallen into:

Looking Where the Light Is: News That Is Easy, Convenient, and Cheap

The rule for lawyers examining a witness in the courtroom is that they must never ask a question whose answer they do not know. The rule for reporters should be something like the reverse. You must sometimes ask questions whose answers you think you know, so as to confirm what you have heard and to compare answers from several sources. But the main work of reporting involves asking questions whose answers you don't know, simultaneously exposing your ignorance but opening up the possibility of learning something new.

Homer Bigart, a renowned reporter for the *New York Times* who was the grand old man of the American press corps in Vietnam, used to tell younger reporters that their first task was to drop the assumption that they understood a story before they reported it. This approach to reporting is harder than it sounds. It is hard psychologically, since it means always working from a disadvantage and posing naive-seeming questions to experts who may not be tolerant of your ignorance. It is hard financially, since it means exploring leads and possibilities with no certainty that they will pay off. It is hard logistically, since it means leaving the desk and your usual list of telephone contacts to meet new people and develop new networks of information. It becomes harder in all ways as reporters get older, because it means breaking away from the familiar precincts where the reporter's name means something to the people he calls. On any given beat, a reporter can, as the years go on, become a very big fish within a limited pond. On a new beat, you have to spell your name and explain whom you work for. You hope rather than expect that your call will be returned. If you're traveling, you spend hours sitting in the hotel room waiting for your calls to be returned. On your regular beat, however, you give your name and hear the surge of recognition from the other end of the telephone line. "Oh, I know the commissioner would like to talk with you, let me get her out of this meeting." The most useful and effective reporters are those who, when well past their hungry and flexible first years in the business, keep exposing themselves to this shock—which is the only way they can have the chance of learning something new.

Famous TV journalists never have to explain who they are, and even print reporters can avoid it as long as they are willing to stick to their comfortable routines of subjects and sources. Many journalists are all too willing to do that. The result is a pattern of news coverage reminiscent of the timeless joke about the drunk who is looking for his lost keys underneath a streetlight. Did you lose them here? a policeman asks as he sees the drunk. No, the drunk says; I lost them over on the next block, but the light is better here. Much of what is in our news is there because journalists are looking where the light is. Coverage that is easy, cheap, and convenient for the news business drives out anything else.

Why does disaster footage make up such a disproportionate share of TV news? Train wrecks, floods, building collapses on the other side of the world, the tornados and hurricanes that predictably rip through mobile home parks. Why is it so easy to get events like these onto the network news, and so hard to get more than ninety seconds to examine a political or economic problem of much greater importance? The obvious reason is that disasters are interesting to look at. But covering disasters is also easy and cheap. You send out a crew, you point the camera at whatever has blown up, and the story tells itself.

In a slightly different way the nightly "standups" from TV correspondents outside the White House or Capitol are also there because they're easy. Unlike footage of floods and tornados, this kind of TV coverage can't be explained away through the excuse that people really want to see it. They don't. Market forces explain the rise of tabloid subjects in the evening news—people love celebrities, violence, and sex—but they can't explain the habits of the journalists who shape national news coverage.

The White House correspondent sits in the pressroom all day, he works the phones and listens to the briefings, and he steps outside to tell what he saw. The work can involve long hours and tiring travel and even the physical strength to push your way to the front of the pack of reporters and yell your question at the president as he walks by. Yes, correspondents can feel they are about to go crazy when they are holed up in the motel at Thurmont, near Camp David, in case the president decides to do anything newsworthy. "And presidential travel!" said Michael Putzel of the *Boston Globe,* who was a White House correspondent for the Associated Press. "Whenever he moves, from his own office to the East Room, or to Europe, it puts the press in a position that grownups do not like to be in. You're herded like cattle, you're penned up behind ropes, you're required to wear what we called our 'jewelry,' the press IDs branding you as someone who has to be kept behind ropes. It is not very dignified. On overseas trips, especially, the crowds are so unwieldy that they want to have you in position literally hours in advance. You can be waiting in the freezing cold for hours. You are there just in case anything is said at the photo op."

In all these ways, and others, the job is hard. It has become even more demoralizing since the first years of the Reagan administration, when more and more of the executive office complex was placed off-limits to reporters and it became impossible to wander down the hall and ask officials what was new. Most White House employees actually have offices in the Old Executive Office Building, a huge, ornate, high-ceilinged palace that sits across an alley from the White House and which a century ago housed the entire departments of State and War. Many of the presidential assistants who work in the OEOB, as it is called (sometimes "Old EOB"), suffer smoldering, low-level discontent about not having one of the handful of offices in the cramped West Wing of the White House itself. They are therefore more grateful for a reporter's attention than, say, the White House press secretary is. Until the Reagan era, reporters could make an appointment to see one person in the OEOB—and then spend the rest of the day going door to door looking for people who would talk with them.

Those days are past, and at the OEOB (as at the Pentagon, the CIA, and many other government installations) reporters are ushered into the building for one appointment and then escorted back out to the main door. Still, correspondents who trade war stories about these hardships often skip past the fact (which Putzel himself emphasizes) that the heart of the job, as defined by most publications, is depressingly easy. If you have the stamina to stick close to the president, you can just summarize whatever he says or does that day.

Why is so much of the news, in print and broadcast alike, about the operational strategy of politics rather than the substance of issues? In part it's because most reporters like the gamesmanship of politics, but that in turn means that the easiest subject for them to discuss is political tactics. Saying whether a new Medicare proposal makes sense or not requires learning something about budgets and health care. Saying whether it helps or hurts Bob Dole can be done off the top of the head. "Rather than putting themselves in circumstances that stretch their experience and views, political journalists find things to talk about that fit what they already know," says Charles Peters of the *Washington Monthly.* "You see this all the time on the talk shows. A subject will come up and instantly it's, 'Well, what will Newt Gingrich say about this?' This approach absolutely minimizes the amount of reporting you have to do outside your own area of expertise—the straight politics of everything. It is *amazing* how rarely the most famous journalists do reporting that plunges them into the middle of new circumstances." It is at least as amazing to see how much political "reporting" is the equivalent of water cooler conversations, in which reporters gather in the corridor after a congressional briefing, or on the press bus after a campaign speech, or in their cubicles after a White House press briefing, and ask each other, "How do you think they're handling this?" or "So, what's your take on it?"

Why, in coverage of politics, do we read so much more about political consultants—the Democrats' James Carville, the Republicans' Frank Luntz—than we ever did before? The main reason is that they have played a larger role in campaign management with each passing year. But it is also true that dealing with the consultants is easy for reporters.

A generation ago, the sign of a crack political reporter was that he knew more county political chairmen than anyone else did. This was how David Broder and Jack Germond got their start. Now the sharpest political reporters are the ones who spend most of their time listening to the handful of hot consultants. Except for police-beat reporters, the people who wrote about politics in the old days prided themselves on having more firsthand contact with the gritty realities of life than anyone else in the news business. Now the consultants realize that their essential job is spending time with reporters, "spinning" the candidate's line (and, not incidentally, getting their own names in print as "savvy" and successful campaign strategists). And reporters can avoid flying to Cuyahoga County and meeting the Democratic officials, if, instead, at a pleasant lunch they can download James Carville's theories of how the Rust Belt will vote. One of the basic litmus tests for whether you're doing a good job as a reporter is to calculate how much of your time you spend interviewing people whose *job* is dealing with the press. The higher the proportion, the easier your daily work is but the less you're likely to learn. Today's consultant-oriented campaign coverage is therefore easier for the reporters but less enlightening for the readers.

Why did so many reporters become computer enthusiasts in the late 1980s, after scoffing at the technology earlier and saying they wouldn't abandon their trusty Underwoods? The main reason, of course, is that computers make it so much more efficient to compose, revise, and transmit their stories. But in the age of Nexis—the age of vast stores of information available over the computer line—computers have also been the key to an easier style of reporting than ever before. With a fax machine, a telephone, and a computer line into Nexis, reporters can attempt to cover any kind of story without leaving their chairs. Nexis is a database of nearly everything published or broadcast over the last fifteen years. In a minute or two on Nexis you can find out whether a politician contradicted today's position five years ago, or what supporters and foes of education reform felt about experimental schools in Chicago, or what the newspapers in Singapore are saying about crime in the United States.

There is of course a place for this kind of data-trawl. When it was done, more slowly and clumsily, with papers or microfilm in a library it was called "research." The danger of a data-central approach is precisely that it is too fast and easy. You can collect the pro-and-con quotes—about experimental schools or for-profit hospitals or emerging businesses—without having any firsthand sense of what you are writing about. You are limited by the things other people have noticed and written and are cut off from the reporter's main asset: his confidence in what he has directly observed.

Time and *Newsweek* have for years applied a strange division of labor, in which reporters—low people on the totem pole—do the interviewing and research for the story, and more highly esteemed writers in New York work it over into newsmagazine prose. "There's a secret to this," one man who has been both a reporter and writer at a newsmagazine said. "This kind of formulaic writing is *so much easier* than the reporting."

> When I write articles I also have reported, I know how hard it is to get the nuance right. It's so much easier to write from other people's reporting. You simply care less if it's accurate. And while the best pieces, in a deep sense, are ones in which you're writing from your own reporting, it is much easier to write 'well' in the sense of superficial style when you're not wrestling with the shadings and complications you've seen through reporting. The pieces I've written that fit most smoothly into the newsmagazine style are the ones I didn't report.

The temptation of the Nexis age is for all journalists to write stories they didn't report. That, in turn, reduces the chances that reporters will ever discover things they didn't know they were looking for. "Every reporter everywhere in the country, as long as he had a laptop computer with a modem, could download the conventional wisdom at 8 A.M. for the day in the most incredible microdetail," Michael Kinsley said of the 1988 presidential campaign, the first one of the Nexis age. "There was no chance that anyone would react independently to the day's events."

In Over Our Heads: Journalists Without the Right Tools

The glory of American society is its flexibility. People take on new roles. Ethnic and occupational groups rise and fall. The other side of this constant mobility has been a greater anxiety in America than in most other societies. If every position is open, then no position is truly secure.

Modern journalism has taken advantage of but has also been affected by this American possibility for shifts in status. Journalism is not a "profession," like law or engineering, since true professional status requires fixed standards for admission and mastery over a specialized field of knowledge. Yet many of its members are now paid as professionals are.

Journalists are not required to have any systematic training in history, the liberal arts, natural sciences, or sociological and economic analysis. Yet they have largely displaced the scholars with such training from the role of "public explainers," who put in context the events of the day.

Journalists are not accountable politically, yet as the rise of talk shows makes clear they have taken more and more of the quasi-political power of judging proposals and setting a tone for political action. The press has always had some of this role, but the distinction between what a congressman can recommend and what a journalist can is eroded when they sit alongside each other trading ideas on *The Capital Gang* or *Crossfire*.

In short, today's journalism has reached a strange twilight zone of status. The media establishment holds many of the powers once reserved to other groups, but it is not bound by the limits, responsibilities, or rules by which those groups are constrained. This can make it more attractive than ever before to be a journalist, and some people have exactly the mixture of talent and training to thrive in this setting. But not everyone does, and some of the media's excesses result from operating in a realm for which it is not really equipped.

For example, during the generation just after World War II, people with a strong connection to academic life played the role of "village explainer" in America (to use Nicholas Lemann's term). Events need to be put in context. As the war ended Americans were debating what their new world role meant; how they could reabsorb the returning GIs; what threats and possibilities the Atomic Age held; how long the old order of segregation would persist; to what purposes America's productive bounty would be put. On these and many other subjects the "village explainers"— largely academics or writers with ties to universities—took the lead.

Vannevar Bush, who had been president of MIT before directing the government's Office of Scientific Research and Development during the war, published a widely discussed article just as the war ended, about the need for continued investment in high technology. (The article, "As We May Think," appeared in the *Atlantic Monthly* in July 1945 and offered an amazingly prescient view of the effect of science on the world economy and of computers on daily life.) James Bryant Conant, the president of Harvard, wrote articles and gave speeches about the need to change American schools. Scholars like Arthur Schlesinger, Sr., Richard Hofstadter, Henry Steele Commager, C. Vann Woodward, and many others, along with scholarly journalists like Bernard deVoto, wrote narrative accounts of American history that were meant to hold the interest not just of specialists but of the general public. Social scientists tried to address broad political and cultural issues, as David Riesman did in his influential book *The Lonely Crowd.* Literary critics like Alfred Kazin and Lionel Trilling taught in universities but wrote articles for readers outside their narrow discipline. And so on.

This tradition is not entirely gone. Stephen Jay Gould,

a paleontologist at Harvard, writes best-sellers popularizing science. Daniel Patrick Moynihan, onetime Harvard and MIT professor, is now in the U.S. Senate. Historians like Simon Schama and Paul Kennedy, and social scientists like James Q. Wilson and Nathan Glazer write books aimed at a general audience. The *New York Review of Books* is full of academics addressing public issues. But many scholars have backed out of the public arena, going more and more deeply into subjects of less and less interest to anyone outside their field.

This is the gap that journalists have attempted to fill, helping readers understand what current trends mean. Garry Wills, who was trained in the classics, writes as a historian-journalist and is well suited to this challenge. The average talk show panelist or newsmagazine writer is not—but is under tremendous pressure to try. On tort reform, on the history of the Balkan states, on the merits of various health-financing plans, commentators are constantly having to take positions on subjects they do not really know about in depth.

This helps explain the tremendous susceptibility of today's opinion-journalism to Big Ideas that sweep through public debate, without the buffers and second thoughts that scholars might apply. During the last fifteen years a number of such ideas have captivated columnists, talk show panelists, and newsmagazine writers, so that they have first been overhyped and then dismissed or dropped.

In the first few months of the Gingrich era, two big ideas were clearly still in the up part of the cycle: that we would soon all live in "cyberspace," and that great big institutions had, like dinosaurs, outlived their moment on earth.

There was something to each of these ideas—computer communications are changing life, much as the telephone, car, and airplane did; for some purposes big institutions have become too cumbersome and unresponsive to do the job.

But scholars would point out the "Hey, wait a minute" factor in each of these trends. "Cyberspace" affects only some people and still is in a gimmicky phase. Relying on big institutions may be a bad way to run elementary schools, but much of the modern world's work will inevitably be done by large, complex organizations—running a telephone system, building jet airplanes or submarines, getting Social Security checks out on time, launching Operation Desert Storm. Therefore, understanding how these institutions work, and improving them, should be as much a part of a "futurist" agenda as Gingrich's emphasis on tiny, decentralized units everywhere. But the writers who celebrated Gingrich for the originality of his thinking (often while criticizing his views as "extreme" or "cruel") applied very little of this common-sense skepticism. They touted ideas which a year or two from now they will surely ridicule.

The worst effect of this cycle is to trivialize issues before they have a chance to be developed, tested, and explored. An idea becomes faddish, it is featured in newsmagazines and TV segments, and then it becomes passé—without ever having passed through the stage of serious attention. The "culture of poverty" was an attractive concept in the 1950s and again in the 1980s, as a way of explaining why poor people stayed poor. It was used as a debating point on talk shows and as the theme for newsmagazine cover stories and columns. But before the political system could focus on what the idea really meant, and what implications the idea held for our school and welfare systems, the idea already seemed "tired" and "behind the curve" to editors and commentators. Who could stand to write about this subject again?

Newsweek has gone further than other mainstream publications in detecting and publicizing hot new ideas, and has also discarded them faster. It ran a major story on the vast implications of Prozac—and then a major story on how

Prozac had been overhyped. In 1995 it took up a potentially important but debatable concept: that America was spawning an "overclass" of highly educated people who were insulating themselves from the crime-ridden downtowns and mediocre schools with which most Americans had to cope. This idea, in various forms, had been propounded by various thinkers for more than a decade—but *Newsweek* handled it by drawing up its "Overclass 100" list. This was a roster of assorted "achievers" which immediately distracted attention from the concept itself. The magazine's editors—and their competitors at *Time* and *U.S. News & World Report*—could tell themselves, *"That* story has been covered" and move on to something else. All they had really done is use up the novelty of the concept without helping readers understand what it might mean.

The up-and-down cycle of Big Ideas has accelerated since the 1970s, mainly because newsmagazines and TV pundits have put themselves more and more squarely in the business of identifying and inevitably hyping trends. During the last two decades, "policy entrepreneurs" with sweeping ideas have sold them, briefly, to an eager press. At the end of the Cold War, the world was said to be flowering with hundreds of new democracies. A year or two later, the world was degenerating into hideous ethnic feuds. At the end of the 1980s, Americans were (the magazines and columnists told us) disgusted by financial excess and greed and ready for a more communal, sharing culture. Midway into the 1990s (the same analysts tell us) Americans live in cocoons, won't tax themselves to pay for schools, and can't come close to saving enough for their retirement years. One year later, Americans are becoming body-conscious and exercise-mad. A year later, they're fatter than ever before. They're going to church in record numbers. Traditional values and the family are falling apart. Judging by what media pundits say, whoever wins each presidential campaign has a remarkably in-

sightful view of what the country needs. Moral probity combined with engineerlike sternness in the case of Jimmy
Carter; bubbling optimism, for Ronald Reagan; the mastery
of world affairs suited for a new world order, in the case of
Bush; a connection to average people and the bounce of a
new generation, for Bill Clinton. A few months later, the de-
fect in each of these visions is laughably obvious to the same
columnists.

Each repetition of this cycle deadens the reader, who
suspects while hearing about any new trend that the exact
opposite will soon be declared true. They have seen the magazines and TV broadcasts cry either "Eureka!" or "Wolf!"
about new trends before. The cycle has also created a market
for the distinct class of "policy entrepreneurs" or "policy
hustlers" who work out of Washington's think tanks and are
forever presenting new "trends" to journalists at briefings
and in research papers. The think tanks—Cato, Heritage,
the American Enterprise Institute, the Progressive Policy
Institute, and so on—present themselves as being quasi-
academic. They are actually bridge groups that blend the
functions of academics, journalists, and lobbyists. Their spe-
cialty is packaging research in a form that fits a columnist's
or commentator's need—and that uses a veneer of scholarship to dress up arguments advancing their political agenda.

For example, during the debates over GATT, NAFTA,
and possible trade sanctions against Japan, the Washington
think tanks turned out studies using the cautionary example
of the Smoot-Hawley tariff. That tariff, passed by the U.S.
Congress in 1930, intensified the effects of the 1929 stock
market crash and helped bring on the worldwide Great Depression. The historical lesson was obvious, these studies implied: even to talk about tariffs was to risk bringing on
another economic Dark Age. By contrast, when academic
economists discuss the pluses and minuses of free trade policies, they rarely bring the Smoot-Hawley Tariff into the dis-

cussion, since every aspect of world trade now is so different that comparisons to Smoot-Hawley are as inapplicable as speculation about the rise of another Napoleon in Europe. (Vice president Gore, unfortunately, took the think tank route by holding up a picture of Messrs. Smoot and Hawley during his televised debate with Ross Perot about NAFTA. He knew the media well enough to understand that this would be taken as a sign of erudition.)

Something similar happened during the brief "democratic spring" in China in 1989. As demonstrators crowded into Tiananmen Square in Beijing, circling around something that looked like the Statue of Liberty, conservative think tanks held forums announcing the inevitable worldwide spread of democracy. Many journalists picked up the theme, which fit the big idea of that moment: the "end of history" and the inevitable spread of Western-style individual rights. "We all, to one degree or another, got sucked in by the prospect that these were the 1980s version . . . the Oriental version of the Concord Bridge," Tom Brokaw said, in explaining the rush to declare China democratized. Very few university-based China scholars were declaring such a sweeping victory for democracy at that time; but it was journalists who were the main explainers of this and many other phenomena, and they went with what they had.

Amortizing Investments: How the Star System Distorts News Coverage

Professional sports teams invest heavily in stars straight out of college and free agents with a number of good years behind them. These investments might more precisely be called "bets," because the most expensive prospects often don't pay off. The Heisman Trophy winner suffers a career-ending injury or proves not to be quite big enough for the pros. The costly free agent coming off five straight All-Star seasons turns out to have no oomph left for a sixth. Since the teams must play to win, they reluctantly swallow the costs, bench whoever is not performing, and field the team that can do best at the time.

Modern journalism also has its free agents and bonus babies, whose contracts affect the way the news is told. But most of journalism lacks the ruthless clarity of win/loss records, batting averages, and points-per-game figures like those in sports. Every news medium has its ad-sales figures and circulation totals to worry about, but only in network TV news is the link between a single performer and overall ratings clear enough to affect the performer's career. Thus in 1995 CBS "benched" Connie Chung, despite her multimillion-dollar free agent contract to coanchor the evening news with Dan Rather, because they were falling behind their rivals in the league.

More typically in print journalism, the free agents are not benched because no one can really prove whether they are performing. Instead they are played—which becomes a problem, since the judgment of what news to cover is complicated by concerns about how to keep the star in the lineup.

How does this affect the news? It works through the phenomenon of the "Bigfoot" at newspapers and especially newsmagazines. The Bigfoot is the star columnist or writer who is paid more than most normal reporters and is happiest when writing about the main story of each week.

There is a well-understood hierarchy of Bigfeet. The biggest of all are the network news anchors—Brokaw, Rather, Jennings—who take over a story when they fly to a riot scene in Los Angeles or a flood site in the Midwest or a summit meeting in Europe and anchor the news broadcast from there. Next biggest are the famous political reporters—David Broder of the *Washington Post,* R. W. Apple of the *New York Times,* the syndicated columnist Jack Germond—who weigh in from Manchester during the New Hampshire primary and from the political conventions when they occur. Next on the scale are the star columnists for the newsmagazines—for instance, Michael Kramer of *Time* or Joe Klein and Jonathan Alter of *Newsweek*—who increasingly are deployed to write about the hottest story of each week. This makes coverage of that one story more interesting but also contributes to the week-by-week jerkiness of newsmagazines as they turn from one subject to another. Next on the Bigfoot chain are the best-known correspondents for any newspaper or broadcast network.

Although there are many individual exceptions, especially at the newsmagazines, the expertise of the typical Bigfoot is pure politics—the way a new proposal will "play" in the Congress, how it will help or hurt the contenders in the next presidential race. The hotter any given issue becomes—tax cuts, immigration, engagement in Haiti or Bosnia or Somalia—the more eager the Bigfoot will be to have a say on it that week. The editors are usually eager to humor him— because of the chummy atmosphere for journalistic big shots, because of the fixed cost of his salary, because they think that readers are looking for his work.

While most of the star correspondents have earned their prominence through diligence and past achievements, the Bigfoot system as a whole discourages other reporters and subtly twists the news. The natural enemy of the Bigfoot is the "beat reporter"—the regular correspondent who covers an agency or a region of the country. Beat reporters have their own vulnerabilities, especially a constant danger of being "captured by," or overly friendly with, the people they cover day in and day out. Their corresponding strength is that they understand the issues they are writing about in a way the visiting Bigfoot cannot. As one newsmagazine beat reporter put it:

Immigration, "unfunded mandates," medical reform—the people who cover it know about this stuff. They have been writing about it for years. But you can't get it into the magazine until Newt Gingrich starts talking about it. And when he does, who do they bring in to write about it?

The answer, he said, was one of his magazine's political Bigfeet.

A beat reporter knows where the weak spots in these new ideas are. The Bigfoot has no idea. So naturally he reverts to what he does know and feels comfortable with, which is the politics in Congress. He can call four or five sources on the Hill and then he's ready to say, "Here's how it's going to play in Congress." And that is what we get about every story that comes up, even though our own magazine contains lots of people who really know the pros and cons.

"The primary currency of reward in newsmags is the byline," another newsmagazine writer said. "More than money or title, a byline is what matters. It is so important to set up a byline system that rewards the values you want. But now the system tends to reward pieces by big-name people with a lot of 'voice.' The perception is that big feet with big attitude get the big bylines. Reporting is thereby undervalued."

And so is coverage that explains the *why* of issues, rather than how they'll affect the next presidential race.

Playing the Game: News as Sports

For years journalists have talked about public affairs using sports metaphors. They cover "horse race politics." Strategists lay out their "game plan." As election time nears the campaign that is behind faces a "fourth and long" situation with "the clock ticking down," so in desperation it tries a "Hail Mary" play.

This is done by habit and no one takes it seriously. But there is a more serious point. For the American media in the 1990s, public life *is* sports. The entire press has become the sports page. The habits that are most annoying and destructive in today's press coverage all make sense if we assume that we have eliminated the differences between news and sports. For example:

"BEING" VERSUS "DOING." Covering sports events is about getting a slot. You are in the broadcast booth for *NFL Monday Night Football,* or you aren't. You are sent by your paper to cover the World Series or Olympics, or you're not. The event is going to happen anyway, and if you don't cover it someone else will. The event itself provides the importance. You live in its reflected glow.

The normal reporter's life should be nothing like this. The world is full of things to learn about and explain. The only limit on a reporter's achievement should be his or her energy and talent—that is, what the reporter *does*—rather than the privileged billets he or she happens to get.

Yet the trend in journalism is in the opposite direction, toward "being" a prominent journalist without doing a reporter's work. "This began to happen after Watergate, and especially the movie about Watergate," William Kovach, a former editor at the *Atlanta Constitution* and *New York Times* who is now curator of the Nieman Foundation at Harvard, has said. "A lot of people started showing up in newspaper offices because they saw journalism as a route toward celebrating themselves. It has greatly increased since then. More and more kids come out of journalism schools wanting to be anchors. They are not that interested in the work of reporting or finding information. They want to be known."

WHAT YOU ARE WRITING ABOUT DOESN'T MAT-
TER, REALLY. During sporting contests we can act for a
few minutes as if it all really matters. Whether Tonya Harding gets through her routine, whether Carl Lewis gets a repeat gold medal in the dash, whether the pitcher going into
the ninth inning with a no-hitter will get the next three bat-
ters out. Concentrating on the outcome for those few minutes is enjoyable even though we know that the result
doesn't ultimately matter. A close game is all suspense,
drama, anticipation, even though it has no permanent consequence. We'll prefer it if the home team wins, but either way
we still must go to work tomorrow. Sports is a metaphor for
life but not the real thing.

Much of today's press acts as if, down deep, they believe
that *none of it matters* in public life either. This indifference
goes beyond the tough exterior that many reporters believe
is part of their professional role. It involves something more
than the fatigue and blur that affects political reporters who
fly from city to city and hear speech after speech while a
campaign is fully under way. It comes through instead in the
increasing instinct of reporters to skip past the consequences
of any trend or event and focus instead on how the game was
played.

- When Mexico's currency collapsed in late 1994, dutiful
  stories on the inside pages of newspapers explored what
  this event might mean for Latin America's future, for
  the long-term prospects of the Mexican economy, for
  the drug trade, for immigration. But the featured coverage—the front-page stories in the newspapers, the
  lead items on the evening news, the subjects of conversation on the weekend talk shows—concerned what
  this event meant for American politics. (Was it embarrassing for the president to have the Mexico "issue"
  flare up so soon after his fight for GATT and NAFTA?

What did Congress's handling of a Mexican bail-out bill show about the relative strengths of Newt Gingrich and Bob Dole? How would it affect the anti-immigrant backlash, and what would that mean for Governor Pete Wilson's chances for the presidency?)

- In June 1994, one day after President Clinton announced a plan to overhaul the welfare system, *all* of the country's major papers devoted their front-page coverage to what this would do politically for Clinton. The reporters were willing to make elaborate arguments, using their best analytical skills, about the question that most engaged them—whether the political gamble would help the president. With a few notable exceptions (mainly Jason DeParle of the *New York Times*) they did not consider the substance of the plan important enough to explain just what it meant.

- As the Republican Congress began trying to control the budget early in 1995, the *New York Times* ran its first big takeout on Medicare. The subject of the story was not Medicare itself but the Medicare *issue*—that is, the way that the "handling" of the Medicare budget would help or hurt the Republicans as they moved toward the next election. "Very little has rattled Republican leaders since they took control of Congress four months ago," the story began, "but their anxiety in recent days has been almost palpable." Substance does of course sneak into the stories. But in public affairs as in sports, *given a choice* most reporters will act as if the "substance" is about as substantial as this year's bowl games.

For a sports reporter, does anything really matter? Indeed it does. Grace. Genius. Determination. Competitive character. The qualities that in their different ways Arthur Ashe, Joe Montana, Martina Navratilova, Jackie Robinson,

Bonnie Blair, Olga Korbut, Larry Bird, or Michael Jordan displayed. Sportswriters are serious in the presence of such greatness and feel honored to see it in use. Political reporters have to rein themselves in, so as not to sound partisan, but what they really respect are the Birds and Jordans of political dexterity, managing campaigns and getting things done at a new level of skill. The same mentality appears in stories by crime or legal reporters who are more wrapped up with the personalities of flamboyant prosecutors and defenders than with explaining the real-world consequences of their cases. It shows up in financial stories that celebrate the wealth and power of Peter Lynch in the 1980s or Lawrence Tisch in the 1990s without asking what their success means for the structure of their industries. It typifies nearly every story about the entertainment industry, most of which glorify whichever dealmaker or star is hottest at the moment without explaining how money is made in the industry, by whom, and at whose expense.

NO CONFLICT, NO NEWS. Sports cannot exist without competition. The thrill of victory. The agony of defeat. You need someone to win and someone to lose. Otherwise, it's not a game but a hobby. Controlled conflict is at the heart of every sport.

Electoral politics is the same way—someone is going to win the race and someone will lose, and the interest lies in the contest between them. But government and public life need not be a series of conflicts. Legislation involves maneuvers and showdowns, but the most important steps often come when people find areas where they can agree.

It is in these areas of possible agreement that most personal, commercial, and governmental progress is made. Yet precisely because they lack the spice of conflict, areas of agreement are as uninteresting to journalists as exhibition games, prearranged not to count, are to sports reporters.

Legal correspondents live for the cliffhanger, 5-4 split decisions from the Supreme Court, which can be analyzed to
show who is the swing vote, which group of justices is acting
as a team, which president has gotten the best and worst value
out of his appointees, and how the next split decision will go.
Usually these tactical dramas get more attention than what
the decision will actually mean for most Americans.

The same tendency applies in international coverage. In
1995, President Clinton traveled to Russia for a series of
meetings. Midway through the journey his advisors sat down
for a background session with the main beat correspondents
who cover the White House. The White House press secretary, Mike McCurry, gave the reporters an overview of the
contentious issues—conflict!—between the United States
and the Russians. Then a senior economic official began to
talk about an economic/strategic deal the administration had
just worked out with the Ukraine. The deal was clever in its
execution and important in its consequences. The U.S. government pledged financial aid and other steps to help the
Ukraine gain economic stability. For its part the Ukraine
government, which had inherited control of part of the former Soviet nuclear missile force, made clear that it would cooperate on nuclear safeguard issues. "I flatter myself that I
was able to make this fairly short and interesting," the official said later. "But you could just see the life go out of
everyone's eyes."

> Then one of the reporters said, "Look, we have a rule
> here. 'No conflict, no story.' If you get Bob Dole to at-
> tack this deal, then we can write about it. Otherwise,
> forget it."

The reporter was joking, but not really.
Less than six months into his term, Bill Clinton went
to Chicago to give the first speech in his Americorps pro-

gram, under which students could earn college tuition by working in national-service projects. A White House aide who went on the trip recalled that during the speech itself, which laid out the details of the service-and-scholarship plan, most of the students in the audience listened with rapt attention. After all, the program the president was describing would directly affect them. As soon as the speech was over, the students in the crowd leapt to their feet and gave Clinton a standing ovation. Through this period the reporters looked on with moderate interest. But then, the aide recalled:

> One of the students asked how Clinton could propose sending troops anywhere when he had not gone to Vietnam. You could see a collective sigh from the press corps. Andrea Mitchell was waving and saying, "Roll tape! Roll tape!" And that was the confrontation that they showed.

"What bothers me is that the hyper-adversarialism that has ruined the American legal system is now really corroding journalism," Jonathan Alter, who has written about the press for *Newsweek*, has said. "It is driven by the TV shows. You get two people who are adversaries and watch them fight. The more they fight, the better TV it is. It conditions people to be adversarial—and unlike in the law, this kind of adversary process is not even useful. It's adversarialism as a pure sport."

MEASURE WHAT CAN BE MEASURED. Baseball has its "seamheads," the statisticians who think that by amassing arcane data they can find the truth about the game. The information in their charts seems so indisputably revealing that seamheads often have no interest in seeing real games played.

Most political journalists enjoy watching the real political game, but they share the crucial seamhead belief that the truth lies in things that can be measured. Because they are not confident expressing judgments about the actual merits of an arms deal with Ukraine or a Medicare cost-control plan, they seek refuge in areas where judgments are unassailable because they can be tied to "hard" data—poll ratings, win-lose records, "gaffes," "flip-flops." It is risky for a reporter to argue that a plan to expand NATO is sensible—or that the plan is foolish. But if the reporter can show that the plan is *different* from what the president recommended six months ago, then he's got a story.

The two worst ramifications of this outlook involve poll results and an emphasis on policy changes and "flip-flops." Polls can mean a lot, or a little, depending on whether the people being polled have any idea what they are talking about. In June 1993, Bill Clinton ordered a missile strike on the headquarters of Iraq's intelligence service, in Baghdad. The strike was intended to punish the Iraqi service for having plotted to assassinate President George Bush when he was visiting in Kuwait. Newspaper stories in the aftermath of the raid said relatively little about the evidence that had led the president to this action, or about how much damage the raid had done. Instead they featured speculation about how this "gesture of strength" would affect Bill Clinton's political standing. For example, the front-page lead in the *Boston Globe* three days after the raid was, "As polls showed him reaping political support in the wake of Saturday's missile attack on an Iraqi intelligence compound, President Clinton said yesterday that he 'took appropriate action' in the national interest by launching the raid."

An overnight poll taken just after the strike, and quickly reported in the *New York Times*, found that 61 percent of the public felt the strike was "a good idea because it teaches Saddam Hussein a lesson"; only 28 percent agreed

that it was "a bad idea because it risks further bloodshed."
At the time this poll was conducted, reports from Iraq were
so fragmentary that the people being polled could have had
no idea about the raid's effect or what response it might pro-
voke. As a result, the poll readings reflected nothing other
than top-of-the-head first reaction, which is often not the
right basis for military commitment. Yet since it produced
precise-seeming results—61 percent pro, 28 percent con—
the poll could be reported as if it represented something real,
whereas the same reactions expressed in a bar might be written off as uninformed guff. Front-page stories about the poll
solemnly noted that the "margin of error" in the results was
plus or minus 4 percent. The real margin of error was closer
to 100 percent.

There is a difference between instant reaction and careful judgment. Yet the daily stories about poll results ignore
this difference altogether. A 53 percent approval rating is
"hard" data, no matter how much or how little those 53 percent may know or how fickle their views may be.

It would be nice to think that there will be some benefit from the barrage of televised murder trials in the 1990s.
If so, it may come through the reminder that people are supposed to wait for evidence and argument before making up
their minds on important matters. If trials were conducted
the way most opinion polls are, the jury would be asked its
opinion on the defendant's guilt or innocence before any arguments were made or any witnesses were called—and then
the attorneys would make their argument match what the
public already believed. When a jury's ruling flagrantly ig-
nores the facts of a case, a judge has the exceptional power to
set the ruling aside. Reporters should exercise similar discre-
tion but generally don't. (For example, they report as "real"
news poll results showing that the public wants to solve the
budget deficit by eliminating foreign aid. According to a
Harris poll conducted late in 1993, most Americans think

the government spends as much on foreign aid as it does on Social Security and medical care. In reality, foreign aid is about 1 percent of the federal budget; spending on Social Security and medical care is nearly fifty times as large. The people who think that the foreign aid budget is as big as Social Security are not "entitled to their opinion." They are grossly misinformed, and their conclusion—that cuts in foreign aid can solve the budget deficit—should not be reported without an explanation of the real budgetary facts.)

The search for "flip-flops" rests on a similar taste for spurious precision. Especially in the age of Nexis, it is easy to find out whether a politician's current views differ from ones he advocated in the past. If they do, the reporter has discovered an "inconsistency" or "flip-flop," which matters more in news terms than do the merits of the views themselves.

For example, during the 1992 campaign, candidate Clinton attacked President Bush for coddling China's repressive government by maintaining trade ties with China. Two years later, Clinton as president decided to extend China's eligibility for Most Favored Nation trade status. The dominant idea of the news coverage was that Clinton had changed his policy—not whether the new policy or the old one made better sense. George Bush might well have chortled about the difficulties Clinton had made for himself with China, but he would have understood the larger predicament caused by the press's hunt for inconsistencies. Bush, after all, never overcame the conflict between his "read my lips" promise in 1988 never to raise taxes and his agreement to a tax increase in 1990. Of course politicians should be accountable for explicit promises that they make, but if reporters worried less about ferreting out inconsistencies and more about explaining what the changed policies mean, and why politicians made the changes, readers would have a clearer sense of how mad—if at all—they should be about the shift in plans.

Politicians who understand the press's "measurability" bias can turn it to their advantage. The most dramatic recent example was Newt Gingrich's strategy for moving the "Contract with America" through the Congress. Just before taking office as Speaker, in 1995, Gingrich set a measurable target for reporters: all ten planks of the Contract would come to a vote in the House within the first one hundred days. The promise did exactly what Gingrich knew it would: it focused political coverage on whether Gingrich was meeting his timetable (as he did), rather than on assessment of what the Contract's provisions would do.

PREDICTION RATHER THAN ASSESSMENT. Anyone who follows sports knows the disproportion between anticipation and aftermath. For the two weeks before the Super Bowl, it is built up as the most exciting showdown in sportsdom. Ex-quarterbacks go on the air with charts and diagrams about what this game's quarterbacks are likely to do. Celebrities make chat on talk shows about which team is likely to win. (When President Clinton was interviewed on NBC TV just before his 1995 State of the Union speech, the final question was whom he favored to win that year's Super Bowl, between San Francisco and San Diego. The president, revealing what it takes to be a politician, said "the team from California.") Newspapers turn over most of their sports sections to position-by-position matchups of the two teams. Then the game begins—and two hours after it's over, the TV analysts are getting ready to talk about the next big event. The only people still interested in the earlier predictions are the bookies and their clients, who must settle up on the basis of how well they guessed.

Public affairs writing largely follows the same pattern. Weeks before an important Senate confirmation vote, months before a congressional election, years before the presidential primaries begin, the most influential figures in journalism spend their time predicting what is going to happen. When the results come in, attention shifts almost immediately to what it all means for the next tests of political strength. The process is like the acceleration of TV advertisement, in which Christmas shopping ads appear just after Halloween. The big difference between political handicappers and those who set the point spread in sports is that in politics there is no payoff day. For pundits there is no financial or professional penalty for being consistently wrong. There can be rewards for being spectacularly right. The main example is Kevin Phillips, who made his reputation while in his twenties, in the Nixon era, by outlining a "Southern strategy" by which the Republicans could win near-permanent control of the white South. But those who are wrong stay in the business to guess another day. On the night of his election victory in 1992, Bill Clinton's supporters played a taped compilation of pundits speaking about Clinton during the previous year. The tape showed nearly every prominent columnist, political analyst, and talk show figure declaring Clinton's campaign dead—after Gennifer Flowers made her accusations, after the draft-board controversy, after "I didn't inhale." Those same experts will be predicting who "can" and "cannot" win in the next election.

"These campaign-coverage jobs are the sexiest jobs in journalism," says a newsmagazine reporter who has covered presidential campaigns. "They pay better. You get more space. The culture rewards you. And they are by far the easiest stories to write. They are the easiest because you cannot get it wrong! It's all just contending theories about who has a better take on what is up and down, and when it's over no one goes back to check."

Bookies would be envious.

"THE ROAD TO THE FINAL FOUR." When the baseball season resumed in 1995, after its disastrous strike, Thomas

Boswell wrote in the *Washington Post* that the previous season might as well be erased from every record book. Each year of baseball had meaning only because it built toward the World Series, he said. That was the final reckoning of the long events of each season, and since there had been no World Series in 1994, every game of the season might as well have not been played.

If Boswell had been a journalism professor, he could have said that the "master narrative" of the baseball year was the race toward the World Series. Each sporting event has a similar overarching theme. From the beginning of the college football season, analysts and handicappers are making picks for the post-season Number One team and the bowl game lineups. Even before the season begins, magazine and newspaper profiles set up a season-long drama about who will win this year's Heisman Trophy. Features about college basketball are typically called "The Road to the Final Four," which gives each game meaning in the context of the NCAA tournament at the end of the season.

Real life rarely offers such clear-cut master narratives. But coverage of public affairs often sounds as if it has the same simple plot line. The narrative cycle in its grand form covers four years, and at each point in the cycle the one truly interesting question is: Who will win the next presidential election? The corollary of this question is, How have the events of the last week changed the odds for the election?

The more esteemed and visible the political correspondent, the more he or she concentrates on the daily and weekly recalibration of prospects for the next presidential election. For example, almost immediately after Bill Clinton took office, the Washington bureau chief of the *New York Times*, R. W. "Johnny" Apple, began declaring that the omens were bad for Clinton's success in office and by extension for his prospects for a second term. Barely ten days into the administration, following Clinton's muffed attempt to make first Zoe Baird and then Kimba Wood his attorney general, Apple wrote that "the new president now desperately needs a victory, as quickly as possible" because of this "painfully public, politically devastating failure."

Updated variants of this pulse-taking exercise, by Apple and others in the *Times* and other papers and networks, have appeared almost daily since then. Republican candidates waited nearly two years after Bill Clinton's inauguration before formally launching their campaigns to unseat him, but journalists were way ahead of them. Within days of his inauguration they were speculating about whether he had the right stuff to finish a first term on a strong note for reelection. By midway point, in January 1995, many had moved into full reelection-analysis mode. In February 1995, when Clinton nominated Dr. Henry Foster to be his surgeon general, the leading journalists were fitting nearly every event into the master narrative of the 1996 campaign. After the Foster nomination, Apple wrote a news story with the headline, "Many Democrats Accuse Clinton of Incompetence." As soon as decently possible it moved from the Foster case to the real subject: whether Clinton would be reelected.

The public sees and hears these stories so often it becomes hard for anyone even to notice them. The implied message of all such coverage is: the four years before elections are a diversion, much like the tedious midseason basketball games. They are interesting mainly for the ways in which they position the combatants for the championship campaign. Although the "Road to the Final Four" mentality is clearest in coverage of political affairs and of sports, it shows up in nearly every form of journalism. Business coverage becomes dominated by the prospect of another big takeover battle. Cultural coverage boils itself down to speculation about whether there will be new government rules controlling TV violence, or new legal restrictions on abortion, rather than examining the details and texture of these issues more carefully.

FLATTENING OF EVENTS. In sports everything is equally engrossing for a brief period. The Super Bowl may be the biggest TV event of the year—but the Olympics is the biggest event for the whole world, or maybe the World Cup is, and the New Year's Day bowl-fest is an orgy of sport, and so on. Each is exciting enough while it is happening that none can really overshadow or outrank the others.

Thanks mainly to television, something similar has happened to public events. Events and trends come in two sizes: those big enough to be on *Nightline* or a CNN live broadcast or the weekend talk shows, and those that can't quite command such treatment. Each "big" event is more important than all the little ones—but no big event is significantly bigger than any of the others. The difference among them, like the contrast between a weeks-long Olympics and a minutes-long heavyweight championship fight, is for how *long* they are big.

The eclipsing American news event of the mid-1990s, the O. J. Simpson trial, demonstrates the point. In early June, 1994, American news outlets were in the grip of a tense-seeming story deserving round-the-clock coverage— but it was not the Simpson case. The United Nations, at the urging of the United States, was demanding that the North Koreans open their nuclear plants to international inspection (in keeping with past treaty promises to do so). The North Koreans said no. American news coverage was intense, because the stakes seemed to be high. Prominent commentators and politicians were saying that if North Korea refused to budge from its position, the U.S. Air Force should bomb it into compliance. Senator John McCain, of Arizona, recommended preemptive air strikes on North Korean facilities. "Get Ready for War," said the headline on a column by

Charles Krauthammer in the *Washington Post*. "Straight 'War Talk' Is Needed Now," William Safire announced in the *New York Times*.

Through May and early June of 1994, the Korean showdown occupied the "Top Story!" slot that had been held at various times in the preceding two years by Ross Perot, Tonya Harding and Nancy Kerrigan, Gennifer Flowers, the Bobbitt family, and the massacre victims of Rwanda. Experts gave the latest updates on *Nightline*. Articles by the same experts appeared the next morning on the op-ed page. Radio talk show hosts gave their views on the weekdays, and on the weekends the panel show pundits argued about how the whole issue had been "handled."

Then, much more suddenly than it had entered the Top Story position, the North Korean "issue" went away. The drama that had seemed so engrossing was barely on the network news or talk shows any more. Three men were responsible for this change. One was former president Jimmy Carter, who had gone to North Korea and bought a few days' negotiating time in talks with North Korean dictator Kim Il Sung. Another was Kim Il Sung himself, who died during those few days. And the third was O. J. Simpson, who so totally captured the attention of the American media that very little of it was left to worry about the North Korean nukes. "When did you know that the moment of crisis had passed?" a South Korean diplomat was asked in 1994. "It was when the O. J. Simpson car chase began," he replied. "As soon as the American media had O. J. to deal with, you could *feel* the weight of CNN and the American pundits come off our shoulders." A celebrity murder case, a potential threat to world peace—they were equally good at filling the slot of the biggest story of the moment.

During its subsequent run at the center of American media attention, the Simpson case was shoved off center stage repeatedly—by the off-year election results; by the congressional showdown over the Contract with America; by the Japanese earthquake and poison-gas attack; by the Oklahoma City bombing and resulting furor over militias and extremists; by the controversy about affirmative action; by the rescue of pilot Scott O'Grady, who had been shot down over Bosnia; and by the actor Hugh Grant's arrest for soliciting a prostitute on Sunset Boulevard. What made the O.J. case unusual is that it kept coming back, not that it was bigger than other stories on any given day. In sports terms it was like a year-round Olympics, always available and diverting but not un-trumpable.

Sports reporters have no particular obligation to tell fans that the NBA playoffs are more (or less) important than the Super Bowl, so the convergence of events suits them fine. But the "normal" media—the branch that covers public affairs—has as one of its main duties helping people understand the trends and happenings that will matter most to them. The more it adopts the sports mentality, channel-surfing from one spectacle to the next, the less it fulfills this fundamental role.

During the baseball season, one loss counts exactly as much as another, whether it is a one-run squeaker in extra innings or a 15–0 blowout. In the sports view of politics, one "gaffe" or "misstep" or "setback" counts as much as another, no matter what the cause. When Bob Woodward wrote *The Agenda*, his inside account of how the Clinton administration made its economic plans, he was careful not to lose his "objectivity" by saying that one approach to balancing the budget made more sense than another. The ironic effect of this evenhandedness was to make *every* problem or disagreement part of one undifferentiated mass of "mishandling" or "disarray." Temper tantrums, legislative miscalculations, historic shifts in economic fundamentals—they all count equally as "losses" or "mistakes."

The political talk shows, which encourage journalists to

sound like color-commentators assessing the performance of players on the field, further blur the distinction between important and unimportant events through the concept of the "good week." The opening question on most of the shows is whether the president had a "good week" or a "bad week," or whether he "won" or "lost" the week's battle over a particular issue. The ingredients that can be thrown into the pot to make each kind of week are amazingly varied. Two of Bill Clinton's cronies use a presidential helicopter for a golf trip, so the president has a "bad week." He signs a treaty with the Russians or the Mexicans and therefore has a "good week." The week is the basic unit of measurement, and as in sports the wins and losses are toted up as if they had equal weight.

"To ask 'who won the week?' is a political act, one that is rarely acknowledged," Jay Rosen, of New York University, wrote in 1993. "The question sets a rhythm to politics that permits the media to play timekeeper, umpire and, finally, judge. It is a question that would not occur to an ordinary citizen." It would, however, come naturally to anyone on the sports beat.

LET THE EXPERTS SET THE AGENDA, BUT MAKE UP FOR IT WITH "ATTITUDE." Sportswriters don't make the schedule. They may complain about the rearrangement of the baseball divisions. They often moan and groan about long playoff series for basketball or hockey. But they aren't making the decisions. They show up for events that someone else has planned.

The writers exercise their control in other ways. They would love to have the players' grace and skill, but they resent the athletes' self-centeredness and man-boy nature. The writers make themselves the players' equals by writing circles around them. When former athletes go into the broadcast booth—Terry Bradshaw, Jim Palmer, Chris Evert—they rarely sound catty about the players still on the field. They have been there themselves. The least athletic sportswriters are often the most biting when a player fails on or off the field.

Increasingly this is the case with public affairs writing too. If politicians decide to fight about an issue, it's news. If not, it's off the front page. In August 1995, President Clinton decided to launch a campaign to reduce smoking by teenagers. Newspapers, newsmagazines, and network TV produced long stories about how many teenagers smoked, why this was a problem, and what could be done about it. They could as easily have done these stories a month or a year earlier, but they let the political leaders define when this became an "issue."

On this and other issues reporters cede control of the definition of "news" to politicians—but demonstrate their control in other ways. Reporters resent countless aspects of their situation relative to politicians, even as most reporters know that they could not do, or could not stand, what the typical politician has to do. "Could not stand" is a more precise way to put it. Most political reporters think that they understand the issues at least as well as most politicians, and can express themselves better. But they could not make themselves give the same speech over and over, or seem enthusiastic when meeting people they will never see again, or choke back any wry or sarcastic comment that might offend some member of some group.

Recognition of what politicians put up with breeds a mixture of admiration and contempt in most reporters. Covering a political campaign is like being backstage with the Wizard of Oz. Each audience hears the applause lines and the pauses to wipe away a tear only once. Reporters hear them six times a day. Reporters see the hair spray going on and the campaign aides whispering in the candidate's ear, "Joe Smith—wife is Annie" seconds before the candidate booms, "Joe! How great to see you! And how's that darling Annie?"

They see the grinding daily need to raise money. They know that most positions come about through compromise and muddle—and the ones that aren't compromises are inevitably a kind of grandstanding. And yet the reporters know that the person who survives this process will end up with the incomparable power of the presidency or the prestige of the Senate.

Reporters might, in theory, put these disgruntled feelings to a variety of constructive uses. They might decide (as some indeed do) that their mission is to understand and explain the issues with which these flawed politicians must cope when one of them wins. They might decide not to let their curiosity be limited by what the politicians decide to talk about and instead explore what they think are the country's real problems. They might decide to be impeccably polite in demeanor, while beneath that courteous guise they are relentlessly tough-minded in exploring a politician's substantive views. But increasingly, they decide to accept the politician's guidance on the subjects they will cover, and to get even for all the indignities through "attitude." If "investigation" was the word for journalism in the Woodward and Bernstein era, attitude and snarl are the words now.

A phenomenon so widespread is hard to illustrate with single examples, but here is a try. On Sunday, May 7, 1995, the story in column 1, page 1, of the *New York Times* had this headline: "Desperately in Need of Winning Streak, Clinton Finds One." This was a "news" story, not an editorial or a "news analysis." Its opening paragraphs said:

> Last Thursday was something of a rarity for Bill Clinton: a good day. Not only that, it was just one of a string of good days this President has had in the last few weeks, with Congress either away on spring recess or returning to Washington to face legislative issues much stickier than those House Republicans dis-

patched in the flush of their first 100 days. . . . Mr.
Clinton has also taken actions that were nothing more
or less than presidential, but that seemed unusually
decisive and rhetorically charged for him.

What's so surprising about this story? In a sense, nothing at all, since it is a representative rather than exceptional
sample of political reporting. But the attitudes behind such
a "news" account are remarkable. Although the story is at
face value complimentary to President Clinton, it drips con-
descension: Bill Clinton is obviously not "presidential," so
merely meeting that standard is a rare accomplishment for
him. A case for that opinion could be made; the significance
of this story is that neither the reporter nor his editors felt
the least obligation to make it. During much of his time in
office, George Bush was subjected to the same reflexively be-
littling comments.

"*Too much attitude* is the main problem of the press
today," another White House correspondent said (shortly before the *Times* story appeared). "One result is that we always
have these slightly irritable-sounding pieces, without going
to the trouble of explaining exactly why they are irritable."

Political journalism encourages a kind of "attitude"
that is more biting than sports commentary except about the
worst cellar-dwelling teams. The newsmagazines have convinced themselves that "edge" is the way to attract attention
and readers. Reporters know beyond doubt that greater
"voice" will get them noticed. "Pieces that are harsh and
snide and critical and quizzical always do better and get bigger play and attract more attention," a newsmagazine writer
has observed.

There is very little risk for a reporter in a not-quite-
perfect attempt to make fun of something. There is tremendous risk in a comparable flawed attempt to make the
positive case for a politician or a program.

"There is nothing that the average journalist fears more than ridicule," Charles Peters has said. "You are really going out on a limb if you say, 'This is a good idea. This is what is good about Bill Clinton'"—or Bob Dole or Newt Gingrich. "Or if you say, 'This is an important idea.' You immediately lay yourself open to people saying that you're being boring, and getting laughed at. One of the real reasons for the vicious pack mentality in journalism is that people are so afraid of ridicule from their peers."

"You can be wrong, as long as you're negative and skeptical," a reporter for ABC said in 1995. "But if you're going to say something remotely positive, you'd better be 150 percent right or you're going to be accused of rolling over."

Different parts of the news culture indulge "attitude" in different ways. In TV broadcasts it comes through in the "witty" final sentence or two of each correspondent's report. In newsmagazines, "The journalistic culture rewards stories with a 'fresh take' and a 'forward spin' on the news," a newsmagazine writer said, which again means attitude rather than argument or analysis. "The pieces that get the most attention are the 'attitude' pieces," Matt Cooper, then the White House correspondent for *U.S. News & World Report* (he later joined the *New Republic)* said. "The ones with the clever turn of phrase—these are the ones that get the buzz. A big reporting piece rarely gets the same response.

"The iconic figure of the press in the eighties was Sam Donaldson shouting his question at Reagan over the helicopter blades," Cooper said. The iconic figure of this era is "a Dowd"—after Maureen Dowd, of the *New York Times*, who was talented enough to get away with a new level of "voice" and chic in what had a decade earlier been a staid paper. "Welcome to the first presidential campaign with an air of Pirandello," she had written during the 1992 Democratic primaries, "an absurdist adventure marked by ironic detachment, existential angst, black humor, and, believe it or not, a vow of celibacy."

The typical sportswriter could probably not pull this off—mainly because he wouldn't have the right literary allusion, but for another reason too. It would apply only to a sport in which he wanted to ridicule not individual participants but the whole enterprise. Which brings us to:

THE BASIC DIFFERENCE. The view of public life that comes through today's press is, finally, less like the Super Bowl, or the World Series, or the Olympics than another sporting enterprise: pro wrestling. To judge by the coverage, everything is a sham. Conflicts are built up and then they blow over, and no one is sincere. As onlookers we can laugh at and look down at the participants, because everyone knows it's all done for effect.

This is the view of public life that comes through the press, with one big difference from any of its sporting counterparts. The tone of coverage affects how this game, the public game, is played. "When the Knicks play the Bulls, what the reporters in attendance say or do has little bearing on the outcome," Jay Rosen wrote in the magazine *Tikkun*. "They may be sloppy, inattentive, or unfair, but the game exists independently of their excesses."

The game of self-government is not independent of the excesses of the media. It is not just a spectacle. And, as we will see, the game is being changed—rigged, weakened—by the way it is portrayed through the media.

Chapter 5

Getting in the Way

The quirks, blind spots, and vanities of today's media may be annoying. But do they matter to anyone outside the business?

They do. During every working day, the conduct of public affairs is shaped—and often warped—by the habits of the modern media. The combined efforts of the country's journalists are supposed to make it easier to cope with our collective problems, but in many cases the media actually get in the way of efforts to deal with important issues. The strange motiveless irritability of today's press has made it harder for us to face complicated challenges, to explore competing ideas, or even to tolerate politicians who are interested in doing more than striking poses. The impact of the media's habits on our efforts to deal with public problems takes several forms:

THE TYRANNY OF TECHNOLOGY. At one time there was such as thing as a daily "news cycle." The story lineup for the evening news shows was set by the early afternoon. If you wanted TV coverage of a speech or announcement, you scheduled it around lunchtime. Newspaper deadlines were just after dinnertime. The next morning, over breakfast, you saw the information in the papers and prepared to respond to it during the day.

Thanks to C-SPAN, CNN, online data services, and radio and TV talk shows, now it is always deadline time. Opinions, events, and accusations crop up ceaselessly through the day. Reporters must keep on top of each new twitch. More importantly, so must the government. The cycle of nonstop news has drawn the government into a stance of nonstop response. A decade ago observers claimed that our public life suffered because politicians had such a short time-horizon, which led to changes in policy day by day. Now a president would be grateful if he even had a whole day to think.

"When we get up in the morning, we are already somewhat constrained by editorial decisions that were made the afternoon or night before," David Dreyer, who worked in the White House communications office during the first two years of the Clinton administration, said early in 1995. By the time the working day began, he said, the president and his staff felt that they had fallen half a cycle behind in the race to cope with breaking news and answer their opponents' criticisms:

> The morning TV shows come on, with pieces by the network correspondents that were finished before they went to dinner the night before. Maybe there is some new footage inserted if there were late news breaks. The newspaper stories we see in the morning were sent in about 8:00 P.M.
>
> The morning agenda for us is set by those morning shows, and the papers, and whatever CNN is vomiting out. We know that at 10:30 or 11:00 A.M. each morning, each of the networks has a conference call be-

tween Washington and New York, to set the lineup for
the evening news broadcasts. What they talk about in
those calls comes off the papers, the morning news
broadcasts, and whatever morsels [press secretary
Mike] McCurry has given out after the senior staff
meeting at 9:00 A.M.

The reporters do their intermediate news gathering between breakfast and the 10:30 calls. Meantime
there are the hourly deadlines for CNN news updates,
and radio news, and the wires. *Hotline*, the faxed political wrap-up, comes out late in the morning. And we
have to respond to all of it, right away, because it will
be plugged back into that evening's news broadcasts
and set up the news cycle for the *next* day. Through this
whole period, radio would prefer to have absolutely
fresh material every hour, and CNN is simply inex-
haustible in its demand for news.

Through the rest of the day, the aide said, the
cycle ground relentlessly on. The White House staff
would schedule some event starring the president—a
bill signing, a handshake with some visiting digni-
tary—for the middle of the afternoon, in hopes that it
would appear on the evening news. When the network
news shows actually occurred, they would create new
charges and questions for the staff to answer—as
would *Crossfire* and *MacNeil/Lehrer,* and sometimes
Larry King, and usually *Nightline.* In the meantime,
Rush Limbaugh would make his new charge of the
day, and the British tabloids would come up with a
Clinton scandal. The White House staff could fill
every hour of its working day simply responding to accusations, queries, and rumors from the press—and
still not answer all of them. It was a challenge that affected every administration regardless of party and that
grew worse year by year.

The most obvious effect of the nonstop news cycle is to force government officials to spend their time in nonstop response. Ideally public officials would be able to think decades ahead, in considering national savings rates and environmental challenges; or years ahead, in planning school reforms and industrial growth; or months ahead about trade negotiations or foreign policy statements; or at least beyond the next weekend's political talk shows with their verdicts on "good" or "bad" weeks.

In reality it can be hard for officials to think more than fifteen minutes ahead, as they look through the mountain of phone slips on their desk and try to answer congressional objections, kill off rumors or leaks, and put their spin on stories in the minutes before the next deadline arrives. A month or two later, most of the issues that had them in a frenzy will be forgotten, but at the time they seem too important to ignore. Trying to carry out long-term plans in this environment is like trying to conduct medical research in a hospital emergency room: conceivable but unlikely. The effect is most intense in the White House but is visible throughout the government.

"It's all so unproductive," a Clinton administration official said in 1995. She said that Anthony Lake, the president's national security advisor, and Warren Christopher, the secretary of state, "had a deal that Lake would not be the public voice or do this sort of thing."

> But after a while even Tony spent hours returning the calls and giving public comments to make a story turn out the right way. Sometimes there is no one else who can kill a story or turn it around except the top gun. And you get killed yourself if other people are talking and you're not telling your side of the story.

Over a period of years, political behavior has naturally evolved in ways that this new media environment rewards.

Since the early 1970s, the U.S. Congress has been converted from a clublike organization run by powerful bosses and committee chairmen into an assemblage of free agents competing for the same scarce commodity: airtime on the network newscasts, the talk shows, or at least C-SPAN.

Newt Gingrich was a pioneering figure in this new approach toward building a political base. Starting in the early 1980s, he became a fixture on C-SPAN, delivering orations that looked impressive to home viewers even though they were surreal when seen firsthand. Through the C-SPAN camera, which was fixed steadily on the podium, Gingrich looked as if he were addressing a packed chamber, with eye contact, pauses, and gestures appropriate to a speaker before a vast crowd. In reality the House was usually empty as he spoke. Gingrich seemed immune to the embarrassment built into this situation. He was one of the first House members to understand that the audience that mattered was the one he could reach through the camera. Gingrich's mastery of press coverage during his own ascent prepared him, when he became Speaker in 1995, to control his party's majority more skillfully than Democratic leaders had managed to do during the preceding forty years when they dominated the Congress.

Bill Clinton also showed his understanding of modern media during the 1992 campaign, with his natural ease in the talk show settings that have become the way in which Americans get to know their celebrities. The public thinks it has a good sense of what Phil Donahue is like as a person, or Oprah Winfrey, or Regis and Kathie Lee, and so by the end of the campaign did they develop a sense of Bill Clinton.

When Clinton became president, however, he had real work to do and decisions to make. The mere force of his personality could no longer play so large a role in relations with the media. He had less time to spend with the press; they had more to write about—and criticize, from squabbling within his administration to his policies on Haiti or China or affirmative action. Because grumbling from the press that the administration was in "disarray" or "faltering" could interfere with all these efforts, the Clinton administration naturally had to figure out ways to shore up its image in the media. Like the Reagan and Bush administrations before it, the Clinton administration seemed to devote at least as much time to selling and "spinning" its policies as to coming up with policies in the first place. The very behavior most members of the press deplore—government dominated by image makers—the querulous press had helped bring about.

"The White House had to operate basically like a big PR firm," one official who worked in the White House during the first two years after Clinton's inauguration said in 1995.

> When I was there, absolutely nothing was more important each day than figuring out what the news was going to be.
>
> No skill was more valued in the Clinton White House than the ability to deal with the press. That is *the* source of power for George Stephanopoulos and Gene Sperling. Others like Bruce Reed and Bill Galston might know a lot more about policy, but they are more hesitant in dealing with the press and therefore less powerful.
>
> We are seeing now the end of what started in the Nixon administration, with the concentration on PR as the center of the presidency. In a generation we've gone from saying that it's important to know how to use the press and PR to having them be the center.
>
> There is no such thing as a substantive discussion that is not shaped or dominated by how it is going to play in the press. You could have a president who started out with a clear, good idea of what he wanted to

do. But it would end up just being driven by the spin of each day's news.

When you put together a press corps that is really only interested in "horse race" and "inside baseball" and a White House staff that is interested only in the press, you've got the worst of both worlds. There is a real motive to do whatever will get the spin in that day's news and worry about everything else later on. It would be unthinkable to let a couple of days go by without crafting a story, because of the fear that if they don't provide something, what the press will come up with will be worse.

This sounds like a partisan complaint, but it is far more important than that. Just as Democratic congressmen must learn from Newt Gingrich's skill in playing to the camera if they want to survive, presidents of both parties must succeed in "operating like a PR firm" if they want a chance to succeed at anything else. During the Reagan and Bush administrations, James Baker and Richard Darman gained strength inside the government through their skill in selective leaking to friends in the press. For example, three weks before the presidential election of 1992, the *Washington Post* published a four-part series by Bob Woodward about economic policy-making in the Bush administration. Richard Darman, budget director in the Bush administration, was obviously a major source for Woodward. The series portrayed Darman as a lonely voice of conscience, warning that big budget deficits would wreck the administration's political prospects and the nation's economic future. Although it seems crude to boil it down this way, the reality is that Darman helped Woodward—and Woodward's series helped Darman, by positioning him as the man who tried to save the administration from itself.

During the Nixon administration, Henry Kissinger and

Alexander Haig played the same game. During the Carter administration . . . no one did, which was part of Carter's problem. While complaining constantly about "image conscious" politicians, the media establishment has ensured that those without "image consciousness" will not survive.

THE DEVIL'S BARGAIN OF "ACCESS." In principle, a government always looking over its shoulder at the media might be a healthy government. The press is supposed to be the voice of the people. So in responding constantly to reporters, public officials might by proxy be getting constantly updated reminders about the popular will. As the reporters have become better informed, on matters ranging from international economic policy to political tensions in the Middle East, their sharp questions might be part of a useful dialog that would lead to the wisest possible political choices.

In some cases the press may have exactly this heightening democratic function. More often, the interaction between press and government has a more destructive, perverse result. The issues a government has to deal with are politically and technically complex. It is morally wrong not to intervene in Bosnia—but what, exactly, would intervention mean, and where and how would it end? It is wrong not to protest prison labor in China—but what leverage, exactly, does the U.S. have over China's policy, and how in the long run can it best achieve its result? It seems suicidal for politicians of either party to talk about limiting Social Security benefits for the wealthiest recipients, or about putting a ceiling on the tax deduction for mortgage interest. Yet all politicians know that the only way to deal with the budget deficit is to offer fewer government benefits to those who are least in need. The press should make it possible for the public to consider these complications honestly—and at brief moments, as when Ross Perot used his balanced-budget charts in the 1992 campaign, the press does so. But most of the time the rules of the game mean that a politician will be punished for "gaffes" or "missteps" if he dares utter a complicated truth. (For example, soon after Newt Gingrich became Speaker of the House, political columnists speculated about the "gaffe" he had committed by hinting that spending for Medicare would have to be limited in some way. Half a year later, columnists and newsmagazines were treating reform of Medicare's financing as a sensible, even obvious idea and chiding the politicians who lacked the "courage" to face this issue.)

Public officials and big-time reporters have worked out an unspoken plan for coexistence that benefits each of them in the short term but makes it harder to solve problems in the long run. At the heart of this understanding is the concept of "access"—a reporter's ability to make contact with a source or public official when the reporter needs to. In the olden days of political journalism, which means the period before the Vietnam War and Watergate, "access" involved a shared establishment consciousness among prominent journalists and the officials they covered. With a few exceptions (notably Walter Lippmann), the journalists of the pre-Vietnam era could not consider themselves the financial or social equals of the senators and cabinet secretaries they dealt with. But they could operate as colleagues in sharing secrets that neither party would divulge to the public, since to do so would not be "in the national interest."

The end of the era of this sort of "access" began on April 17, 1961, with the aborted and disastrous attempt to invade Cuba at the Bay of Pigs. James Reston, of the *New York Times*, had known about the invasion plans in advance but did not share the news with his readers. He soon decided that he had made a historic mistake. John Kennedy reportedly came to agree with him, and to wish that the plans had been debunked in public before they led to embarrassment and bloodshed. More than a generation later, the old-style "access" system of broadly shared secrets is almost unimaginable. In its place has come a vast series of person-to-person "access" deals.

What the reporter needs from today's access deal is, simply, *material.* If he is a talk show regular, he needs to be able to call up a State Department official on Friday morning and get a nugget about Iraq or China he can use on that weekend's shows. If he is a twice-weekly columnist, he needs to be able to talk with an assistant to Newt Gingrich or Bob Dole, who will tell him who is scheming against whom within the party. If he is a regular beat reporter, he needs contacts who will tell him how the White House's proposal for welfare reform will be different from the plans being drawn up in the Department of Health and Human Services. If he is a bureau chief, he wants to know a cabinet secretary or prominent senator who will accept his invitation to be a guest at the publication's table at the annual press banquets, as living proof of the bureau chief's clout. If he is a regular on the speaking circuit, he needs a constant supply of anecdotes beginning, "I was talking to Bob Rubin last week, and he said . . ." to throw into his talk.

This is what the journalists want from "access," and it is what the sources can give. But as in any other exchange, value must flow both ways. From the public's point of view, the problems of the "access" system arise from what the reporters must give in return.

At the crudest and least harmful level, what journalists give back is flattery. The columnist and talk show stalwart Robert Novak has long been notorious for this practice. His regular informants are portrayed in his column as "dynamic," "rising," "thoughtful," and so on. William Safire does the same thing in a slightly subtler way.

During his tenure in the Clinton White House, David Gergen demonstrated a variant of the access-for-adulation exchange. Very soon after his arrival in early summer 1993, Gergen realized something that Clinton and his advisors should have figured out earlier: that the administration was hurting itself by creating an "anecdote crisis." Modern political coverage, especially in the weekly newsmagazines, relies heavily on anecdotes and specific, telling details to give life and insider sizzle to its minute-by-minute "tick-tock" accounts. An ideal behind-the-scenes story might say:

> As he toyed with his breakfast of fried Spam drenched in Log Cabin Lite syrup, the weary president sighed twice and said, "Gosh darn it Hillary, we've been outsmarted by that Bob Dole."
>
> "I hate to hear you talk that way," Hillary Rodham Clinton replied, as she, with practiced hand, wiped an inch-thick gob of syrup from her husband's size 46 all-cotton sweatshirt, still dripping with moisture from his 4.2-mile morning run. "Let's talk to that nice Mister Gingrich about a balanced-budget agreement."
> And thus was born the budget compromise of 1995.

Theodore White introduced this style to political journalism with his *Making of the President* books in the 1960s, and for better or worse it is here to stay. During a political campaign, it's no problem to get these scene-setting details, since reporters are right there amidst the syrup and the Spam. But in the White House most action occurs beyond reporters' views. The reporters must therefore rely on access to get the vivid if meaningless details they need.

Until David Gergen's arrival, almost no one in the White House seemed to have realized how desperately reporters needed the inside dope. Gergen, a veteran of the Nixon and Reagan White Houses, understood perfectly. When the Gergen era began, so did the flow of anecdotes—and with the charming twist that many of them featured

Gergen in the savior's role. For instance, early on Gergen's watch the front page of the *Washington Post* reported this vignette: Senator Robert Kerrey is in agony about how to vote on the administration's budget proposal in 1993. His telephone rings. It's David Gergen! Gergen asks, "Would it help if we talked?" After a meal with Gergen, the senator sees things clearly and goes along with the president.

The flood of similar ennobling anecdotes caused much bitter humor among Gergen's rivals in the White House but was essentially harmless. (Gergen himself staunchly maintained that this emphasis was the reporters' own doing and that he had not engineered his own spin.) The real danger of the access bargain lies in stories that are the converse of Gergen's—that is, what happens to officials who do not allow "access" when some of their colleagues are providing it.

As "insider" accounts of political decisions have become more common and have appeared earlier in each successive administration's term, officials have in effect been blackmailed into providing "access" for self-protection. Until roughly the beginning of the Reagan administration, officials usually waited until they had left office before providing firsthand accounts of who had said what to the president, and why he had finally decided the way he did. Arthur Schlesinger's *A Thousand Days* and Theodore Sorensen's *With Kennedy* were two well-known illustrations of this genre. Both of these books came out when John Kennedy's reputation was virtually unsullied, and they contained relatively little score-settling about the administration's decisions. As time went on and presidencies in general became more embattled, aides writing memoirs went to greater lengths to explain why they had not been responsible for what went wrong. An old Washington joke held that the generic title for such memoirs should be, *If Only They'd Listened to Me.*

Political aides have for decades leaked information about pending decisions to newspaper reporters, as a way of enhancing their own reputations and improving the chances that a decision will turn out the way they want. (To give one simple example: If President Clinton were deciding whether to accept a Republican proposal to cut domestic spending, aides who opposed the cut could leak word that the president was in danger of "capitulating" to right-wing interests, or that the decision was being viewed by his liberal base as a sign of whether he would "betray" them.)

The leaking process acquired a new velocity by the time of the Clinton administration, as books describing internal struggles appeared while the administration was still finding its feet. Bob Woodward's *The Agenda*, which was published sixteen months after Bill Clinton was sworn in, and Elizabeth Drew's *On the Edge,* which came out a few months later, described policy struggles among combatants who were nearly all still in office. Those who had provided "access" to the authors came out far better than those who hadn't. The payoff for those who cooperated lay not so much in explicit flattery (although the adjective "thoughtful" is a nearly foolproof sign that an official has helped the author) as in having their side of the story told. Neither Ira Magaziner, the ill-starred health-reform coordinator, nor Warren Christopher, the secretary of state, cooperated in the Woodward or Drew accounts. Each came off much worse than his bureaucratic rivals did.

Because the access bargain is going on even as an administration is making policy, it distorts what people say, think, and do. "The Woodward book really changed the atmosphere," an official of Clinton's White House said six months after the book appeared. "There was a different feeling in the meetings, especially involving the president, because people were very self-conscious about thinking how anything could look if taken out of context. I went to a meeting with ten people sitting against the wall, all of them taking notes. In a cabinet-level meeting about government spending Clinton said something like, 'Civil servants, we don't need 'em!' A minute or two later he was careful to go back and correct himself for the record, so that his joke would not be misunderstood."

In short, the access bargain has become journalism's equivalent to plea bargaining in court. The authorities can make things easy for you or make them tough, depending on how much you cooperate with them. But there is another, less obvious effect of access bargaining, which may be more significant and damaging. To use the courtroom analogy, it involves the offenses that the authorities agree to overlook, in return for cooperation on petty crimes.

If public officials give reporters what the reporters need, from "tick-tock" details to attendance at the annual press banquets, they can to a surprising degree limit or direct what else the reporters will do. The officials cannot of course control the usually nasty tone of press commentary, nor can they shut off the incessant tactical commentary about whether the administration has committed a "gaffe" or a "flip-flop." They are constrained from laying out the complications that make almost any presidential decision a difficult one (if it were an easy or obvious decision, someone would have made it before it got to the president) for fear that the full story will make the president look "wishy-washy" or "indecisive." Nonetheless, in most cases officials can keep reporters from ever looking too deeply into the areas of greatest vulnerability: the substantive merits of what the administration is trying to do.

On television in particular, which for most Americans is now the main source of news, officials have nearly perfected the art of deflecting attention from the substantive weaknesses of their policies. "There's essentially a 'two question' rule in preparing officials for TV interviews," explained a former White House official. "Because of the enormous time constraints on television, if you can seem to give credible answers to two question on any subject—the first question and then the follow-up—you can use up the time without saying anything you don't want to say. It never fails. After two questions, the interviewer moves on to something else."

The importance of a "two question" rule predated the Clinton administration. Marlin Fitzwater, who had been White House press secretary under presidents Reagan and Bush, revealed after he left office that a variant of this rule had helped his presidents move through press conferences unscathed. The White House press corps had insisted that each correspondent who asked a question at a presidential press conference should be allowed to ask a follow-up as well. The reporters thought this would give them a better chance of pinning down the president. In reality, Fitzwater wrote in 1995, giving each correspondent two questions had the opposite effect. "The follow-up question allows the president time to more fully consider his first answer, and then to leave the issue with just the right words." In a typical thirty-minute news conference, a president must handle about twenty-six questions—but because of follow-ups, the questions will cover only thirteen topics. Fitzwater pointed out, "If everyone got a separate question, [the president] would have to cover twenty to twenty-five different subjects, a much harder task." Some reporters realized that the follow-up rule played into an administration's hands. But as long as press conferences were televised, Fitzwater concluded, no reporter would pass up the chance to ask a second question. To do so would mean giving up the network airtime that gives reporters "fame, power in the eyes of their peers, recognition by their families, ego gratification, and lecture fees from the Storm Door and Sash Associations of the world."

The "toughness" of today's media is mainly a toughness of demeanor rather than real toughness of reporting, investigation, or substantive change. The hostile tone of press briefings and the "attitude" of political coverage coexist with the media's willingness to give politicians a free pass on many issues of substance. The result is like the classic dysfunctional family; in exchange for enduring abuse, one partner gets to make most of the decisions. Journalists succeed in making government officials look like liars, and in the process make themselves look like self-righteous scolds.

"You could *always* outguess what reporters would ask at press conferences," a former employee of the Clinton White House said.

> Inside the government you are always worrying about
> what you can get away with in the press, and how this
> or that decision is going to play in press coverage. But
> you almost never have to worry that you'll be called on
> the substance of an issue.

Another official who had worked in the Clinton administration made the crucial point: "I don't know how the average person feels he has *any* way of making a decision, based on what's in the press."

LEARNED HELPLESSNESS. Press accounts are supposed to give us more and more realistic pictures of the world, allowing us to make more and more sensible decisions in private and public life. In areas ranging from foreign affairs to the condition of American cities the effect is often the reverse. Misleading coverage has made it hard to take sensible steps, or any steps at all.

Most of what the American press reports about the world outside our borders has less to do with the daily realities of life in China or South Africa or Chile than with projections of American concerns, neuroses, and assumptions onto other parts of the world. Much of what goes wrong in American foreign policy arises from a touching but misguided belief that world events can be shoehorned into concepts derived from American domestic politics. One obvious example is Japan. For half a century American press reports have been predicting a consumer revolution or youth rebellion in Japan that would slow down its productive machinery much the way the upheavals of the 1960s changed the United States. Protests against government power in Mexico, the Philippines, China, and elsewhere are portrayed as if they are direct descendants of the Minutemen at Lexington and Concord. The struggle in South Africa was seen as an extension of the U.S. civil rights struggle. Terms like "liberals" and "conservatives" are thrown around for the former Soviet states as if they had some resemblance to American conditions. In rare cases these perceptions may match the on-the-ground realities. Usually they leave the U.S. government and public chronically surprised at the mismatch between their expectations and unfolding events.

Like sports coverage, with its emphasis on the upcoming contest and lack of interest in previous games, and like weather reports, with a new supply of precise-seeming forecasts even though the old forecasts were laughably wrong, coverage of international affairs spends more time hypothesizing about what might happen than understanding what has already occurred. "Our system for covering foreign policy is tremendously powerful at issuing warnings and casting blame," Jonathan Clarke, a former diplomat who now writes about foreign policy, has said. "But there is almost no provision for going back and saying, 'We were wrong about the warnings! The plan worked.'" Clarke used the example of the Clinton administration's decision to invade Haiti in 1994. Press and political opinion had turned against the move by the time Bill Clinton decided to go ahead with it. Nonetheless, a year after it was undertaken, the exercise worked far better than most of the critics had feared. Press coverage of foreign policy very rarely reassesses such events to say, "This worked, and that didn't," Clarke observed. "It's a matter of warning about today's emergency and then warning about tomorrow's."

"The cumulative message on TV today is that the rest of the world is a confusing and dangerous place filled with civil war and ethnic and nationalist hatreds," Tom Rosenstiel wrote in the *Los Angeles Times* in 1994. The world is indeed confusing, but not quite in the way that news implies. He pointed out that year-by-year coverage has become shorter and more violence-driven as if what is going on in the world outside were one big drive-by shooting. In the mid-1990s, the major networks spend an average of six minutes per day on news outside the United States. Ten years earlier, international news represented nine minutes of the typical evening broadcast—a significant difference, on a show with twenty-four total minutes of news—and most of the stories were about economics, social developments, and political or diplomatic trends, rather than the natural disasters or bloodshed that provide a "news peg" for most foreign stories on TV now. The world events that appear on American TV mainly involve famine, warfare, shellings, communal violence, and other spasmodic episodes that evoke an all-or-nothing response from the United States—short-term humanitarian or even military intervention, or simply forgetting about it.

The standard coverage of urban affairs has been strangely parallel to foreign reporting. Both convey the message that the world being described is inexplicably and uncontrollably perilous. The logical conclusion in either case is that the individual citizen can do nothing at all about the dangers except to avoid any entanglement in them.

Much of the emphasis on catastrophe comes from TV stations' emphasis on ratings, which in turn reflects the belief of most local TV news operations that they must compete with pure entertainment programs head-to-head. Local TV news is the most immediately ratings-driven part of today's news business. Local stations across the country take advice from the same teams of ratings consultants, who have worked up formulas for holding the viewer's interest in this age of channel-surfing. Because of the consultants' influence, the local TV news is surprisingly similar from Boston to Seattle to San Antonio. The broadcast usually starts with crimes, fires, or auto wrecks, on the principle of "if it bleeds, it leads." Then there is political news, almost always in the context of horse race politics—the mayor is criticizing his opponents, the city council is arguing with the mayor. There are teases for the weather forecast—"We'll hear what kind of a weekend Bob has in store for us"—and for the latest sports results, details of which will come only near the end of the show. Even more than broadcast coverage of national or world events, local TV news suggests an environment of generalized menace that cannot really be understood but that viewers should try to insulate themselves from. If destructive events are placed in any perspective at all it is usually the perspective of raw politics—for instance, whether a shooting at a high school means that the superintendent of schools must step down.

Ralph Nader, the longtime consumer activist, has recently been studying the effect of news coverage on citizen attitudes. Suppose, he has said, that you are part of a group of parents trying seriously to improve public schools; or a group of merchants trying to change the tattered image of the downtown shopping district; or a group of neighbors trying to find activities other than drinking or watching TV for teenagers to do. "You might get a patronizing story every six months or so on some inner-city school that's working," Nader has argued.

> But in the meantime, you've been bombarded with homicides, rapes, child abuse and runaway-kid custody cases. What does it all amount to? It means a huge collective demoralization for the people who are masochistic enough to watch the TV. . . .

Nader said that the conventions of local news have defined as insignificant most events that don't end in violence. What qualifies best as news was, in Nader's words, "something that jerks your head up every ten seconds, whether that is shootings, robberies, sports showdowns, or dramatic weather forecasts." The accumulated impact of this kind of news, he concluded, was to give citizens a nightmarish view of life in their own community—or to tempt them to ignore the news altogether, since it was likely to be so horrifying.

"The effect of local news coverage on American crime policy since 1970 has been catastrophic," David Bruck said late in 1995. Bruck is the South Carolina lawyer who was in the national spotlight earlier in 1995 when arguing, successfully, that Susan Smith should be sentenced to life in prison rather than being executed for drowning her two sons. According to Bruck, between 1970 and 1995, the United States underwent a "punishment boom"—involving longer sentences for criminals and dramatically higher prison populations—that was unprecedented in American history. The main force behind this boom, he said, was "the media-created illusion that rare, spectacularly violent crimes are actually commonplace and proliferating." He added:

> Local TV causes the public to look at each unusual occurrence through the wrong end of a telescope. When one parolee out of 1,000 commits a terrible crime, the media act as if the only policy question were the stupidity of paroling that one aberrant individual. The conclusion, naturally, is to deny parole to everyone else. But the local news says nothing about the enormous costs of keeping the other 1,000 in jail.

Journalists continue to insist that they are merely holding up a mirror to an imperfect society. There is, however, increasing evidence that their cynical handling of political issues and their contextless presentation of violent events make society's problems harder to solve than they would otherwise be. In May 1995, the Times Mirror Center of the People and the Press released the results of a major study of the public's attitudes toward journalists and journalists' view of themselves. The results received muted coverage in the national media—a story on page D7 of the *New York Times,* another on the inside pages of the *Washington Post,* nothing on the major network programs. By comparison when a similar study a few months later showed widespread public loathing of politicians from every party, the *Washington Post* ran it on the front page.

"The news media has a generally positive view of itself in the watchdog role," the authors of the Times Mirror report said, "ranging from the way it feels it has covered Bill Clinton to the way it sees its own ethics." "I think we're doing things pretty well," a network news executive told the survey group. "We're covering things better, and we're covering more subjects. . . . The investigative work I think we're doing better and better." The rest of the country strongly begged to differ:

> The outside world strongly faults the news media for its negativism. . . . Top business executives, members of Congress, and local leaders from all around the country also think the press is more critical of them than it has been in the past. The public goes so far as to say that the press gets in the way of society solving its problems, an opinion that is even shared by many leaders.

By far the most telling part of the study compared "cynicism" levels among reporters and members of the public. How firmly was each group convinced that politicians were all in it for self-promotion, that government was one big racket run for powerful interests, and that there was not much chance of public life leading anywhere good?

Perhaps surprisingly, the survey showed that journalists, in their private beliefs, were not very cynical at all. Many of them said they respected individual politicians. A majority (53 percent) thought public officials as a class were more honest and more honorable than the general public was! Journalists, according to the survey, viewed the American democratic process as a flawed but basically decent means of reconciling different points of view and solving collective problems.

But that is not what their stories said. The view of public life that came through most print and broadcast accounts was an unrelieved tableau of posturing officeholders and ever-failed attempts to make any problem any better. Because of the conventions of modern "attitude" journalism, because of the fear of losing the public's attention if they stopped sounding snappy for even a moment, because of the ratings experts' advice that coverage of disasters and crimes would keep viewers hooked, because of a lack of a sense of responsibility for how public life turned out, the leading journalists of the 1990s presented a view of public life that was much bleaker than the journalists themselves believed to be true. And this relentlessly despairing message had the predictable result. According to this survey, members of the American public—who necessarily rely on press accounts for information about the general course of public life—were enormously cynical about American politics. Four-fifths of the public believed that politicians' morals were worse than those of the average citizen. Four-fifths thought that political authorities could "never" be trusted to do the right thing. (In the early 1960s, 70 percent of Americans thought the government *could* be trusted to do the right thing.) Real life had changed in ways that justified additional cynicism, but the tone of the media had changed even more. A belief in possibility may not by itself be sufficient to overcome obstacles. An assumption of impossibility is self-fulfilling.

In the early 1990s, researchers at the University of Pennsylvania's Annenberg School of Communication conducted a study to see how the tone of news coverage affected public attitudes toward politicians and government. The experiment involved readers in six cities other than Philadelphia, all of whom were given stories to read about the 1991 race for mayor of Philadelphia. Half of the readers were shown real newspaper and TV stories that emphasized standard horse race style political reporting. These stories featured poll results, charge and countercharge, examinations of the candidates' potential "character problems." The other readers were given an invented set of stories that concentrated on the candidates' proposals for dealing with the city's problems. "The results were clear," the supervisors of the study said. "Those who read and saw the 'strategy-based' reporting were more likely to conclude that the candidates were posturing, deceptive, self-interested, and unconcerned with the welfare of the city." They were also less likely to believe that there was any hope for progress through civic involvement.

The clearest sustained example of how the habits of the modern press can get in the way of the nation's business occurred between the spring of 1993 and the fall of 1994. It involved the Clinton administration's attempt to change the nation's health-care system. Bill and Hillary Clinton are usually presented as the losers in this struggle. What they lost legislatively was trivial compared to the damage to public life.

On its merits the plan may or may not have deserved to pass. Yet it confronted obstacles that said less about the plan's merits or demerits than about the destructive instincts of today's media. Political leaders of any party, as they decide whether to tackle any major national problem, must consider the impact of these same instincts. Many leaders decided that the obstacles are so great that it is not worth even attempting a serious discussion of problems that require more explanation than fits into a sound bite or a talk-show riposte.

There were many significant and interesting aspects to the Clinton administration's plan, any of which the press might have emphasized in helping the public decide whether it wanted to take this step. Before looking at what the press chose to concentrate on during the health debate, it is worth reviewing what it underplayed or ignored—the guts of the plan itself, the logic and trade-offs behind it, and the choices Americans really had about a future health system.

The Press's Vietnam War: The Health Care Debate

In October 1991, Governor Bill Clinton of Arkansas announced that he would run for president. One month later he held an internal debate among his advisors to work out his position on health care. Clinton had already decided that the issue was important both in substantive and in political terms. For more than a generation, health-care costs had risen about twice as fast as prices in general. Starting in the mid-1980s, big American companies began reporting that the most expensive part of their products—the biggest single component in the cost of a new car, for instance—was medical insurance for their employees. Sooner or later every serious plan for dealing with the government budget deficit involved controlling the cost of medical care, since the costs of Medicare (for people over age sixty-five) and Medicaid (for people who are poor) were by far the fastest-growing parts of federal, state, and local budgets. Politically the issue had suddenly heated up. A combination of rising insurance costs and increasing corporate layoffs meant that the percentage of Americans with no health insurance, which had fallen for decades, was going up again.

As Clinton was deciding whether and how to discuss health care in his campaign, policy experts from both parties had reached agreement on a surprisingly broad range of issues. The starting point for all discussions was a shared understanding that the "market" for medical care did not operate in the same way as markets for imported cars, or houses, or anything else.

It differed from other markets in that people were not allowed to be priced out of it all together. No one believes that every person has an absolute right to a car or a laptop computer or even a telephone, but politicians of all parties agree that people rich and poor have some equal right to medical care when they urgently need it. And our political system is set up on this premise as well: after a traffic accident or a drug overdose, hospitals are supposed to treat people even before they check the insurance forms.

It differed from other kinds of markets in that customers don't have the time or the knowledge to "shop" sensibly by themselves. They know what they are getting when choosing a Camry rather than a Lexus, but most patients have no way of assessing what they are buying when they pay for more expensive care, or what they give up when they pay less. What they do know about the medical market only increases their sense of not being able to "shop" there as they would for other products. People suspect that, in some specialized, high-tech corner of the American medical establishment, there is an advanced treatment for almost any disorder, but because these treatments are so expensive, people believe that insurance companies and health maintenance organizations will try to discourage patients from finding out about or using them.

The health-care market differed from other markets in that people don't even do the paying themselves, at least not at the time they get the care. In a perfect market situation, the purchaser will have free choice among many alternatives; he will have full knowledge about the selections; and he will have an incentive to economize. In the medical market, the customer often has none of those things. Doctors and nurses make most of the decisions about what treatments to use, which patients barely know how to second-guess. Insurance companies have the incentive to save money, but they either learn about decisions after they are made or try to anticipate all of them with hugely cumbersome Stalin-like lists of what is covered and what is not. The patient is usually the object of this process rather than a participant in it.

And medical care differs profoundly from other markets in the way that the main private corporations involved, the insurance companies, make their money. Most service companies—FedEx, McDonald's—can profit by economizing on the way that they provide their services. The best way for insurance companies to make money is simply to avoid insuring people who are going to get sick. You can save far more money in medical care by covering only young and healthy people than you can by figuring out more efficient ways to care for people who are old and sick. The problem, of course, is that everyone (except for those who die young) is eventually going to get old or sick, so every company has an incentive not to provide coverage for services that everyone will eventually need.

These oddities of the medical market had been well and thoroughly discussed by academics and policy experts in the years between Medicare's enactment in 1965 and the beginning of Bill Clinton's campaign in 1991. By the time Clinton began discussing health-care reform when campaigning in New Hampshire in 1992, all the indicators of prevailing opinion—statements from think tanks, comments on talk shows, asides in newsmagazines, speeches by politicians of both parties—suggested that some significant change in the health-care system was inevitable, and coming soon. The contending politicians and policy experts naturally disagreed about exactly what that change should be, but nearly all of their speeches and recommendations seemed to proceed from three shared observations about the American medical system:

First, that one way or another, the country had to control the overall cost of medical care. Businesses were in a panic about medical expenses, and so were any public officials responsible for a budget. The United States spent twice as large a share of its national income on medical care as the average for other developed nations. The money bought the world's most advanced and high-tech treatment for certain maladies, but it also left the U.S. with a higher infant-mortality rate and a lower life expectancy than in other advanced societies.

Second, that one way or another, the country had to offer coverage to everyone living within its borders. You could think of this as a "human dignity" issue if you wanted, but it was also a matter of practicality. People who got sick without insurance were still taken care of, but they were treated in the least efficient way possible—in hospital emergency rooms, after they had become severely sick. The insurance companies' efforts to shed any customers who had ever been ill was widely resented by the public. While sensible for the companies it was costly for the whole nation, since these uninsured patients would eventually be cared for in emergency circumstances too.

The ultimate logic of the insurance companies' approach was to offer rock-bottom rates to twenty-five-year-olds with no prior illnesses (many of whom would skip coverage anyway, since they probably would not get sick)—and to raise premiums for those forty-five years old and above and for people of any age with a history of illness, so as to cover their real cost of coverage. Those premiums would be too high for many people to pay, so they would be back in the emergency room. "Universal coverage" was a means not simply of protecting families against bad luck—a disabling accident, a premature child—but also of averaging the costs of a lifetime's medical care over a whole lifetime.

Third, the reform plans reflected the belief that one way or another, the experience of receiving medical care had to be changed in such a way that patients considered, but were not crushed by, the cost of the treatment they received. When patients received heart transplants, heroic treatment very late in life, experimental drugs, and other extremely costly forms of medical care, *someone* eventually paid the cost. That someone was either the taxpayer, covering mounting costs for Medicare and Medicaid, or those who paid insurance premiums. None of the reformers was proposing that the entire burden of these costs be placed back on the patients receiving care, which would defeat the purpose of insurance. But in various ways they tried to build more cost-awareness into the doctors' and patients' behavior.

Republican and Democrat, think tank expert and practicing physician—nearly all of the experts involved in medical policy could by the early 1990s agree on these three points. The disagreement involved the best way to realize these goals.

The ideas for dealing with medical problems fell into two large categories: "single-payer," and everything else. A single-payer system would essentially mean extending Medicare to cover people of all ages. Everyone would receive the same basic coverage, which they could supplement with additional insurance if they wanted. The same doctors, clinics, HMOs, and other organizations that now provide care would continue to do so. But all the money would go through one source—a "single" paying agency, run like the Medicare system by the federal government.

Single-payer systems were often described during the health debates as if they represented a radical step toward big-brother government, even though Medicare is exactly such a system. (Medicare is such a fixture of American life

that many people don't realize that it is a single-payer system, or even that it is run by the government. In town meetings during the health-care fight, representatives of the
Clinton administration often heard complaints along the
lines of, "The government should keep its hands off my
Medicare!") What would be radical and big-brotherish is a
single-*provider* system, in which the government did not
simply pay for but also delivered all medical care. This is the
way that Veterans Administration hospitals are run, with
government-owned hospitals and government-employed
doctors, but it was not part of Democratic proposals for
changing the health-care system.

The strongest argument for "single payer" is, strangely,
that it would be antibureaucratic. The great administrative
nightmare in American medicine is the need to keep track of
dozens of reimbursement forms from dozens of insurance
companies, each with its own rules about payment rates and
authorized courses of care. When Medicare was debated
thirty years ago, doctors feared the burden of coping with
government paperwork. Coping with private-insurance paperwork is a far greater burden on them now. "Single payer"
would also ensure universal coverage, as Medicare does for
retirement-age Americans, and as with Medicare it gives the
payer bargaining power to hold down costs.

The main argument against a single-payer system is that
it would require a new tax. People and companies would no
longer have to pay insurance premiums, but they would have
to make up the difference (and more, since more people
would initially be covered) in taxes. Moreover, to many people "single payer" sounds like another Democratic scheme for
expanding the reach of big government. And—of great political significance—the insurance companies would be sure to
fight ferociously against it, since it would simply put them
out of the enormous business of providing medical insurance.

All other proposals for reforming the health-care system avoided funneling money through the government, in single-payer fashion, but tried to create other incentives to hold down costs. Many alternatives had been proposed in the half-dozen years before Bill Clinton ran for president, but the one that became the most important was "managed competition." This was a hybrid scheme that left all existing parties—insurance companies, doctors, HMOs, and so on—in business but controlled what rates they would charge, what coverage they must offer, and whom they must insure.

The relevant politics of the health issue began in November 1991, a few weeks after Clinton announced that he would run for president and immediately after the Democratic candidate, Harris Wofford, won the off-year Senate election in Pennsylvania with a platform emphasizing health-care reform. As he did on a number of policy issues, and as politicians routinely do, Clinton invited proponents of different approaches to debate in front of him, after which he would choose. After listening to their cases he concluded that "single payer" was the simpler and more logical solution to health-care problems—but that it was politically unrealistic, since it would require a big new tax. Instead he began working toward a "managed competition" plan similar to the one his task force ultimately proposed in 1993.

In the three years between Clinton's in-house debate over "single payer" in 1991 and his admission in late 1994 that his health-reform effort had failed, the American political system went through one of its great exercises in decision making. A problem had emerged; political leaders proposed solutions; the people's representatives made their choice. In this case the choice was to reject the president's proposal, and the lesson that is generally taken from the experience is that the Clinton administration bungled the affair from beginning to end.

The evidence is at least as strong, however, for another interpretation: that the media failed in a historic way to help Americans understand and decide on this issue. Even those who were dead set against this plan should not feel good about the way in which it was defeated. The habits of mind that the media revealed in covering this fight will be equally troublesome for Republicans trying to present their agenda. These habits get in the way of anyone trying to do anything.

How, specifically, did the press affect this episode? As a matter of press performance, the health-care drama had seven acts. In each of them the media illustrated one of the problems it creates for public life.

THE EMERGENCE OF THE HEALTH-CARE "ISSUE": HORSE RACE POLITICS ONLY. In a way, the most fateful choice Bill Clinton made about health care was the one he made at the beginning of his campaign. It was not simply that he would stress health reform as a campaign issue but that he would not choose "single payer." This may have been wise politics (although it is hard to see how a single-payer bill could have fared worse than the one he presented). It may have been foolish. Regardless of whether it was right or wrong, it had enormous implications for the way health-care reform would progress if Clinton won the election— and these implications were barely mentioned in campaign coverage.

Senator Robert Kerrey, of Nebraska, supported a single-payer plan. As long as he remained in the Democratic primaries, as an opponent to Clinton, the single-payer issue remained on the political radar screen. It was, after all, one of the issues about which Clinton and Kerrey criticized each other and therefore was part of the political game. But in political sex appeal it could not begin to compare to the more visible difference between the candidates: the severely wounded war hero versus the notorious noncombatant. Once Kerrey dropped out of the race, leaving Clinton and Paul Tsongas competing for the right to challenge George Bush (and Ross Perot), the single-payer option was barely mentioned again, since none of the remaining candidates was espousing it. During the general election, most stories described the health-care "issue" that Clinton would use in attacking Bush, rather than considering the pluses or minuses of what each candidate proposed to do.

NOT INVITED TO THE CHRISTENING: THE PRESS GETS EVEN. By the time the Clinton health-care bill had finally been rejected in 1994, a standard list of explanations for its failure had entered the conventional wisdom. The list usually began with the complaint that the health bill had been "conceived in secrecy," by a coven of egghead advisors led by Hillary Clinton and the secretive Ira C. Magaziner. "The health-care task force of 500 'experts,' a kind of policy ship of fools, labored in secret while divulging nightly news bites of misinformation," said an analysis in the *Washington Post* in late August 1994. "Opponents of Clinton-style reform used the secrecy issue to cast the first real doubts on the effort," said another *Post* wrap-up two months later. "Clinton's eager health-care legions—having concocted their plan in secrecy—never were savvy enough to see they'd have to settle for a good start" rather than a comprehensive plan, *USA Today* said in an editorial after the Clinton administration had conceded defeat on the bill.

It is interesting that few people registered the complaint when the health-care task force was actually doing its work. The task forces that Magaziner and Hillary Clinton directed worked on a tight schedule and behind usually closed doors during the first few months of the administration. But that is what administrations *always* do when drawing up their initial legislative plans. Ronald Reagan did this with his budget proposals. Jimmy Carter did so with his en-

ergy plan. Richard Nixon did so with his proposals for welfare reform. Franklin Roosevelt of course pioneered the approach of rush projects to develop legislative agendas. Some
of these previous examples may suggest that secrecy does not
make for wise policy, but they also suggest that the Clinton
health-care team was not some aberration.

Moreover, while they were drawing up their plans, the
task forces were anything but secret with the groups whose
approval would ultimately be most important: the congressional committees that would consider a health-reform plan.
The specialized publications that cover Washington politics,
such as *Congressional Quarterly* and *National Journal,* emphasized how extensive the administration's consultations with
Congress had been. A typical headline from *CQ* in May 1993
said, "Clinton Task Force All Ears on the Subject of Overhaul." "Most members of Congress give the president high
marks for laying the political groundwork necessary for his
proposal to get the careful consideration of both parties," the
article continued. "Clinton has been playing the health-care
issue with an eye to keeping everyone at the table, at least at
the outset." In late September 1993, when Hillary Clinton
appeared before five congressional committees to explain the
rationale behind the bill, not a single legislator complained
about "closed" or "secretive" deliberations.

What went wrong? It seems that there was one important group that was truly excluded from the task force's deliberations: the Washington press. During the brusque, early
weeks of the Clinton administration, George Stephanopoulos
was walling reporters out of the White House press office
and the administration thought it could take its message directly to the public through radio appearances and interview
shows. As part of the same strategy, Magaziner was instructed
by Stephanopoulos's communications office that he and his
associates must not let reporters know what was going to be

in the new bill. All information was to flow through a single spokesman, Robert Boorstin. This didn't stop leaks, of course, but it gave Magaziner a lasting reputation among reporters as a man who liked to operate in the dark.

When the battle was all over, Magaziner and Hillary Clinton realized that stiff-arming the press had been a huge blunder. "Even though we had a process unlike any other that has drafted a bill—more open, more inclusive—we got labeled as being secretive because of our failure to understand the additional requirement of feeding the press along the way," she said in August 1994, as the health bill neared death. "That was something that we just missed. . . . We were not aware of how significant it is to be part of the inside story in Washington, in order to make the case for whatever your policy is."

The more alarming point that the administration "just missed" is how many of the reporters view treatment of *them* as a proxy for treatment of the nation as a whole. Of course there are cases in which reporters really do represent the broader public's right to know, and if a mayor or a general or a foreign leader or a sheriff refuses to speak to them, by extension he spites the entire public. But there are other cases in which the press confuses its own interest in needing to know with the public's interest in having events turn out well in the long run. As a *tactical* matter the Clinton officials were idiots (as they later admitted) to think it made sense to banish leaks and deny reporters their gruel of daily background briefings. But the press made this mistake sound like something worse: a deliberate decision to exclude the rest of the nation from deliberations leading to a health-reform plan.

"POLICY DEVELOPMENT": THE TYRANNY OF LEAK AND SCANDAL. The health-care task forces began their work even before the administration took office in January 1993. The 1600-page fruit of their effort, the Health Security

Act of 1993, was presented to the Congress that September. During those nine months, the administration's concerns about press coverage and reactions to the habits of the modern media played nearly as big a role as legislative, financial, or medical concerns in dictating the progress of the proposals.

The administration's initial hope had been to apply the hallowed "Hundred Days" example of Franklin Roosevelt with his New Deal legislation and Ronald Reagan with his tax-cut schemes, and ram a health bill through the Congress right away. Coming up with the right proposals was not, they thought, the main obstacle to doing so—their ideas had been in gestation for a long time. The trick would instead be one of legislative maneuvering. If the main principle of their health plan could be attached to the first "budget reconciliation" bill that Congress acted on in 1993, then its passage would depend only on a majority vote. In theory it takes fifty-one votes to get a bill through the Senate, but in modern reality it takes sixty votes to end a filibuster, which was more than the Democrats had in 1993 (or the Republicans in 1995). Budget bills, however, come to the floor under rules requiring only a fifty-one-vote majority for passage.

The plan of attaching health legislation to the budget bill had been endorsed by the Senate's majority leader, George Mitchell, but it was torpedoed by Senator Robert Byrd of West Virginia, the Senate's de facto parliamentarian. The administration then decided that it would have the health plan in the pipeline and introduce it just as soon as its budget bill, with tax increases and spending cuts designed to reduce the federal deficit, got through.

That was the rub. The budget bill, with its big deficit-reduction package, was seen by "everyone" in Washington as the major, early test of the administration's strength. The budget fight dragged on much longer than Bill Clinton hoped or planned. With each passing week, the schedule for introducing health legislation was pushed back not by a single week but by two or three, because even the final decisions about health policy were delayed for fear of inevitable leaks. In the beginning of June 1993, when the administration's health negotiators had hoped to be working out specific legislative plans with congressional staff members, Tom Foley, the Speaker of the House, specifically asked that they not "share paper" with anyone in the Congress until the budget fight was over. The details of any measure they were considering, from payroll taxes to increases in the levies on wine and beer, would immediately leak to the press, and groups who were upset about any of these proposals would try to hold the budget bill hostage.

The administration's budget bill finally passed in August. Only then did the administration once again "share paper" containing specifics of what the health plan would cover, how much it might cost, and where the money would come from. The details were publicly presented in late September, first by Hillary Clinton in her week of congressional testimony and then by her husband in an address to a joint session of the Senate and House. The immediate reception— from press, politicians, and initial public-opinion polls— was strongly favorable. An article in *Time* magazine shortly after the president's speech said, "Politicians almost unanimously agree that public sentiment so strongly favors some kind of health-care reform that many Congress members dare not run for reelection in 1994 without having voted to enact any." "The reviews are in and the box office is terrific," the political analyst William Schneider wrote just after the plan was presented. "President Clinton's health-care reform plan is a hit. . . . The more people read and hear about the plan, the more they seem to like it." But as Congress prepared to consider what to do with the plan, the scandal-and-spectacle switch was thrown again by the press.

Bill Clinton had planned to spend virtually the whole month of October traveling and speaking about the health plan, replicating the all-out push he had previously given the NAFTA treaty. As he was flying to the first event in this sequence, a labor convention in California, news came that American soldiers had been killed in Somalia. Clinton flew back to Washington after the rally and spent most of the next four weeks dealing with what seemed at the time to be the transcendent urgency of the showdown in Somalia. On talk shows, pundits said that this misadventure might plague Clinton's presidency, much as the failed rescue of hostages in Iran in 1980 had become a symbol of Jimmy Carter's luckless quality in office. Given the media's relentless concentration on what the "misstep" in Somalia would mean for Clinton's political prospects, Americans would remember the horrific picture of a GI's corpse being dragged through dusty foreign streets long after the event occurred. They would have had a harder time remembering or explaining exactly what U.S. troops were doing there.

The Somalia crisis eventually came to an end, but the media coverage left the impression that the Clinton administration was once again "floundering" and "in disarray." While Clinton was still embroiled in Somalia, the business group with the most to lose if the Clinton plan were enacted—the Health Insurance Association of America (HIAA), representing many of the nation's health insurance companies— launched its advertising campaign against the plan. Most of the HIAA's television ads featured two actors, a man and woman who appeared to be prosperous and in their forties, talking about how government-run health care would take away the choice and flexibility they valued so highly.

These characters, never named in the commercials, became known as "Harry and Louise" in the countless news accounts of the HIAA's campaign. The campaign was expensive—by the HIAA's own estimate it invested at least $14 million in advertisements—but its greatest power lay in its shrewd understanding of the press. The "Harry and Louise" ads did not appear even once on broadcast network TV. They were, instead, concentrated in the places where journalists and politicians might be expected to see them—on CNN and on local stations in the home cities of key legislators who would vote on the health-care bill.

If you were a political reporter based in Washington, you seemed to run into the ads all the time. They showed up on the political talk shows, on the local TV news, and on CNN whenever you checked in to follow breaking stories from Somalia. It was natural for reporters to assume that their fellow citizens were being exposed to a similar avalanche of ads, and many newspaper and TV reporters began referring offhandedly to the "Harry and Louise" campaign, which most Americans had never seen. Hillary Clinton, who apparently also overestimated the scope of the advertising campaign, elevated its importance by criticizing "Harry and Louise" in a speech. Network news broadcasts showed clips from the "Harry and Louise" ads, allowing the HIAA to reach for free a much larger audience than it had paid for. An academic study of the health-reform fight concluded that these press references to "Harry and Louise" were far more valuable to the HIAA than the purchased ads themselves.

As the HIAA campaign was gaining momentum (at least as far as reporters in Washington could tell from what they saw on TV), White House press attention shifted to "Troopergate." Allegations that Bill Clinton, as governor, had used Arkansas state troopers to procure women broke just before Christmas time of 1993. The administration responded to the Troopergate and Whitewater allegations at this point with a stonewalling policy that only heightened the media's interest in the subjects. The cumulative result of these problems—Somalia, counterattacks on health care, "Troopergate," continued rumblings on talk radio shows about whether the Clintons' confidant, Vince Foster, had really committed suicide (as opposed to being murdered) in the summer of 1993, plus the assorted loose ends of the Whitewater affair—was to give the Clinton administration a series of "bad weeks" late in 1993. The president's popularity, which had bounced up after his budget victory in the summer and gone even higher after he won the NAFTA fight in the fall, was on its way down again.

None of these difficulties had any logical or direct connection to the future of health care in America. But since the press had instinctively cast the health-reform fight as yet another test of the president's "clout" and popularity, a weakened president meant an imperiled health-care bill.

So it was at the turn of the year Republican strategists changed their assessment of the prospects for health care. Through 1993 they had believed that passage of *some* health-reform bill was inevitable. Their task was to work with the Clinton administration to tailor the bill to their party's tastes. As late as the fall of 1993, Bob Dole had made joint appearances with Hillary Clinton to support the need for universal coverage. But by the beginning of 1994 they had concluded that they could in fact kill the bill outright, not because anything had changed in the proposal but because emergencies and scandals, detailed in the press, had made the administration weak. William Kristol, a former aide to Vice President Dan Quayle who had become an influential Republican strategist, sent a memo to party leaders near the end of 1993 saying that President Clinton had become newly vulnerable. A defeat of his health-care program would be a mortal political blow to the president. Therefore, Kristol concluded, Republicans should oppose passage of any plan proposed by the administration, "sight unseen."

FEAR-MONGERING: THE EMPHASIS ON SINGLE-INTEREST POLITICS. By the time the health plan was unveiled in the fall of 1993, another factor had begun to work against its passage. The work of one influential reporter,

Robert Pear of the Washington bureau of the *New York Times,* was at the center of this effect.

Pear had concentrated for years on the substance, rather than the party politics, of domestic issues—immigration, welfare, economic policy, and, during the Clinton administration, health care. His forte had been smoking out documents that revealed what government agencies were considering or what plans might soon be announced. During the misguided "secret" stage of the administration's health deliberations, he displayed the same skill. Each time a new idea was floated for changing health coverage or limiting costs, Pear usually found out about it and reported its implications on the front page of the *Times* the next day.

Individually many of the stories were impressive feats of reportage. Collectively they had a peculiar effect, especially because of their prominent play in the *Times.* Over the last generation every commentator in America has bemoaned the rise of "single-interest" politics, in which people ask "What's in it for me?" about each proposal and never ask anything else. The *Times's* coverage of the health deliberations, driven by the prominent play of Pear's stories, fed exactly that mentality.

One of his earliest stories reported, on the front page, that the Clinton panel was considered doing away with Medicare and making it part of the new national plan. Whether or not this approach might have made sense in logical terms, politically and journalistically the "threat to Medicare" became an "incident" and "gaffe." The pro-Medicare lobby took up arms to defend its program; the administration spent time calming their fears.

Over the next few months, *Times* stories singled out, one by one, the groups that might suffer tiny losses because of changes in the status quo. Headlines in the *Times,* over Pear's byline and often on the front page, gave a stream of warnings like:

"Health-Care Costs May Be Increased $100 Billion a Year," May 3, 1993, page 1;

"Medicaid and Medicare Cutback Sought to Finance Health Plan," September 9, 1993, page 1;

"Premium Limits in Health Plan Draw Criticism," September 18, 1993, page 1;

"Clinton Care Plan May Cut Benefits to Some Children," October 11, 1993, page 1;

"Influential Group Says Health Plan Slights the Aged," October 24, 1993, page 1;

"In Noting Absence, A.M.A. Sees a Snub," December 7, 1993, page 24; and so on.

The *Times,* on its editorial page, often emphasizes the need to look at the big picture and rise above a collection of special-interest concerns. But the paper's coverage did that much less frequently and much less prominently than it warned people that their subsegment of the population might suffer.

Because the *Times* casts such a huge shadow not simply over other papers but over network news operations as well, the rest of the news machine soon began covering the health deliberations as if they were a continuation of the presidential race—that is, mainly a contest for the support of balkanized interest groups. In an article in the *Washington Monthly,* the authors Tom Hamburger, Ted Marmor, and Jon Meacham described how profound the influence of Pear and the *Times* had been. In 1994, they said:

> A group of reporters were drinking beer and lamenting what had already become apparent: The coverage of health care resembled nothing so much as the hasty horserace stories of a political campaign. What could we do?
>
> "Shoot Robert Pear," said one network television reporter, referring to his enterprising colleague at the

New York Times who was breaking story after story on
the health beat. The comment produced a roar of laugh-
ter from the table; everyone there had had an angry editor demanding a follow-up on a Pear piece. . . ."

There may be no better reporter at scooping the
competition than Robert Pear. But get-it-first journalism was not what America needed during debate over
the most ambitious social legislation since the New
Deal.

This is not really a complaint about Pear himself, who
is conscientious, honest, and an extremely diligent reporter.
He has said that he recognizes the legitimacy of concerns
about the impact of news on public policy. But he pointed
out, with citations to James Madison's warning against the
role of "factions" in *The Federalist Papers,* that American politics had been vexed by special-interest pressure from the beginning. And he added that he was uncomfortable basing
his reporting on "what America needed," as the authors of
the *Washington Monthly* critique of his coverage had put it,
since "that implies a more instrumental or teleological view
of journalism" than he felt was appropriate.

These are reasonable views. Yet they leave us with a
concept of news that rewards diligence in figuring out which
group will suffer which losses—but is lackadaisical about
explaining consequences for the public as a whole.

THE BUM OF THE MONTH. At the beginning of the
health-reform fight, Kathleen Hall Jamieson, dean of the
Annenberg School for Communication at the University of
Pennsylvania, began a study of press coverage of the deliberations. In 1994, as part of this work, she sat with reporters
who had come to Philadelphia to watch Hillary Clinton
make a presentation of the plan.

Mrs. Clinton was onstage for nearly two hours. During

that time, she described the rationale for reform in the medical market, detailed the reasoning that went into the administration's plan, and took questions from the audience at length.

"She went into the substance of the plan, and took on virtually every argument that had been raised against it," Jamieson said. "You may disagree with her answers. You may say that the plan was not right for the country—I had objections to it myself. What I'm discussing concerns the behavior of the reporters."

> What was interesting to me was the physical sensation of being in the middle of the press corps during the different parts of the presentation. When she was talking about her plan, the reporters had clearly heard all of this before and found it completely uninteresting. They were talking to each other, passing notes around.
>
> But as soon as she made a brief attack on the Republicans, there was a physiological reaction, this surge of adrenaline, all around me. The pens moved. The reporters arched forward. They wrote everything down rapidly. As soon as this part was over, they clearly weren't paying attention any more. They were writing on their laptops as they began constructing the story of how the First Lady had attacked her opponents.

What Jamieson saw that day was a small illustration of a much larger truth. Once the administration had laid its health proposal before the Congress, the press treated the plan as if it were a candidate in an election. A variety of other bills had been proposed before the administration formally submitted its plan, and as time went on more and more politicians presented their own health-reform alternatives. A horse race was under way again, and the drama lay in seeing whether the Clinton bill would hold its lead against the Chaffee bill, or the Cooper bill, or whatever other dark-horse bills might enter the race.

Jamieson called this style of coverage "conflict frame" or "political strategy" reporting, as opposed to substantive reporting about what was *in* the various health plans. Her survey of print and broadcast coverage found that the media concentrated overwhelmingly on who was likely to "win" the health fight, rather than what the consequences of winning or losing might be for the public. (She found that 67 percent of all broadcast coverage of health reform, and 62 percent of all print coverage, was in the "conflict frame." Typical headlines for this approach would be "Dole attacks Clinton plan" or "Contests for seniors' vote as health-care showdown nears.")

The emphasis on "conflict" turned press coverage into a moving spotlight. From the fall of 1993 through the summer of 1994, a variety of alternatives to the Clinton plan emerged and receded. The "Cooper bill" became the "Clinton Lite" plan became "Cooper/Breaux/Grandy." Senators Kennedy, Dole, Moynihan, Gramm, and Mitchell each had plans with their names attached. So did Representatives Stark, Dingell, Michel, Gibbons, Gephardt—to name a few. As each politician came up with a new scheme, the politician and his plan briefly moved into the center of news coverage, until they proved unable to dislodge the Clinton plan and the next contender appeared.

The process resembled the "Bum of the Month" parade of palookas challenging established heavyweight champs like Joe Louis or Muhammad Ali. While the Clinton plan did not exactly enjoy the status of a champ, the news coverage had the same tone of weekly showdowns forgotten nearly as soon as they had occurred. Whoever was attacking the president most stridently was usually attacked in return— and the press, in "conflict mode," gave those fights far more attention than moderate attempts to find agreement. In the summer of 1994, Newt Gingrich declared on the David Brinkley show that having universal coverage would mean creation of a "police state." This was hardly mainstream Republican doctrine—Bob Dole had called universal coverage "indispensable" less than a year earlier—but because it was flamboyant, and because the White House counterattacked, it dominated the news for a few days.

Jamieson's analysis of published survey data indicated that, despite a year's worth of news coverage, the public remained confused on basic factual issues about the contents of the Clinton plan and the alternative proposals. Jamieson and her colleague Joseph N. Cappella ran an experiment to test how informative press coverage had been. Subjects in their experimental group read fifteen news articles about the health-reform process. Subjects in the control group read one article about health reform—and fourteen articles on another topic. The groups were then tested to see not which plan they preferred but how well they understood what various plans would do. The group that had read fifteen health articles did not do better on this test than the group that had read only one.

"The problem with raising any of these problems is that people will say, 'Oh, you just wanted the Clinton plan to pass.'" Jamieson commented after describing her findings.

> In fact, I didn't think the plan was such a good plan.
> But I also don't think that it was dismissed based on
> any reasoned deliberation in a public sphere.

MISINFORMATION. Hillary Clinton, thanks to her position in the government, was one of two women with the greatest influence on the health debate. Elizabeth McCaughey, because of the quirks of the press, was the other.

Early in 1994, she was a researcher at the Manhattan

Institute, a conservative think tank in New York that usually specialized in welfare and other domestic issues. One year later, as Hillary Clinton licked her wounds and backed away from public debates because of her health reform defeat, McCaughey (pronounced "McCoy") was sworn in as the Republican lieutenant governor of New York.

In between these two moments McCaughey had a dramatic impact on the course of debate about the health plan. The February 7, 1994, issue of the *New Republic* carried an article by McCaughey about the Clinton health plan. The title was "No Exit," and the article's premise was that an outside observer (that is, McCaughey) had, for the first time, mustered the stamina and clear-headedness to read through the health proposal and see what it actually contained. Her discoveries were terrifying, and McCaughey wanted to share them with her fellow citizens before it was too late.

The article began with a series of claims about the radical changes the bill would bring to the American medical system, accompanied by convincing-seeming citations to pages in the bill:

> The law will prevent you from going outside the system to buy basic health coverage you think is better, even after you pay the mandatory premium (see the bill, page 244). The bill guarantees you a package of medical services, but you can't have them unless they are deemed "necessary" and "appropriate" (pages 90–91). That decision will be made by the government, not by you and your doctor. Escaping the system and paying out-of-pocket to see a specialist for the tests and treatment you think you need will be almost impossible.

And so on. People didn't know about these limits, she said, because, unlike her, very few had taken the trouble to read the whole bill and therefore they were vulnerable to politicians' distortions. "If these facts surprise you, it's because you haven't been given a straight story about the Clinton health bill," McCaughey said.

As it happened, it was McCaughey herself who had not grasped the straight story about the bill. Her article contained two kinds of misinterpretations which together gave a completely distorted picture of what the bill would do. One distortion came from her apparent unfamiliarity with the way medical care works even without the Clinton bill. Early in her piece McCaughey professed to be shocked by the idea that the plan would offer coverage only for what the government deemed "necessary and appropriate" treatment. It would have been far more amazing if the plan did not include such a limiting clause. Medicare covers only "necessary" and "appropriate" treatment right now, and it pays for it only according to schedules set by the government. Private insurance plans also include such "necessary" and "appropriate" limits (as do plans for auto insurance, theft insurance, and most other reimbursement systems). Part of the idea behind revising the health-coverage system was holding down overall medical spending, which is hard enough in any case but would be impossible if "unnecessary" and "inappropriate" treatment were included. McCaughey also found it outrageous that, under the Clinton plan, patients would have to show proof of coverage when they went to a doctor's office or hospital. This is the way most hospitals and HMOs have operated for years.

Behind complaints like these was a deeper attitude that had little to do with the Clinton bill. McCaughey's objection to payment limits, identification cards, and the other traits of bureaucratized medicine would apply just as bitingly to most medical care that is delivered today, through HMOs and managed-care organizations. In a "can you believe it?" tone she wrote that if the Clinton plan took effect,

price controls on premiums will push most Americans
into HMOs and pressure HMOs into sharply cutting
access to specialists and effective, high-tech cures.
Price controls on doctors' fees and regulations tying
doctors' hands will curb the care physicians can give
patients.

Price controls and limits on care may not sound attractive, but most Americans realize that this is where medical
care is headed, with or without any intervention by the government. Of all Americans who have health insurance coverage, at least two-thirds are now enrolled in some kind of
managed-care system (as opposed to traditional "fee for service" treatment). As business organizations continue to shift
their employees' coverage to some form of managed care, the
proportion of Americans enrolled in managed programs continues to go up. The essence of "management" is limits.
Since the amount of money that could be spent on medical
care rises much faster than the amount the government, private companies, or individual people are willing to spend,
someone has to put on the brakes. Someone will be double-
checking a patient's request for care rather than automatically paying the bill. Medical "gatekeepers" will check a
patient's complaints before approving a visit to a specialist.
Insurance companies will declare certain expensive procedures "experimental" and refuse to cover the costs. This is
the real world of medical care that most Americans have
known for the last decade, and which they will know more
intimately in the future. In suggesting that managed care
was an avoidable evil, McCaughey not only revealed her
naiveté about medical economics but also misrepresented
the range of choices America has in designing a future medical system.

The other great misrepresentation came from either an
accidental or a deliberate failure to grasp certain legal

points. The overriding theme of McCaughey's article (and of two follow-ups by her, in response to outraged letters of protest) was that the health reform would lock everyone into an inflexible, centrally planned, no-options medical system, much as if the whole country had been conscripted into the network of VA hospitals. The title of her first article, "No Exit," summed up the theme. Your only choice under the plan would be the "choice" that bureaucrats deigned to offer you. This, McCaughey concluded, would almost certainly not include the one kind of medical care she approved of— "traditional"-style "fee for service" care, in which you visit one physician (rather than a clinic or HMO) and pay him or her directly. No matter how much money you had, you'd be stuck in the clumsy centrally run system. Doctors under the "single-payer" system would operate under draconian price controls, which soon would drive them out of business altogether. "We've been told that the government won't be putting price controls on doctors, but the bill limits what health plans can pay physicians and prohibits patients from paying their doctors directly."

This sounded alarming, but it overlooked one fundamental point. Nothing in the bill "prohibits patients from paying their doctors directly." What it prohibited was patients paying doctors extra for services that *the health plan was already paying for.* If you wanted to see a specialist, get daily treatments, have a magnetic-resonance image of your sore knee, but the bureaucrats didn't like it—no problem! All you had to do was pay for it yourself. But if a doctor was already billing a managed-care plan for the procedures, he couldn't bill you extra too. As Mickey Kaus pointed out in the *New Republic* a year later, the situation is analogous to education. All taxpayers are required to help cover the cost of the public school system, and all taxpayers and employers would be required to contribute to the cost of the new national health-care system. "But if you don't like the public schools, you can use your own money to send your kid to private school," Kaus wrote. Similarly, anyone who was unhappy with the choices offered by the Clinton plan could use his or her own money to get extra care.

The distinction McCaughey missed was between what the government would *pay for* and what it would *outlaw.* She acted as if anything that was not paid for under the plan was therefore prohibited—which, again, is like imagining that private schools are against the law.

McCaughey's article contained some of the schoolboy-howler errors that make many journalists sit up nights worrying ("What if someone sees that I misunderstood the bill?") and that convince most magazines, although not the *New Republic,* to hire fact-checking staffs. Yet for more than a year after its publication, McCaughey's article received very little critical scrutiny. Its central "no exit" claim was passed on by spokesmen who reached much larger audiences than the hundred thousand or so subscribers to the *New Republic.* George Will embellished the claim with a "patients in jail" scenario. ("It would be illegal for doctors to accept money directly from patients, and there would be fifteen-year jail terms for people driven to bribery for care they feel they need but the government does not deem 'necessary.'") In fact, the "bribery" provisions of the Clinton bill are similar to those under today's Medicaid and Medicare law: they are meant to punish people who defraud the government through false billings. People who wanted care the government did not deem necessary would be in just the same position they are today, if their insurance company does not deem the care necessary. They can pay for it themselves.

Rush Limbaugh broadcast the same police-state theme to a much larger audience. As McCaughey's claims took on momentum and a life of their own—as politicians cited them in speeches and they became taken for granted on talk shows—a journalistic establishment devoted to helping

Americans resolve this issue would have examined criticisms of the plan, as well as the plan itself.

A tiny minority of journalists did this. Michael Weinstein, in a short editorial-page item in the *New York Times,* argued that "Ms. McCaughey's analysis is careless, misleading and wrong" and said that "her fear-mongering falsehoods . . . threaten to warp the debate." One week after McCaughey's article appeared in the *New Republic,* Michael Kinsley said in the same magazine that "Perhaps she has spent too much time buried in those famous 1,342 pages [of the health plan] and not enough observing the world around her." (McCaughey responded to Kinsley and other critics mainly through assertions that her reading of the bill had, in fact, been right. For example, in direct response to Kinsley's article she wrote, "Anyone who reads the bill will see that it expressly prohibits Americans from buying the kinds of extensive, high-quality health plans that many now choose.")

Most coverage of McCaughey's article did not examine its premises but instead passed along her conclusions as true—or, to be precise, it did something more important and damaging than that. It viewed them as being "interesting" and "in play." Because McCaughey and her arguments had affected the prospects for the rest of the participants, they could be talked about without ever being examined. The articles about McCaughey herself were generally "cute" and "bright" feature pieces, especially when she entered the lieutenant governor's race. (Good-looking Park Avenue socialite stirs up big policy mess! Political novice plunges into New York political scramble!) It was not until more than a year after her piece was published, when the National Association of Magazine Editors took the dumbfounding step of awarding McCaughey the prize for "Excellence in Public Interest," that her articles got another look. (The most effective of these reappraisals was by Mickey Kaus, in the *New Republic*—which was cheeky, considering that the magazine was the official recipient of the award.)

The award represented the magazine world's adoption of the standards of the talk shows. The citation said that Mc-Caughey's "carefully researched" pieces had "transcended the coverage in most of the press. More than any other single event in the debate, what she wrote stopped the bill in its intellectual tracks." The standards for this award (and many other "public service" awards in journalism) place heavy emphasis on hard political results—an investigative work could be brilliant, revealing, and spellbinding, but if it doesn't lead to Congressional hearings or put a politician in jail, it doesn't count. McCaughey's article revealed the opposite side of this logic. A work could be defective by normal journalistic standards, but if it causes a stir, it has met the test. It didn't matter that much of what McCaughey said was wrong, or that if anything her articles retarded the national effort to decide where to strike a balance between controlling costs and preserving individual choice and freedom. The articles attracted attention. They affected the debate. They had buzz and impact. That was enough.

OUT OF SIGHT, OUT OF MIND. With the collapse of the Clinton plan in the summer of 1994, press and political attention moved elsewhere. In October 1994, two months after the administration conceded defeat in its attempts to change the health-care system, the Republicans unveiled the "Contract with America" on which they would base their nationwide congressional campaign. The contract did not include a single word about controlling the cost of medical care.

Ignoring the issue did not make it go away. When the congressional Republicans returned, victorious, in 1995 they soon found that all their efforts to reduce the federal budget deficit were imperiled by the ceaseless increase in Medicare spending. The inflation rate for medical spending, private and public, had fallen from its peaks in the early 1990s. But for at least three decades, the annual rise in medical costs had been about three percentage points higher than the overall inflation rate. That gap grew slightly wider in 1994. As corporate "downsizing" continued, the proportion of Americans with no medical insurance whatsoever also rose. Yet the "medical" issue virtually vanished from TV news and retreated from most front pages, except as it involved the Republicans' difficulties in "handling" the Medicare "issue."

Sooner or later, the American public would have to accept some arrangement for balancing its interest in advanced technology, individual choice, and manageable cost. For the previous two years, the political and journalistic systems had devoted tremendous attention to this issue. And at the end of the process there was no sign that the public was closer to understanding the problems it faced or the choices it would have to make than if the whole exercise had never occurred.

Chapter 6

News and Democracy

In the decade after World War I, Americans debated the connection between information and democracy more seriously than they have ever done since. The war coincided with the birth of the new science of "public relations." In the years just before the war a former newspaper reporter named Ivy Lee had convinced the Rockefeller interests and other major corporations that they should invest time and money improving the "image" held of them by the public. Toward that end he advised them about how to deal more skillfully with reporters and how to control the information they did and did not release about their activities.

During the war, the U.S. government undertook a program of information management that was sophisticated by the standards of the times. Abraham Lincoln's administration had censored the news during the Civil War, but under Woodrow Wilson the U.S. government enlisted the nation's artistic and intellectual classes in a broad campaign to build support for the war. The modern age of propaganda is usually considered to have begun with World War I. British and

French posters depicting atrocities by "the Hun" were part of a more serious effort to sway mass opinion than governments had attempted during previous wars.

After the war, a number of American intellectuals expressed second thoughts about how thoroughly they had embraced the pro-war effort. Their self-examination was motivated by their dawning awareness of the power of "public relations"—and by resentment that one of their own, the scholar and former president of Princeton, Woodrow Wilson, had condoned the campaign.

In 1922 Walter Lippmann, then a young editorial writer for Joseph Pulitzer's *New York World*, published a book called *Public Opinion*. It used the experience of censorship and information-control during the war as the starting point for an argument that the nature of democracy had fundamentally changed. Modern civilization, with its vast scale and great technological advances, had become too complex to be governed by old-style mass democracy, Lippmann said. The intricacies of science, economics, diplomacy, the law, and a dozen other areas were so refined and specialized that no ordinary citizen could possibly keep up with them. Government based on informed consent by a fully participating public was simply no longer feasible. Events were too diverse and unfathomable. The possibility of manipulating news and images was too great, as the handling of war news had shown. The only hope for effective modern government lay in cultivating a group of well-trained experts, who would manage the country's journalism as well as its governmental affairs. The newspapers and magazines produced by these experts would lay out conclusions for the public to follow, but no one should expect the public to play more than a passive, spectator's role.

In later works Lippmann backed away from such a stark endorsement of rule by an expert elite. Yet through his long and enormously influential career as a columnist (he was a major force in journalism through the mid-1960s, when he was in his seventies), he embodied the idea of the journalist as expert. He consulted privately with his fellow experts in government and shared his conclusions with readers through his column, "Today and Tomorrow." If he declared, in his column, that a certain policy was wise—or foolish—he could, through force of his authority and logic, often sway political opinion virtually by himself.

There was, however, a challenge to Lippmann's view of the relation between information and public life. It came from the philosopher and educator John Dewey, who was a generation older than Lippmann (Dewey was in his late fifties during World War I; Lippmann in his late twenties) and was nowhere near Lippmann's match as a clear and forceful writer. In a series of magazine articles and in his numerous books, the best-known of which was *Experience and Nature,* published in 1925, Dewey argued that a healthy *process* of democratic self-government was at least as important as an efficient result. Indeed, he said that unless citizens were actively engaged in the large decisions any society had to make, the results of those decisions would inevitably be flawed.

Therefore, Dewey contended, those in charge of both the government and the press had a responsibility to figure out how to engage the entire public in the decisions that would affect them all in the long run. If the public was confused, alienated, pessimistic, or hostile to government, that was only partly the public's fault. Dewey's work also indicated that the government and the nation's system of transmitting ideas—its educators but also its journalists—had not done their job of involving people in the ongoing process of democratic decision.

The implication of Dewey's work was that democracy was too fundamental a value to abandon simply because technology was moving fast. In the long journey from the Greek city-states through the Magna Carta to the American Constitution and the efforts to expand democracy by ending

slavery and giving women the vote, the concept of democracy had endured strains and changes far more traumatic
than those created by twentieth-century science. The citizens, teachers, political leaders, and communicators of each
era saw themselves as having an obligation not to abandon
the concept of active, democratic self-rule but instead to find
ways to make it work in the circumstances of their age.

Nearly seventy-five years after the appearance of *Public Opinion*, the argument between Lippmann and Dewey is the basic
argument about the roles of government and press. Some parts
of Lippmann's analysis have stood up well. What was complicated about science and technology in the early 1920s—when
there was no knowledge of DNA, nuclear bombs, or the
transistor and the semiconductor chip—is a thousand times
more complicated in the late 1990s. What was confusing to
understand about a world dominated by a handful of great
colonial powers can seem nearly impossible to comprehend
in a world with some two hundred sovereign states.

One practical implication of Lippmann's advice—that
journalists must be well educated—has been embraced at
least by the print-journalism establishment. By the early
1960s, when it had become clear that TV would take away
much of the newspaper's traditional function of reporting
the previous day's events, papers began wondering what new
service they could offer—and turned to better-schooled,
more "expert" journalists as one response. James Reston of
the *New York Times*, a one-time protégé of Lippmann's who
guided the *Times*'s Washington operations in the 1960s, re-
cruited avidly from Ivy League schools in the belief that
modern journalism required a more elite staff. Strobe Tal-
bott, who studied Russian at Yale, roomed with Bill Clinton
at Oxford, covered Soviet affairs through two decades at
Time, and became deputy secretary of state in the Clinton ad-

ministration, exemplified the sort of expertise and inside connections that Lippmann hoped to see in journalism.

A broader implication of Lippmann's argument was that journalism should always be a leader rather than a follower of public opinion. Citizens may know enough about specific, local issues to have an informed view, but on bigger, longer-term questions—How should we feel about China's government? Is the earth's atmosphere heating up or not?—their opinions are often based on misinformation or partial truths. Editors and reporters therefore have a duty to tell people not what they want to hear, or what they already suspect to be true, but what they *should* understand about these complicated issues (based, in turn, on the journalists' more expert knowledge).

To some extent this advice makes even better sense at the end of the twentieth century than it did when Lippmann wrote. Many things that "everyone knows" are actually not true—or, to be more specific, are not what the experts have been able to determine. When they believe the public is wrong, reporters and editors have a duty to say so and try to change people's minds. For example, Americans have believed for years that Social Security benefits merely represented a return of the money workers contributed while they were employed. Any reporter who has learned about Social Security knows that it does not work that way. Benefits for people who retired at some point from the 1950s through the early 1990s were 200 percent to 2000 percent larger than their contributions would have justified. (The "windfall" proportion of Social Security benefits will fall sharply for retirees of the late 1990s and onward.) Journalism should "lead" the public by pointing out realities of this sort; otherwise, it will be impossible to make sane choices about Social Security or any other difficult issue. This leadership is an exercise of elite Lippmannesque power. Journalists are saying:

We have looked into this issue, and based on our specialized knowledge, we have something you need to know.

Walter Lippmann is one of the few journalists whose influence has outlived the regular appearance of his byline. Yet from the perspective of the end of the twentieth century, Dewey's analysis seems to hold up better than Lippmann's. The issues he was concerned about seem more fundamental than Lippmann's, and his recommendations are more useful in our times.

Today's journalistic establishment has tried harder to meet Lippmann's challenge—the need for expert accounts of complicated issues—than it has to accomodate Dewey's concern about the impact of journalism on democracy. Reporters operate as experts, or at least insiders, in their field, and they often act as if their real audience is made up of the other reporters or government officials they consider their peers. The system does not work with as much refinement as Lippmann would have hoped, but the public anger at journalism does not arise from the gap between today's journalism and Lippmann's ideal.

Instead, the anger comes from the problem that John Dewey identified: the public's sense that it is not *engaged* in politics, public life, or the discussion that goes on in the press. The media establishment seems to talk *at* people rather than with or even to them. When anchormen travel to the site of a flood or bombing or hurricane, when correspondents do standups from the campaign trail or the White House lawn, they usually seem to be part of a spectacle, competing to hold our attention for a moment, rather than part of a process that would engage us in solving or even considering shared problems. Politicians seem to dance above the real concerns the public has, rather than doing anything serious to cope with them. The public therefore comes to view the media largely as an irritant, which can be resented or ignored. And it comes to view politicians as mere diverters or entertainers, on a par with the other celebrities competing for our attention on TV each night. There is little sense of the media as a crucial tool for understanding the forces shaping lives, or of politicians as partners through whom we can resolve issues that affect all of us.

The American politics of the 1990s have amounted to wave after wave of revulsion against whatever group is in power. George Bush was wildly popular in early 1991 and kicked out of office eighteen months later. Bill Clinton was celebrated during his campaign "buscapade" and reviled within a year. Even the majority of reporters who were skeptical of the contents of Newt Gingrich's "Contract with America" celebrated his strategic mastery when he and his Republican majority took control of the House in 1995. Within six months he was belittled for having reached too far too fast. The sharp swings of these reactions are the way we respond to *entertainers*—to a pop group that has overstayed its moment—rather than to leaders with whom we are seriously engaged. The cycle of boom and bust in political reputations makes itself steadily worse, since in these circumstances no political leader can hold our attention long enough to make serious headway on national issues. The elections that are supposed to be the basic instruments of democracy become outlets for serial frustration and little more.

Both Walter Lippmann and John Dewey were prescient about strains on modern society. In the late 1990s, we confront countless issues, from definitions of "life" and "death" to emerging patterns of economic competition, that, just as Lippmann warned, are too complicated for most people to spend the time necessary to understand. Yet Dewey's fear, that democracy could not function well if citizens feel estranged from political life, touches a more profound modern concern. People are unhappy with the political system— which is to say, with the structure of democracy—because they feel they have no control over it and that it has no connection to their lives. When a leader or an institution seems to offer even a flicker of hope for engagement, potential supporters flock in with touching enthusiasm. The early stages of the Perot campaign of 1992; the late stages of the Clinton campaign that same year, with people lining the bus routes; the hoped-for campaign of Colin Powell; the communities that have grown up around talk radio programs, which give a sense of shared concerns and the possibility of "participating" by calling in; the similar communities based on Internet groups—these causes and activities boomed in popularity, at least temporarily, because they offered what normal politics does not. They allowed people to think that they could play some part in a larger activity, even if their part was nothing more than tuning in Rush Limbaugh each day; and they made people believe that the outcome of this activity would make some difference in their lives. Normal political activity seems to offer these qualities only in the weeks just before and just after a major election. The rest of the time it's a game to be played by insiders and pros.

These include the insiders and pros in the press. Reporters and editors tell themselves that they have to dress up the news and make it sexy to get the attention of an increasingly hostile public. But if anything is clear, it is that the mainstream press is pathetically out of touch with what people want to hear. At the end of the 1992 campaign, political reporters mocked George Bush's hopeless attempts to get people interested in him. Couldn't he see that no one wanted to buy what he had to sell? Yet these same reporters and analysts, with their X-ray vision of Bush's failings, cannot see the reaction that their endless harping on insider politics evokes. Just at the time of the 1992 election, scholars from the University of Chicago released a study of how news coverage shaped people's sense of politics. The group said that its findings suggest that at least part of the public's limited interest in the official side of national and international affairs results from a profound sense of powerlessness. Ironically . . . the style of what is usually considered journalism at its best may reinforce this sense of powerlessness through an emphasis on irony . . . [or] the hopeless complexity of issues.

The media branches by themselves could not entirely correct the sense of cynical mistrust that threatens American politics. This requires the efforts of politicians and of the public as well. Journalists could, however, recognize how much they are contributing to a mood of fatalistic disengagement. If they recognized that this mood was the fundamental challenge not just to a functioning democracy but to their own professional survival as well, many other decisions would fall into place. They would understand why they should take public complaints seriously. They would understand the importance of changing their habits soon. And they would have an idea of the kinds of changes they should make.

The changes would all be in the direction of making it easier for citizens to feel a connection to their society's public life. This would mean an improvement in politics, for reasons that John Dewey had outlined in his essays. It would also mean salvation for the press itself. The truth that today's media establishment has tried to avoid seeing is that it will *rise or fall with the political system.*

The ultimate reason people buy the *New York Times* rather than *People*, or watch *World News Tonight* rather than *Entertainment Tonight,* is a belief that it is worth paying attention to public affairs. If people thought there was no point even in hearing about public affairs—because the politicians were all crooks, because the outcome was always rigged, because ordinary people stood no chance, because everyone in power was looking out for himself—then news-papers and broadcast news operations might as well close up shop too, because there would be no market for what they were selling. If people have no interest in politics or public life, they have no reason to follow the news. It doesn't con-cern them. They might as well spend their time going shop-ping or watching baseball. They might as well confine their viewing to sitcoms and daytime talk shows, and their read-ing to computer magazines and diet books.

Mainstream journalism has made the mistake of trying to compete with the pure entertainment media—music, TV celebrities, movies—on their own terms. But this is a losing game. Between January and September of 1995, the network news programs devoted an astonishing amount of airtime to the O. J. Simpson trial. News about O. J. made up fully 15 percent of the *NBC Nightly News* during this period. (It was 13 percent for the *CBS Evening News,* and 9 percent of *ABC's World News Tonight.*) Yet no matter how much time the net-works dedicate to the Simpson trial—or the Menendez brothers, or Tonya Harding, or whatever future scandal oc-cupies our attention—they can never match *Hard Copy* or *In-side Edition.* They are locking themselves into a competition they are bound to lose. If the public is looking for pure celebrity or entertainment, it will go for the real thing. If public life continues to lose its claim on America's attention, so—inevitably—will journalism. What will be left is more restrained versions of *Hard Copy.*

WHEN DEMOCRACY WORKS. In 1993 the Kettering Foundation, based in Ohio, released a study of the way in which people decide to act as "citizens" and take a role in public life. The study was called *Meaningful Chaos: How Peo-ple Form Relationships with Public Concerns*, and it was based on extensive interviewing, focus groups, and other attempts to determine why people did and did not get involved in community or political affairs.

The study came up with a list of traits that distinguished groups and communities with healthy, active political life from those where people felt estranged and cynical. The most interesting aspect of the list is that all the traits that distinguished a successful political community were at direct odds with the norms of mainstream journalism.

For instance, the Kettering study emphasized the importance of "connection." Citizens understand that issues run together—that the problems of schools are connected to family structure, which is connected to the changing job market, which is connected to taxes and trade and countless other matters. But by journalistic convention these are treated as separate "items" on a political or legislative agenda. The press presents these issues as being connected mainly when political circumstances bind them together: "President Clinton, still reeling from a setback on the school prayer issue, faced new trouble with disappointing unemployment statistics for the month."

Another trait that citizens valued, according to the survey, was "ambivalence." Difficult public issues stay with us precisely because they are difficult. Most people who are opposed to capital punishment can understand (though they give less weight to) the desire for retribution that motivates the other side. Most people who support capital punishment understand the grimness and gravity of the act. A few people on either side of the abortion debate have clear, uncomplicated views of what is right and wrong. Most people view it as a balance of competing rights—or wrongs. (Polls have consistently shown that most Americans disapprove of abortion but believe it should be legal.) Yet the tendency of mainstream journalism is to present issues in stark yes-no form. An episode of *Crossfire* or *The Capital Gang* does not work if everyone is agreeing that the issues are tangled and impossible. Journalistic showdowns are presented instead as contests of expert opinion, each of which is trying to rub the other out. This makes for "energetic" television but is directly contrary to the way effective public life works. In real life, people disagree but consider the possibility of consensus; in polarized talk-show life, they score points off one another and don't even pretend that there's a possibility one combatant might change his mind.

In his 1991 book, *Why Americans Hate Politics,* E. J. Dionne, Jr., wrote that each political party had an electoral incentive to push issues toward unrealistic extremes—on affirmative action, gun control, almost any subject. Most voters were left feeling that they didn't like any of the available choices and condemned politics as a whole. Journalism now reinforces this trend. "Journalists keep trying to find people who are at 1 and at 9 on a scale of 1 to 10, rather than people at 3 to 7 where most people actually are," Cole Campbell, editor of the *Norfolk Virginian-Pilot,* has said. "Journalism should say that the people from 3 to 7 are just as newsworthy and quotable as those at either end of spectrum lobbing bombs toward the middle."

Yet another ingredient of healthy political communities, according to the study, was the existence of "catalysts" and "mediating institutions." Catalysts were people who went out of their way to make an organization run, whether the organization was the local PTA or a presidential campaign. Mediating institutions were churches, neighborhood groups, amateur sports leagues, or any other group that gave people a connection to each other and allowed them to act together or resolve differences. When local institutions appear in the media, the tone is usually patronizing and dutiful. Institutions typically make the news only when they are controversial—the Citadel for excluding a woman candidate, black student organizations only when they invited Louis Farrakhan to speak.

There were many other items on the Kettering Foundation's list, all of them ingredients of healthy political life, all of them ignored, downplayed, or actively thwarted by today's press coverage. The situation is perverse. The press, which in the long run cannot survive if people lose interest in politics, is acting as if its purpose was to guarantee that people are repelled by public life.

"Public Journalism": An Attempt to Connect the Media with the Public

During the U.S. military's darkest moments just after the Vietnam War, a group of officers and analysts undertook a "military reform" movement. Rather than papering over the deep problems that the Vietnam years had revealed, and rather than searching for external sources of blame, this group attempted to locate the internal problems that had weakened the military so that the problems could be faced and solved. The "military reformers'" record of success was not perfect, but at their instigation the U.S. military coped with more of its fundamental difficulties than any other American institution has.

Since the early 1990s, a group of journalistic reformers has launched a similar attempt to cope with the basic weaknesses of their institution. As was the case with the military reformers, their efforts have been scorned by some of the most powerful leaders of the current establishment. As with the military reformers, they do not have the complete or satisfying answer to all of today's journalistic problems. But, like the military reformers, they are more right than wrong. At a minimum their ideas point the way to a media establishment that is less intensely scorned than today's is.

Those involved in the "public journalism" (sometimes called "civic journalism") movement stress its cooperative, collaborative nature. But several people have played large roles in developing its ideas.

One is Davis Merritt, a man in his late fifties, who since the mid-1970s has been editor of the *Wichita Eagle* in Kansas. The cover of his 1995 book *Public Journalism and Public Life* says "by Davis 'Buzz' Merritt," and he has the laconic, unrushable bearing one would associate with a test pilot or astronaut named "Buzz."

Merritt started out in newspapers in the 1950s, working as a reporter and editor in North Carolina, Washington, D.C., and Florida. By the time of the Watergate upheavals in the early 1970s, when Merritt was in his late thirties, he had become news editor of the Knight newspapers' bureau in Washington. In 1975, after the recently merged Knight and Ridder newspaper chains had acquired (among other papers) the *Wichita Eagle,* Merritt went to Kansas for what he thought would be a short-term job as the *Eagle*'s editor.

The *Eagle* at that time illustrated much that was wrong with traditional small-town journalism. It played favorites in its coverage of local political fights, in keeping with the financial and personal interests of its owners. After buying the paper from its local owners, Knight-Ridder assigned Merritt there as part of a resuscitation drive.

Over the next decade, Merritt felt that the paper's coverage was improving by all objective measures—it won national awards, and journalism reviews cited it for its quality. But even as the paper moved ahead, it fell behind, with fewer and fewer people in town bothering to buy it or read it. The public mood in Wichita soured during those same years, with polls indicating that people there (as in most of the rest of the country) were mistrustful of political leadership and pessimistic about resolving important public problems.

People involved in the public journalism movement

often talk of "epiphanies" or transforming experiences that convinced them that a different course was necessary. Merritt says that his came just after the 1988 presidential election campaign. His paper was carrying the predictable wire stories: about the Dukakis campaign's response to the Bush campaign's attacks, about Gary Hart and his girl friends, about what Willie Horton did or did not do, about what Michael Dukakis would or would not do if his wife was raped.

Merritt says that as he put these stories into his paper each day, he found himself asking, Why are we publishing this? What are we doing? The accepted style of political coverage, he thought, was bringing out the worst in every participant in public life. It drove out serious candidates. It rewarded gutter-fighting. It disgusted most of the public. It embarrassed even the reporters. It trivialized the election— and it made everyone feel dirty when it was done. With the election experience fresh in his mind, Merritt began thinking about how journalists could use all their traditional tools of investigation, explanation, fair-mindedness, and so on in a way that was less destructive to the society in which journalists and readers alike had to live.

Soon afterward Merritt encountered another prominent figure in the public journalism movement, Jay Rosen of New York University. Rosen was trained in communications theory. His doctoral dissertation was about the struggle between Dewey and Lippmann over the role of an informed public in American political life. "This was a debate that Lippmann won, with a cynical view of what was possible for the public, but that Dewey should have won," Rosen has said.

Rosen believed that the Dewey–Lippmann debate had ongoing relevance for the American press, and on the basis of his academic work he was invited to speak at the Associated Press Managing Editors' conference in Des Moines in 1989. There he gave the working journalists an updated version of John Dewey's contention that in the long run the success of the press and the success of democracy depended on each other. Democratic government could not exist without a functioning press, but journalism (as opposed to pure celebrity-based entertainment) could not survive if "public life is not going well." This phrasing—"public life going well," drawn from the Harvard philosopher Michael Sandel—turns up again and again in public journalism discussions. It means a shared sense by citizens that they have *some* connection to and control over the institutions that make the big decisions, and therefore that they need the information journalism provides about public life.

Rosen received a surprising amount of response to the speech, mainly from reporters and editors who shared his sense that the sinking ship of public life was taking them down too. He corresponded with Jack Swift, editor of the *Ledger-Enquirer* newspaper in Columbus, Georgia. At the *Ledger-Enquirer,* many editors had grown frustrated with the familiar ways of covering the city's problems and were experimenting with new approaches. Swift's version of the "transforming experience" that led him to public journalism was the reaction to a series of which the paper itself was very proud.

The series examined the economic threats Columbus faced, as its traditional textile economy fell apart and new service industries hesitated to move into town because its school system seemed too weak. The reaction to the series, which the editors considered a model of its kind, was . . . almost no reaction.

The paper's editors began thinking of other ways to engage their city in decisions about its future—not pushing any particular policy but urging politicians, civic groups, and ordinary citizens to come up with *some* policy. The *Ledger-Enquirer* convened a "town meeting," at which three hundred Columbus citizens talked about the city's future. Some of the citizens were from established civic groups but many had had no previous organized involvement in public affairs. On the basis of this meeting, an independent civic organization called "United Beyond 2000" was created. It sponsored future meetings and task-force work and eventually took the newspaper out of the role of directly backing civic-action efforts. A state court judge, John Allen, contacted Swift to suggest that they work together to set up networks of private citizens in Columbus. Like Swift, Allen was a Vietnam veteran; unlike Swift, Allen was black, and the networks were designed to increase contact across racial lines.

Swift died in 1991, as the project his paper had set in motion was still developing. Yet even by that time what the *Ledger-Enquirer* had done (in the words of an article written by Jay Rosen after Swift's death) was to

> reconstrue the position of the journalist within politics. Instead of standing outside the political community, and reporting on its pathologies, they took up residence within its borders. This was a courageous move that made a difference to the citizens of Columbus. And it is an example others in the press might follow.

The Columbus project had attracted the interest of David Matthews, a former secretary of health, education, and welfare in the Ford administration who had become president of the Kettering Foundation in Ohio. Matthews and Kettering had supported projects designed to improve the operating mechanics of American democracy—better ways of disseminating information, new schemes for resolving political issues through "deliberation" rather than confrontation, standoff, and threat. The Kettering Foundation and the Poynter Institute for Media Studies, based in Florida, began bringing reporters and editors together to compare their concerns about "traditional" journalism and the new approaches they had tried.

In 1991 the fledgling movement got an important

boost when David Broder of the *Washington Post,* probably the best-respected political reporter of his time, gave a lecture in California implicitly endorsing their approach. His statement was seen as significant not simply because of his personal stature but also because he had had contact with the public-journalism advocates and had come to a conclusion like theirs on his own.

In a speech sponsored by the Riverside, California *Press-Enterprise* and the University of California at Riverside, Broder said that coverage of public affairs had become a cynical and pointless insiders' game. Political consultants—rather than candidates—had come to have a dominant role in politics, Broder said. And these hired guns, "these new political bosses, have become for those of us in political journalism not only our best sources but, in many cases, our best friends."

The two groups got along because they both loved the operating details of politics, Broder said. They felt a distance from the slightly comic, sweating candidates who had to give speeches and raise money and submit themselves to the voters' will. For these poor candidates, Broder said, election day really was a judgment day. But for the reporters and consultants, no matter what the results of the election, they could play the game over and over again.

There was a more disturbing similarity between the groups, Broder said. "We both disclaim any responsibility for the consequences of elections."

> Let me say again, for emphasis: We disclaim ANY responsibility for the consequences of elections. Consultants will tell you they are hired to produce victory on Election Day. Reporters will tell you that we are hired to cover campaigns. . . . I've often said to our White House reporters, "My job is to deliver these turkeys; after they're in office, they're your responsibility."

What this means in less facetious terms is that a very large percentage of the information that the American people get about politics comes from people who disclaim any responsibility for the consequences of our politics.

After spending nearly four decades in this activity, Broder said, he felt uneasy about the consequences of his life's work. By concentrating on the operations of politics and disdaining the results, reporters "have colluded with the campaign consultants to produce the kind of politics which is turning off the American people." By the early 1970s—the time of movies like *The Candidate* and books like *The Selling of the President*—journalists began to realize that the most important part of a political campaign was the ads a candidate put on radio and television:

> So we began to focus on the ads, and we began to write about them. We began to write about the people who made the ads, the campaign consultants and media advisers and pollsters. We wrote about them so often that I think we have turned some of them into political celebrities in their own right. We have helped to make them both famous and rich.
>
> In all of this, we forgot about the people who were the consumers of these ads, those who had the message pushed at them, willingly or not, every time they turned on their radio or television set. We forgot our obligation as journalists to help them cope with this mass of political propaganda coming their way.

The line Broder had drawn—between accepting and ignoring the consequences of what reporters wrote—was to be the main dividing line between the public journalism movement and the "mainstream" press. Even before this speech, Broder had written a column issuing a similar challenge to journalists. "It is time for us in the world's freest press to become activists," he wrote in 1990, "not on behalf of a particular party or politician, but on behalf of the process of self-government."

Toward the end of advancing this kind of "activism," Broder laid out in his speech recommendations for future campaign coverage that would pay less attention to tactical maneuvers and more to the connection between the campaign and real national problems. One specific suggestion, which seems obvious now but had rarely been done before Broder proposed it, was that reporters cover campaign ads not from the candidates' point of view but from the voters'. That is, instead of emphasizing what each campaign was trying to accomplish with the ads—how they were exploiting their opponents' vulnerabilities, which interest groups they were trying to peel off, and how—the reporters should examine how truthful and realistic the advertisements were. One immediate effect of Broder's recommendation was the rapid spread of "Ad Watch"-type coverage in campaign coverage, in which correspondents examined political ads for smears and misrepresentations.

PUBLIC JOURNALISM IN PRACTICE. Through meetings coordinated by Jay Rosen's Project on Public Life and the Press (which is based at New York University and funded by the Knight Foundation), public journalism became a "movement" by 1993. Its main base of support was in regional newspapers and some broadcast stations, usually working in partnership with the papers. By 1995 more than 170 newspapers had taken part in some activity tracked by Rosen's center. A conference in the spring of 1995 included representatives from papers or broadcast stations in California, Mississippi, Virginia, Wisconsin, Florida, Minnesota, Pennsylvania, Massachusetts, New Jersey, Maine, and elsewhere. Several books now exist chronicling these efforts.

Editors and reporters at these news organizations attempted to produce coverage that would make people feel reconnected to the public life of their community. The goal was not to promote one political party or one vision of economic or social policy, any more than *Sports Illustrated* coverage, while promoting interest in sports as a whole, is intended to promote one team. But, as Buzz Merritt put in an editorial before the Kansas gubernatorial elections in 1990, his paper would have "a strong bias: we believe the voters are entitled to have the candidates talk about the issues in depth."

The best-known project in public journalism's short history is probably the *Charlotte Observer*'s approach to covering the North Carolina elections in 1992. The paper's editors, who had carefully studied Broder's proposals and Merritt's 1990 election coverage in Wichita, didn't want their coverage to be driven by the issues that each candidate thought would be tactically useful in the election. Instead, they began an elaborate effort to determine what issues the state's people believed were most important, and what other issues might have the greatest impact on the state's future welfare even though the public was not yet fully aware of them. The paper commissioned a poll of more than a thousand area residents (not merely subscribers) to ask their views about the public issues that concerned them most. The poll was not a yes-or-no survey but involved extensive discussions to explore the reasons behind the respondents' views. After the initial polling, the *Observer* arranged for five hundred residents to serve as an ongoing citizens' advisory panel to the paper through the election season.

Based on the issues that emerged from the polls and panel discussions, as well as from efforts by the paper's reporters and editors to judge the trends that would affect the state, the paper drew up lists of topics about which the public expected answers from the candidates. These citizen-generated issues were not the same as the ones on which many of the candidates had planned to run. For instance, the citizen panels showed a widespread concern about environmental problems caused by Charlotte's rapid growth. Politicians had not planned to emphasize this theme, but the paper decided to push for statements on this and the other issues the citizen panels had recommended. At the same time, it ran fewer stories about advertising strategies, about horse-race-style opinion polls, and about other traditional campaign techniques.

The moment of truth for this new approach came early in the campaign season, and it involved a question that a newspaper did *not* ask. After the citizens' panel had stressed its interest in environmental issues (among other concerns), the *Observer* prepared a big grid to run in the newspaper, showing each candidate's position on the questions the panel had raised. At the time, the long-time Democratic office-holder Terry Sanford was running for the Senate. The *Observer*'s editor, Rich Opel, has described what happened next:

> Voters are intensely interested in the environment. . . . So our reporters went out to senatorial candidates and said, "Here are the voters' questions." Terry Sanford, the incumbent senator, called me up from Washington and said, "Rich, I have these questions from your reporter and I'm not going to talk about the environment until the general election." This was the primary. I said, "Well, the voters want to know about the environment now, Terry." He said, "Well, that's not the way I have my campaign structured." I said, "Fine, I will run the questions and I will leave a space under it for you to answer. If you choose not to, we will just say, 'Would not respond' or we will leave it blank." We ended the conversation. In about ten days he sent the answers down.

Most political reporters for most newspapers know how they would instinctively respond when a candidate told them he was delaying discussion of an issue. "That's interesting," they would say. "What's the thinking behind that?" Like a campaign consultant, the reporter would be instantly engaged in figuring out why the issue would be useless against other Democrats in the primaries but would be useful against Republicans in the general election. By responding as proxies for the public rather than as consultants' manqués, the reporters evoked the discussion their readers wanted to hear.

"This is not a way of being 'tough' on a candidate for its own sake, but of using toughness in service of certain public values," Jay Rosen has said of the Charlotte project. "It is also a way of adding some civility, since there are rewards to balance the penalties that dominate today's campaigns. In normal campaign coverage, candidates get praised and criticized, but on the basis of what values? In this case the paper said: *here* are the issues the public wants to hear about. We'll judge you on whether you respond to these views." Most newspapers, he said, also judge candidates by a set of values—but never lay out clearly for the reader or the candidate exactly what those values are. (In practice, they are usually tactical values—"handling" issues well, and so forth.)

Newspapers in Miami, Spokane, and Dayton have sponsored a series of community meetings to find the areas where citizens most disagreed—and agreed. They found that the very act of asking people their views made most of them feel more committed to the community and more hopeful. A coalition of news organizations in Madison, Wisconsin, including the *Wisconsin State Journal* and statewide TV and radio outlets, held a mock legislature in which citizens tried to deal with the state government's problems.

The *Virginian-Pilot* in Norfolk took reporters and editors who had been covering schools, city hall, the police, and politics and assembled them into a "public life team." The mission statement for the team was, "We will revitalize a democracy that has grown sick with disenchantment. We will lead the community to discover itself and act on what it has learned." This philosophy had an immediate effect on the paper's coverage of local elections. Previously it had reported them the way most national campaigns are now covered—as an exchange of accusations and charges between politicians trying to outmaneuver each other. Instead, the paper presented the politicans as "job candidates," who were "applying" for positions of great importance to the town's future. Rather than giving main emphasis to the candidates' comments about each other, the paper described the duties of each office; laid out the résumés and past records of the candidates; repeatedly published information about how citizens could contact the campaign themselves; and collected questions from readers that it then presented to the candidates for their answers. This approach obviously had potential pitfalls, but so does the customary "tactics-oriented" approach to campaign coverage, and indications were that the readers felt better served by the new coverage. The reporters and editors also underwent a long process of self-education and internal debate and discussion about the connection between news and democracy, using texts that started with de Tocqueville and led to recent works about how the public makes up its mind. Hard-boiled veterans of other newsrooms might laugh at this process, but those involved seem to have taken it as a serious intellectual and moral exercise.

After David Duke, the former Ku Klux Klan leader, was nearly elected governor of Louisiana in 1991, the *New Orleans Times-Picayune* undertook a mammoth, year-long effort to explore race relations from a "public journalism" perspective. Rather than reporting on what the most extreme white racists said about blacks, and what the most publicity-seeking black nationalists said in return, the paper involved twenty reporters in an effort to understand the historic, economic, and political roots of the city's racial tensions. Black and white reporters on the team tried for a while to exchange lives with each other, putting themselves as much as possible into the other's racial position and seeing their community through the other's eyes. The results of their work, which were published over a six-month period, drew a tremendous public response. Some sixty-five hundred people called the paper's voice-mail line to comment on the series and on racial issues; the paper published nearly a thousand of these comments. After the Rodney King upheavals in Los Angeles, the Akron *Beacon-Journal* undertook a similar sweeping inquiry on racial tensions in its community. After the first installment appeared, the paper received strong community reaction, saying that it should continue its work. For its work the *Beacon-Journal* won the Pulitzer Prize for public service.

In 1993, the *Chicago Sun-Times* collaborated with a local PBS station and charitable foundations in promoting a "schools summit" to cope with the obvious failings of the city's schools. At the three "summit" sessions, representatives of all relevant groups—parents, teachers, students, the school board, and even the mayor and governor—met to determine where they agreed and disagreed. The sessions were broadcast live on radio and TV; the *Sun-Times* gave extensive coverage to the schools' problems and the possible solutions before and after the meetings.

There are scores of other examples from scores of other cities. Some have been more successful than others in sustaining public involvement and improving public debate. In the most successful efforts, editors and reporters have listened carefully to public concerns—but have balanced what they learned that way with their own best judgment about the issues of greatest long-term significance to their readers. The editors and news directors who have launched these projects seem unanimous in one finding: that a public-journalism emphasis has drawn far *less* criticism from the public than their normal coverage has, and that it has attracted far *more* praise, interest, follow-up community activity, and other indicators that the journalists are on the right track.

COMPLAINTS FROM THE MEDIA ESTABLISHMENT.

There has, however, been one important source of backlash against the public-journalism approach. It has come from the editors of the country's largest and most influential newspapers. Leonard Downie, executive editor of the *Washington Post,* has said the movement's basic premise is "completely wrong." Max Frankel, the former executive editor of the *New York Times,* has expressed a similar hostility—as have others, including William F. Woo, editor of the *St. Louis Post-Dispatch.*

The crux of their unhappiness lies with the concept of "objectivity." One of public journalism's basic claims is that journalists should stop kidding themselves about their ability to remain detached from and objective about public life. Journalists are not like scientists, observing the behavior of fruit flies but not influencing what the flies might do. They inescapably change the reality of whatever they are observing by whether and how they choose to write about it.

From the nearly infinite array of events, dramas, tragedies, and successes occurring in the world each day, newspaper editors and broadcast producers must define a tiny sample as "the news." The conventions of choosing "the news" are so familiar, and so much of the process happens by learned and ingrained habits, that it is easy for journalists to forget that the result reflects *decisions,* rather than some kind of neutral scientific truth.

At the national level, the daily public-affairs news concentrates heavily on what the president said and did that day; how well- or badly organized his staff seems to be; whether he is moving ahead or falling behind in his struggle against opponents from the other party; and who is using what tactics to get ready for the next presidential race. Each time the chairman of the Federal Reserve opens his mouth, he usually gets on the front page of the newspaper and on the evening network news. Each month, when the government releases its report on unemployment rates and consumer-price increases, papers and networks treat this as a genuine news event. Each summer when the leaders of industrialized nations hold their G-7 meeting, the news gives us a few minutes of prime ministers and presidents discussing their latest economic disputes. When the local school board selects a new superintendent of schools, that announcement, and the comments of the new superintendent, are played prominently in the local news.

A case could be made that some or all of these events are really the most important "news" that a broad readership needs each day. But you could just as easily make a case that most of these official, often ceremonial events should be overlooked and that a whole different category of human activity deserves coverage as "news." Instead of telling us what Newt Gingrich will do to block Bill Clinton's spending plans for education, the "news" might involve the way parochial schools work and ask whether their standard of discipline is possible in public schools. Instead of describing rivalries on the White House staff, the "news" could treat the presidency the way it does the scientific establishment, judging it mainly by public pronouncements and not looking too far behind the veil. The simplest daily reminder that the news is the result of countless judgment calls, rather than some abstract truth, is a comparison of the front page of the *Wall Street Journal* with that of almost any other major newspaper. The "news" that dominates four-fifths of most front pages is confined, in the *Journal,* to two little columns of news summary. (Here is an alarming fact: Those two columns represent more words than a half-hour TV news show would, if written out.) The rest of the front page represents the *Journal*'s attempt to explain what is interesting and important about the world, though it may not be at the top of the breaking "news." The two great journalistic organizations that illustrate how creatively the "news" could be defined are in fact the *Journal*'s news (not editorial) sections and National Public Radio's news staff. Each of them covers the breaking news but does so in a summary fashion, so it can put its energy, space, and professional pride into reports that are not driven by the latest official pronouncement.

"It's absolutely correct to say that there are objectively occurring events," says Cole Campbell, of the *Virginian-Pilot*. "Speeches are made, volcanoes erupt, trees fall. But *news* is not a scientifically observable event. News is a choice, an extraction process, saying that one event is more meaningful than another event. The very act of saying that means making judgments that are based on values and based on frames."

It might seem that in making this point, Campbell and his colleagues had "discovered" a principle that most people figure out when they are in high school. There is no such thing as "just the news," and that's why editors are both necessary and powerful. But the public-journalism advocates have pushed this obvious-seeming point toward a conclusion that has angered many other editors. They have argued that the way modern journalists *choose* to present the news increases the chance that citizens will feel unhappy, powerless, betrayed by, and angry about their political system. And because the most powerful journalistic organs are unwilling to admit that they've made this choice, Rosen says, it is almost impossible for them to change.

"I couldn't disagree more with that view of newspaper journalism," Leonard Downie of the *Washington Post* has said in discussing the public-journalism theory that reporters should be actively biased in favor of encouraging the community to be involved in politics:

I think our job is to report the news. To come as near as we can to giving people the truth, recognizing that the truth is multifaceted and that it changes from time to time as we learn more. I know that is what we do at the *Washington Post*. I know there are times when individual feelings among reporters and editors may cause them to want to take a side. We work very hard here to try to drive that out of our work.

Downie says that this approach is hard on his reporters, who in an attempt to suppress their personal feelings about an issue must "pretend to be less fully human than they really are." (Downie himself takes this belief to such an extreme that he *refuses to vote* in elections, feeling that this would make him too involved in the political process.) He admits that the newspaper's claim of "objectivity" is not convincing to many readers, who believe that the paper has its own angle on many stories. But he says that wavering even for a moment from the pursuit of "objectivity" would be disastrous.

Where I am most bothered is when a newspaper uses its news columns—not its editorial page or its publisher—to achieve specific outcomes in the community. That is what I think is wrong, and very wrong. That line is very bright, and very sharp, and extremely dangerous. It is being manipulated by academics who are risking the terrible prostitution of our profession. Telling political candidates that they must come to a newspaper's forum, or that they must discuss certain issues—that is very dangerous stuff. That is not our role. There are plenty of institutions in every community to do this sort of thing. If newspapers are lax in covering these activities—if we are guilty only of covering crime and horse-race politics, then we should do our job better. We shouldn't change our job.

This defense of pure, detached "objectivity" drives many public-journalism advocates crazy. Rosen, Merritt, Campbell, and others say that when papers and TV stations have taken a more "engaged," less "objective" approach, they virtually never receive complaints from their readers or viewers. "*All* of the resistance to public journalism has come from other journalists, not from the public or politicians," Jay Rosen has said. "The resistance is always in the name of the community, but it is hard to find anyone in the community who objects." In its several years of public-journalism projects, the *Virginian Pilot* has received one hostile letter to the editor, claiming that its new approach to the community's problems meant abandoning the old standard of objectivity. But that letter came from a retired newspaper editor; the paper says it has received no similar complaints from readers without a professional axe to grind.

"I think Len Downie is right when he says that public journalism is an 'ideology,'" says Cole Campbell. "There are *two* ideologies, and he is unself-conscious about the ideology that drives his kind of journalism.

> The ideology of mainstream journalism is, When there is conflict, there is news. When there is no conflict, there's no news. That is ideological. It is out of touch with how people experience life.

Buzz Merritt elaborated on this point in *Public Journalism and Public Life:* "It is interesting that journalism's binding axiom of objectivity allows, even requires, unlimited toughness as a tool as well as a credo, yet it rejects *purposefulness*—having a motivation beyond mere exposure—as unprofessional. Without purposefulness, toughness is mere self-indulgence."

THE HIDDEN CONSENSUS. Beneath the apparent gulf that separates the public-journalism advocates from their elite critics is a broader ground of hopeful consensus. Although Leonard Downie objects vehemently to public journalism in theory, he has said that he respects most of the actual journalistic projects that have been done in its name. "The notion that in political campaigns you should shift some of your resources away from covering consultants and toward reporting the issues voters are primarily interested in—that is simply an evolution of good political journalism," he said.

> These are not new ways of reporting. Using public opinion surveys to find out what people think about their own communities, doing solutions reporting to see what things are working in solving societal problems—this is all part of what I would see as normal newspaper reporting.

But why, Downie asks, call this "public journalism"? Why not just call it "good journalism" and try to do more of it?

Other editors who have been on the warpath against the public-journalism concept, including William Woo of the *St. Louis Post-Dispatch* and Howard Schneider of *Newsday,* have also said there is "nothing new" in the concept of public-spirited reporting. It's what papers should have been doing all along.

The public-journalism advocates might take this as a sign that they are winning the battle. In the 1970s and early 1980s, the military reformers in the Pentagon knew that the tide had turned their way when their opponents began saying that there was "nothing new" in the reformers' analysis. After all, its principles had been in circulation since the time of Douglas MacArthur, or Robert E. Lee, or for that matter Genghis Khan.

The rancor surrounding the public-journalism debate actually seems to arise from two misunderstandings. One concerns the nature of journalism's "involvement" in public life. When Leonard Downie and Max Frankel hear that term, they seem to imagine drumbeating campaigns by a newspaper on behalf of a particular candidate or a specific action-plan for a community. What the editors who have put public journalism into effect mean is "just good journalism"—that is, making people care about the issues that affect their lives, and helping them see how they can play a part in resolving those issues.

And when big-paper editors hear that the public journalists want to "listen" to the public and be "guided" by its concerns, the editors imagine something that they dread. This sounds all too similar to pure "user-driven" journalism, in which the marketing department surveys readers to find out what they're interested in, and the editors give them only that. This version of public journalism sounds like an invitation to abandon all critical judgment and turn the paper into a pure "feel good" advertising sheet. It misrepresents the best conception of public journalism, which is that editors and reporters will continue to exercise their judgment about issues, as they claim to now, but will pay more attention than today's elite journalists do to the impact of their work on the health of democracy.

"I think the people who make this criticism have not looked closely enough at what public interest journalism is doing," William Kovach, of the Nieman Foundation, said in 1995. "Papers are using surveys, but they are very careful surveys; they're doing a lot of work in neighborhoods. It's not a politically designed opinion poll to take a snap judgment." The editors who have undertaken public-journalism projects say they are using their best reportorial skills to determine not what people want to hear but what issues concern them most, and then applying that knowledge in their coverage.

Leonard Downie is right: This approach is "just good journalism." The real questions it raises are not hair-splitting quarrels about what it should be called but the practical work of implementation.

Journalism in the Public Spirit

Today's journalists can choose: Do they want merely to entertain the public or to engage it? If they want to entertain, they will keep doing what they have done for the last generation. Concentrating on conflict and spectacle, building up celebrities and tearing them down, presenting a crisis or issue with the volume turned all the way up, only to drop that issue and turn to the next emergency. They will make themselves the center of attention, as they exchange one-liners as if public life were a parlor game and make fun of the gaffes and imperfections of anyone in public life. They will view their berths as opportunities for personal aggrandizement and enrichment, trading on the power of their celebrity. And while they do these things, they will be constantly more hated and constantly less useful to the public whose attention they are trying to attract. In the long run, real celebrities—singers, quarterbacks, movie stars—will crowd them off the stage. Public life will become more sour and embittered, and American democracy will be even less successful in addressing the nation's economic, social, and moral concerns.

But if journalists should choose to engage the public, they will begin a long series of experiments and decisions to see how journalism might better serve its fundamental purpose, that of making democratic self-government possible. They could start with the example set by public journalism and work on the obvious problems and limits of that model.

For example, most of its innovations have occurred at medium-sized papers in cities the size of Norfolk or Wichita. There the reporters and editors have a natural bond to their community that will never exist between, say, Ted Koppel and his viewers around the world.

Journalists, who have coped with changes before, could recognize this challenge of scale as a challenge, not a fatal obstacle. Political leaders have experimented with ways to create a sense of community on a national scale. Franklin Roosevelt did so with his "Fireside Chats"; Bill Clinton was, for a while, successful with his *Donahue* show-style talk programs that made an audience feel he was listening to them.

Journalists should be even freer to experiment—and some successful experiments are in place. ABC's *Nightline* program represents both a technological and a commercial breakthrough. The technical breakthrough, based on satellite communications, was the ability to have multiple guests on screen at the same time, talking with one another from different corners of the globe. The commercial insight was that a late-night audience for hard news existed. ABC and Ted Koppel used this innovation to create a kind of dialogue that did not exist before. Although the program's guest roster runs too heavily toward familiar expert talking-heads, and although it virtually never addresses economic issues, *Nightline* is a successful experiment. Ted Koppel has also experimented with ways to turn his own celebrity to productive purposes. He has held town meeting-style dialogues in strife-filled locations from South Africa to south central Los Angeles. People may have watched these dialogues merely because Koppel is famous, yet he decided to use his fame for something more than an interview with Michael Jackson and Lisa-Marie Presley or a series of lucrative lecture dates.

In 1970, nearly a decade before the creation of *Nightline*, the *New York Times* invented a space for public discussion when it created its op-ed page. Until that time, newspapers published their own editorials, syndicated columns, and letters to the editor, but there was no established place in which outsiders could have a say. The op-ed form, like *Nightline* and most talk shows, is dominated by the usual suspects from government and think tanks. Still, journalism would be even less engaging if this space did not exist.

It is impossible to predict in advance where other experiments would lead. But if journalism took the need for innovations seriously, its offerings could change as rapidly and richly as, say, those in the computer software industry. These are, after all, energetic and creative people. When competing to be first and best at a set task, they can reveal phenomenal resourcefulness and daring. The problem lies with the task that is set. Too often it amounts to being the first to detect the blood in the water around a wounded politician or being the best with a one-line summary of the events of the past week. No one who has seen a pack of journalists descend on Little Rock (during the Whitewater investigation) or watched them jostle for position at news conferences can think they are lazy or undetermined. They are merely misdirected.

If they recognized that their purpose was to give citizens the tools to participate in public life, and recognized as well that fulfilling this purpose is the only way journalism itself can survive, journalists would find it natural to change many other habits and attitudes. They would spend less time predicting future political events, since the predictions are so often wrong and in any case are useless. They would instead devote that energy toward understanding and explaining what had already occurred—and its implications for the future (which are different from guesses about who will win the straw poll in Florida). They would spend less time on sportscaster-like analysis of how politicians were playing their game, because they would realize that very few people care. Many journalists care, and their friends in politics care, but when they make this chat public they become as boring and irrelevant as any other group of insiders talking shop. They would feel less compelled to flock to the spectacle of the moment, in hopes of following the audience's fickle interest, and instead act as if the real challenge in journalism was that of making important matters seem sexy and intriguing. Broadcasters will always need to think about ratings and publishers will always need to think about circulation. But the evidence is clear: The "canny" tactical analysis on which today's political reporters pride themselves is *not* valued by the public. If it were, the press would have become more popular as it has grown more pundit-like.

If they held themselves as responsible for the rise of public cynicism as they hold "venal" politicians and the "selfish" public; if they considered that the license they have to criticize and defame comes with an implied responsibility to serve the public—if they did all or any of these things, they would make journalism more useful, public life stronger, and themselves far more worthy of esteem.

Epilogue

In the summer of 1995, as I was interviewing reporters, editors, and broadcasters about the decisions and trade-offs they had made in their careers, I met Jim Wooten in Washington. Through most of the 1970s, Wooten had been a star political correspondent for the *New York Times*. In 1979, after a brief stint on the staff of *Esquire* magazine, he joined ABC News. Although he has never become one of the network's most recognizable celebrities, he has been involved in all its presidential campaign coverage as well as reporting war and revolution from the Middle East, Central America, Rwanda, Somalia, Bosnia, and other troubled corners of the world. At the *Times* he had been known as a stylish writer, and his TV reports often have a distinctive edge. While reporting from Sarajevo in 1993, he produced one story in which he said nothing for 55 seconds—an eternity on air—while the camera moved across scenes of wartime devastation.

Wooten had turned to television because he needed the money. His first wife had died after a long, excruciating illness. Wooten had lost his job at *Esquire* and his medical insurance there when the magazine was purchased by two young, cost-cutting entrepreneurs, Christopher Whittle and Philip Moffett. He ended up deeply in debt from his wife's medical bills. When he joined ABC, the mighty Roone Arledge, head of ABC News, arranged to ease that burden. ABC lent Wooten the money to pay off his debts, and then with generous contract renewals and raises enabled him to repay the loan. By 1995 Wooten's salary was several hundred thousand dollars per year.

Near the end of our discussion, he put his hand into the inside pocket of his blue blazer and brought out a half-sheet of white paper, folded over so many times it was the size of a matchbook. He unfolded it and pulled on his glasses so he could look again at a few lines in extremely small print. "I don't really need to look at it," he said. "I know it by heart."

The words on the paper were from a letter to the editor of the *Huntsville Times,* published when Wooten worked there as a cub reporter in the mid-1960s. Bobby Kennedy had just made a well-publicized trip through the rural South, and had declared himself shocked by the poverty and misery he had discovered there. Wooten, who had grown up all across the South as the son of a minister, decided to reexplore locally what Kennedy had found in Mississippi.

"I did a five-part series about poverty in and around Huntsville," Wooten said. "The paper, to its credit, ran every story on the front page above the fold, even though I'd found some devastating examples. After it was published, the paper got this letter. I never met the man who wrote it, but I still think about him. And I carry his letter with me every day."

Wooten handed the paper, with its tiny printing, to me. As I struggled to make out the minuscule type, Wooten began to read along from memory:

In the apparent absence of any community conscience, Mr. Wooten has stepped into the void to serve as a conscience for us all—to see and to hear and to feel for the rest of us and then, as any good reporter should, to tell us the reality that is beyond our reach or that we thoughtlessly have overlooked or purposefully neglected.

Give the man a raise.

Wooten laughed at the last line, and laughed again in saying, "There were *other* letters too, which I don't keep." It was easy to envision what a series by a young reporter, determined to make his mark and shake up the community, might have been like. Wooten would probably cringe if made to read it thirty years later. Since he, like every reporter, had had to learn how to shrug off letters from readers who were angry, he knew he couldn't take praise at face value either.

But it wasn't praise for this series that had stuck with him, or that impressed me. It was the device this reporter had chosen to remind himself that the work he did mattered. It was not just entertainment. It was not just a way to make as much money as he could—though he has gone on to make a lot of money now. It was a serious responsibility, a public trust, which deserved the very best that was in him to give.

Notes

Unless otherwise attributed, all material in direct quotations in the text comes from interviews conducted by the author.

Introduction

4 **Big Three floundered:** This change is a main theme of David Halberstam's book *The Reckoning* (New York: William Morrow, 1986).

1. Why We Hate the Media

20 *Meet the Press* **transcript:** *Meet the Press,* March 19, 1995. Official transcript from Burrelle's Information Service, Livingston, New Jersey.

21 **Questions from "ordinary people":** Thomas E. Patterson discussed this pattern in *Out of Order* (New York: Vintage, 1994), pp. 55–56.

22 **Teenagers' questions:** White House transcript of "Remarks by President Bill Clinton at Roundtable with the Mayor's Youth Council, Boston, Massachusetts, January 31, 1995."

23 **Peter Jennings's questions:** ABC World News Tonight, January 6, 1995, ABC Transcript 5005-7.

24 **Dan Rather's questions:** CBS Evening News, January 26, 1995. Transcript by Burrelle's Information Services.

24 **Tom Brokaw's questions:** NBC Today interview with President Clinton, January 27, 1995. Transcript from Federal News Service.

26 **"Twenty-six years":** "Clinton on Spot on Vietnam Issue" by Todd S. Purdum, *New York Times,* June 26, 1995.

30 **Bill Bradley interview:** Inside Politics, CNN, August 17, 1995.

33 **"Brit Hume":** "The Snooze at 11; White House Correspondents Wait While Nothing Happens" by Howard Kurtz, *Washington Post,* March 24, 1995.

37 **Sam Donaldson's ranch:** These and related episodes are described in "Newscaster Feuding with Newspapers" by Alan Wolper, *Editor and Publisher,* May 6, 1995; "Ranch Hand: Donaldson Unfair," Associated Press Online, March 29, 1995; "Donaldson Fires Injured Ranch Hand," *Phoenix Gazette,* March 28, 1995; and "When the Press Outclasses the Public" by Howard Kurtz, *Columbia Journalism Review,* May–June 1994.

38 **George Will:** "A Conflict of Wills? Pundit Kept Quiet about Wife's Role as Lobbyist" by Howard Kurtz, *Washington Post,* May 23, 1995.

39 **Members of the Punditocracy:** Eric Alterman popularized this term in his book *Sound and Fury: The Washington Punditocracy and the Collapse of American Politics* (New York: Harper Collins, 1992).

41 **"All Mush and No Message":** Richard Cohen, *Washington Post,* January 26, 1995.

41 **"An Opportunity Missed":** David Broder, "Some Hear Echo of Past Success in Clinton Speech," *Washington Post,* January 26, 1995.

41 **"If self-discipline":** "Some Hear Echo of Past Success in Clinton Speech" by David Broder, *Washington Post,* January 26, 1995.

45 **Movies and TV shows:** "Hollywood's New Villain: Journalists" by Antonia Zerbisias, *Toronto Star,* September 12, 1993.

45 *Saturday Night Live* **skit:** "The journalists were portrayed as ignorant, arrogant, and pointlessly adversarial. By gently rebuffing their ludicrous questions, the Pentagon briefer [on SNL] came off as a model of sanity." From "Cynicism Works—If You're Bogart; Reporters Think They're Doing Their Job by Being Adversarial, But to the TV Viewer It Looks Like Unmerited Arrogance" by Jay Rosen, *Los Angeles Times,* May 30, 1991.

46 **Survey about media:** "Ordinary Americans More Cynical Than Journalists: News Media Differs with Public and Leaders on Watchdog Issues." Washington: Times Mirror Center on the People and the Press, May 22, 1995.

2. What Changed

47 **"The function of a good newspaper":** Henry Fairlie referred to this comment of Scott's in the *New Republic,* April 30, 1977.

49 **Polls of reporters:** According to an exhaustive poll of media attitudes released in 1995, members of the national press were about twice as willing to accept homosexuality as the general public was. When asked whether homosexuality should be "accepted" or "discouraged," 83 percent of respondents from the press corps said "accepted"; 4 percent said "discouraged." For the general public, the figures were 41 percent "accepted," 53 percent "discouraged." They were also far less likely to be regular churchgoers, and far more accepting of abortion. "Ordinary Americans More Cynical than Journalists: News Media Differs with Public and Leaders on Watchdog Issues," Washington: Times Mirror Center on the People and the Press, May 22, 1995.

50 **Coverage of Clinton:** The Times Mirror study released in May 1995 explored reporters' attitudes toward the Clinton administration. According to this survey, 32 percent of national press representatives (reporters, editors, and broadcasters surveyed) approved of the Clinton administration's performance in office. 44 percent of the general public approved. "Ordinary Ameri-

cans More Cynical than Journalists: News Media Differs with Public and Leaders on Watchdog Issues," Washington: Times Mirror Center on the People and the Press, May 22, 1995.

50 **"failed Clinton presidency":** "The Year in Review" by Dave Barry, syndicated column, December 31, 1992.

50 **Profile of George Stephanopoulos:** *Time,* November 30, 1992.

52 **Vaclav Havel's speech:** Commencement Address, delivered at Harvard University, June 8, 1995.

56 **"But at *60 Minutes*":** Halberstam's elaboration on his views of the long-run effect of *60 Minutes*-style journalism. Mike Wallace, he said, has an instinctive sense of how he should be "cast" in each story,

> I think in that sense he's perfect for Don Hewitt. No wonder that marriage (the two of them) is so successful and has lasted so long. I think what has happened is that a line has been moved in television journalism, and it's going to get worse every year, and the people who come after them will move the line even more, and we'll probably eventually be nostalgic for Hewitt and Wallace.

After his comment that Wallace should simply "do fewer" TV stories, Halberstam said:

> I said I'd make a lot more money if I did my larger books in two years instead of four or five, and even more if I could do them in one year. But the only thing you have is your signature—that you vouch for what you put your name over. The terrible thing is that they still managed to get the context of the story wrong. Yes, Westy cooked the books—but the real question is why he did it. Because Mike didn't do his legwork—he got it completely wrong. He has Westy cooking the books and misleading Lyndon in the process. But Westy didn't do it to mislead Lyndon. He did it to mislead Johnson's (and therefore his own) *principal domestic critics,* the Congress and the press. Westy was always a Boy Scout compared to Lyndon Johnson. Anyone who knew anything about how the war was run knew that. *Westy was giving Lyndon exactly what he wanted.* That's a very big mistake—it's hard to get a story more wrong than that.

In print signature reporters have always done their own work and if they became stars, like Harrison Salisbury or Homer Bigart did, it was largely within their own private world and it was because the cumulative value of their careers was so stunning, the ability on story after story to surface as the best journalist around, that even their colleagues were in awe. But on television, there's a need for stars, and a belief that the delivery system, that is the reporter as an entertainment instrument—is more important than the substance of the story. That's why they use a tiny handful of stars on 60 *Minutes* and keep the producers, who are often excellent and do the heavy lifting there, in relative anonymity. And that's why Diane Sawyer, because of a perceived sense of her cosmetic attractiveness, is handed to us as a signature journalistic figure before we can even tell whether she's a particularly good reporter or not. I am afraid in television the old value system, where the opinion of your peers mattered so much, is largely gone. The only thing which matters is getting the ratings. Get the ratings and you're forgiven all else. The sin there is not being inaccurate. The sin is being boring. I think Mike is very talented, he's really good at that particular show and occasionally he'll do a terrific piece of work. But I don't think of him as a journalist, and I don't know many senior print people in this business who do.

57 **"In fact, of the nearly 500 stories . . .":** Calculations based on author's tally of 60 *Minutes* program logs from January 1990 through December 1994.

62 **Recent opinion polls:** The most influential of these polls, the *Times Mirror* study released in May 1995, said that citizens are actually *more* cynical about politicians than journalists are. The analysts said that this indicated a stylistic bias in today's reporting. Even though journalists do not believe that all politicians are shallow and insincere, the conventions of reporting lead to stories suggesting that—and these stories, in turn, shape the public's view of politics. "Ordinary Americans More Cynical than Journalists: News Media Differs with Public and Leaders

on Watchdog Issues," Washington: Times Mirror Center on the People and the Press, May 22, 1995.

63 **"They'll look you straight in the eye"**: Joe Peyronnin quoted by Stephen Budiansky, *U.S. News & World Report,* January 9, 1995.

64 **"President Clinton returned"**: "Oxford Journal: Whereas, He Is an Old Boy, If a Young Chief, Honor Him" by Maureen Dowd, *New York Times,* June 9, 1994, p. 1.

71 **Mark Willes interview:** "Business Outsider Is Moving in at *Times Mirror*" by William Glaberson, *New York Times,* May 3, 1995.

72 **Cheerios:** *"Times Mirror* Chief Stresses Primacy of Newspapers" by James Sterngold, *New York Times,* July 28, 1995.

3. The Gravy Train

78 **"It is not entirely surprising"**: "Washington's New Ruling Class: Clincest" by Jacob Weisberg, *New Republic,* April 26, 1993.

79 **"Was I using the opportunity . . . ?"**: Howard Fineman quoted in "They're Being True to Their School" by Howard Kurtz, *Washington Post,* January 15, 1993.

79 **"Most journalists"**: Jonathan Cohn, "Perrier in the Newsroom," *American Prospect,* Spring 1995.

80 **"Ten thousand dollars?"**: Recounted by Steven Waldman in *The Bill: How the Adventures of Clinton's National Service Bill Reveal What Is Corrupt, Comic, Cynical—and Noble—About Washington* (New York: Viking Penguin, 1995), p. 70.

80 **Clinton's plan was treated as insignificant:** Jonathan Cohn discusses this and related incidents in "Perrier in the Newsroom," *American Prospect,* Spring 1995.

82 **Talk show appearances:** I have some experience in the talk show world. More than a decade ago, in the early years of *The McLaughlin Group,* I was a guest panelist on the show three times within a six-month period. This experience provided one

priceless memory. While sitting with the other panelists waiting for the taping to begin, I watched in amazement as Robert Novak, a *McLaughlin* regular, pounded out his newspaper column on a portable computer. "I realized I was losing too much damn time this way," he said. Nonetheless, I became uncomfortable with the show because of the need to express opinions on subjects I knew little or nothing about—that week's developments in the Middle East, for instance, or an emerging crisis in some Third World country I had never reported on or visited. Since that time I have not appeared on panel shows and have confined my TV appearances to subjects I have reported and written about.

Through my journalistic career I have done—and enjoyed—a limited amount of public speaking. In a typical year, I will give twenty to twenty-five speeches, most of which will be for free. These are to such audiences as World Affairs Councils, government institutions, and high schools. The paid engagements, five or six a year, are mostly at universities. These are for university programs related to subjects I have written books or magazine articles about. With one exception, the most I have received for a speech is $6,000, and the average is much less. The most I have made in a year from speaking is $26,000.

Here is the exception: In 1992 the producers of William F. Buckley's *Firing Line* series organized a televised two-hour debate on international trade policy. The team arguing that unrestricted free trade could cause problems consisted of former governor Jerry Brown of California; Lester Thurow of MIT: Representative Dick Gephardt of Missouri; and me. The members of the other team arguing in favor of free trade were Buckley; former secretary of state Henry Kissinger; former congressman and Cabinet secretary Jack Kemp; and Representative Dick Armey of Texas. The debate was moderated by Michael Kinsley.

I welcomed the chance to participate in this debate, which was to take place at the University of Mississippi before an audience of thousands of people. It involved the very issues about which I had been reporting and writing throught the previous decade, especially when I was based in Asia. The presidential campaign of 1992 was nearing its climax, and the question of which trade strategy would best enhance America's economic interests was an important theme. I had written many times that American economic debate often got stuck at the level of banalities from introductory economics courses. The chance to move the discussion beyond those truisms, in a nationally televised discussion with several august figures, is one I eagerly seized. No one mentioned a fee to me when the preparations were under way. I assumed that participation in the event was to be its own compensation.

Two months after the debate, a check for $15,000 arrived from Buckley's production company. After calling to make sure that this was not a mistake—that it wasn't meant to be $1,500 to cover airfare and other travel expenses—I gave $5,000 to charity, paid the expenses, and kept the rest.

In the last two years I have been paid fees for speaking to six organizations. These groups have been: the American Institute of Architects; the alliance of Japanese pharmaceutical companies called PharmaForum; Fisher Scientific International; the United Technologies Corporation; the Association for Manufacturing Technology, which is the organization of American machine toolmakers; and the employees association of a firm in Alabama called Vulcan industries.

85 **"Let's use fictional numbers":** Joe Cosby, originally quoted in James Fallows, "The New Celebrities of Washington," *New York Review of Books,* June 12, 1986.

87 **Cokie Roberts's Junior League engagement:** This is discussed in "Take the Money and Talk" by Alicia C. Shepard, *American Journalism Review,* June 1995.

96 **"You can now aspire":** Jeff Greenfield, originally quoted in Fallows, "The New Celebrities of Washington," *New York Review of Books,* June 12, 1986.

97 **David Gergen's speaking income:** James M. Perry reported on this disclosure in the *Wall Street Journal,* April 15, 1994.

97 **"Being paid more than you're worth":** "Confessions of a Buckraker" by Michael Kinsley, *New Republic,* May 1, 1995.

103 **"If the Insurance Institute of America"**: Ben Bradlee quoted in Shepard, "Take the Money and Talk," *New American Journalism Review,* June 1995.

103 **"You tell me"**: Alan Murray quoted in Shepard, "Take the Money and Talk," *New American Journalism Review,* June 1995.

104 **American Bankers Association convention**: James Warren reported on this engagement in "Sunday Watch," *Chicago Tribune,* October 30, 1994.

105 **"No group I've spoken to"**: Kinsley, "Confessions of a Buckraker," *New Republic,* May 1, 1995.

108 **"sends out one of those messages"**: Brian Lamb quoted in Shepard, "Take the Money and Talk," *New American Journalism Review,* June 1995.

111 **"The Most Exciting and Influential Leaders"**: There were four other featured speakers: Tom Peters, coauthor of *In Search of Excellence;* former cabinet member Elizabeth Dole; former surgeon general C. Everett Koop; and entertainer Mark Russell.

113 **"it's not something"**: Alicia C. Shepard reported this response, related by ABC spokeswoman Eileen Murphy, in "Take the Money and Talk," *New American Journalism Review,* June 1995.

114 **"But I do it"**: Kinsley, "Confessions of a Buckracker," *New Republic,* May 1, 1995.

114 **"This is not writing"**: "Squawking Heads: Are TV's political talk shows too glib for our own good?" by Mark Jurkowitz, *Boston Globe,* April 27, 1995.

114 **"People generally don't take the McLaughlin Group"**: Fred Barnes quoted in "Thinking Out Loud: Journalism's Talking Heads Find It Pays to Have an Opinion" by Howard Kurtz, *Washington Post,* October 4, 1994.

119 **"He's not terribly eager"**: Cokie Roberts on NPR, June 12, 1995.

120 **"Who had a better week . . . ?"**: "Mighty Mouths" by James Wolcott, *New Yorker,* December 26–January 2, 1994.

122 **"The less you know"**: Margaret Carlson quoted in Kurtz, "Thinking Out Loud: Journalism's Talking Heads Find It Pays to Have an Opinion," *Washington Post,* October 4, 1994.

123 **"We didn't know"**: Mark Gearan quoted by Tom Rosenstiel, *New Republic,* August 22, 1994.

125 **Promotional flyer for Roberts's column:** The United Feature Syndicate flyer was widely distributed to newspapers and was first quoted by James Warren in the *Chicago Tribune,* August 28, 1994.

126 **"their regulars' own luxury-skybox view"**: Wolcott, "Mighty Mouths," *New Yorker,* December 26–January 2, 1994.

4. Bad Attitude

129 **Why do we need the news?**: Michael Schudson, a professor at the University of California at San Diego who is a prominent academic theorist of the news, has used the thought-experiment of a news establishment that suddenly vanishes, in order to show the real value of journalism.

Suppose, Schudson has said, that the elite press, which filters the news in a way many people dislike, went out of business sometime in the near future. Suppose further that, thanks to imminent advances in technology, each person could get exactly the information he or she wanted, with none of the annoying "spin" from editors or commentators. With a vastly expanded system of cable TV, each viewer could watch sessions of each congressional committee, each state legislature, each city council. Through the Internet, people at home could instantly find the latest research reports about heart disease, or AIDS, or the effectiveness of different exercise schemes. Through fully indexed online versions of the *Congressional Record,* they could find out what any congressman said about any theme. On Court TV and its many channels they could follow all the major legal battles. If they wanted to know the crime rates for each part of town or the crash rate for each commuter airline company, they could pull up that information too. The media establishment as we know it would seem to be short-circuited. And yet, Schudson wrote in his book *The Power of News,* "Journalism—of some sort—would be reinvented."

> People would want ways to sift through the endless information available. What is most important? What is most relevant? What is most interesting? People would want help interpreting and explaining events. . . . It is hard to picture the contemporary world, even in the face of a technology that makes each of us potentially equal senders and receivers of information, without a specialized institution of journalism.

From *The Power of News,* Michael Schudson (Harvard University Press, 1995), p.2.

131 **Morning Edition:** For the record, I have done commentaries for National Public Radio's *Morning Edition* since 1987.

131 **Twice as many stories about Whitewater:** This is on the basis of a Nexis search.

135 **"This week we can talk":** Sam Donaldson quoted in "Dire Judgments on Clinton Started Just Days into Term; Competition among Analysts and President's Risky Agenda Played Roles in Drumbeat of Early Criticism" by David Shaw, *Los Angeles Times,* September 16, 1993.

135 **Presidents' performances:** George Bush had his greatest moment in the second half of his term, when leading an international coalition against Saddam Hussein. (Agree or disagree with the policy, Bush carried it out with great skill.) Different groups have different nominations for Bush's worst moment— breaking the "read my lips" pledge; letting his post–Gulf War popularity melt away rather than using it to enact domestic reforms; nominating Clarence Thomas—but all took place at least eighteen months into Bush's term.

Jimmy Carter's greatest achievement came near the end of his second year in office, late in 1978, when he persuaded Anwar Sadat and Menachem Begin to sign the Camp David peace accords. His greatest failures—the Iranian hostage disaster, the panicky-seeming cabinet reshuffle, the failure to ratify the strategic-arms treaty after the Soviet invasion of Afghanistan—all occurred in the second half of his term.

Richard Nixon's major positive legacy was his opening to China, which he visited three years after his inauguration. His obvious failure was to be forced out of office, for events that began in the fourth year of his first term. Lyndon Johnson's flurry of legislative activity, in 1965, began more than a year after he became president. His fateful decisions to escalate in Vietnam began at about the same time.

Ronald Reagan is the one apparent exception to this pattern, since the tax cuts he enacted in his first year in office were his major accomplishment, for better or worse. (Gerald Ford served for too short a time to fit this scheme.) But even Reagan's case illustrates how hard it is to predict how a presidency will end from the way it begins. In his first two months in office Reagan was called a "stumbling" and "uncertain" leader; his job-approval rating at the start was only 51 percent. His approval rating rose after he survived John Hinckley's assassination attempt—but had fallen far enough by mid-1982 that he ran far behind Walter Mondale in presidential-preference polls.

137 **Exchange between Amanpour and Wallace:** *60 Minutes,* May 14, 1995. The exchange was also described in a preview of the *60 Minutes* show by Richard Huff in the *New York Daily News,* May 12, 1995.

137 **"Our remaining correspondents":** "Parachutes, Bigfoot, and Parochialism: How the American Media Cover the World" by Larry Martz, *Dateline,* Overseas Press Club, 1995.

138 **Comparison of Taiwan and South Korea:** The Korean export economy, for instance, is dominated by huge industrial combines—Daewoo, Samsung, Gold Star—much as Japan's is by Mitsubishi, Matsushita, and NEC. Taiwan has almost no industrial giants—the biggest is the little-known Evergreen—but hundreds of thousands of tiny family-owned firms. Korea's relationship with Japan is bitter in part because the cultures are so similar; Taiwan's is more relaxed, even though like Korea it was under Japanese colonial rule. Korea and Taiwan feel in different ways threatened by China, but for Taiwan ties

to the mainland Chinese market are the center of all commercial hopes for the future. And so on.

143 **Homer Bigart:** James Wooten discussed Bigart's legacy in "The Ambassador's Terrace: A Brief Memoir of Itinerant Journalism," the 1995 Joe Alex Morris, Jr., Lecture, delivered at Harvard University. Reprinted in *Nieman Reports,* Summer 1995.

148 **Basic litmus test for reporters:** I am grateful to Nicholas Lemann for this rule of thumb.

149 **"Every reporter everywhere in the country":** "Washington's Influential Sources: Opinion Leaders Dictate the Conventional Wisdom" by David Shaw, *Los Angeles Times,* August 26, 1989.

156 **"We all . . . got sucked in":** Tom Brokaw quoted in Shaw, "Washington's Influential Sources: Opinion Leaders Dictate the Conventional Wisdom," *Los Angeles Times,* August 26, 1989.

162 **Coverage of Clinton's plan to overhaul welfare system:** Tom Rosenstiel described the welfare-reform episode in "The Myth of CNN: Why Ted Turner's Revolution Is Bad News," *New Republic,* August 22–29, 1994.

162 *New York Times* **Medicare story:** "Congressional Memo: G.O.P. Feels the Heat. The Furnace: Medicare" by Robin Toner, *New York Times,* May 5, 1995.

164 **"The interviewer moves on to something else."** The White House official gave an illustration of how this process works:

> Suppose you're the President and you're taking questions about the deficit, say, during your first two years in office. You know the first one will be something like, "Mr. Clinton, how can you say you're serious about the deficit when it will remain at least $200 billion even if all your proposals are enacted?"
>
> You answer, "After twelve years of rising deficits, we'll be the first to actually get the deficit headed down for three years in a row. I think that's serious by anyone's definition."

The next question will be something like, "But isn't entitlement spending still soaring?"

You come back with, "Yes—and that's why we've proposed health care reforms to help control those costs, which as you know are driving our long-term budget problems."

That will do it! You've answered truthfully, as far as it goes. But no reporter asks the key next question that would expose the real problem: that under the Clinton health plan's own assumptions, spending on health would rise from 14 percent of GDP today to 20 percent and more in the next century, meaning the budget problem would only get worse! Being ready with two questions' worth "talking points" gets you past any embarrassing fact like this.

165 **Marlin Fitzwater comments:** "Television: An Opiate for Journalists" by Marlin Fitzwater, *Washington Monthly,* October 1995.

165 **"called on the substance of an issue":** The official said there was one important exception that proved the rule. This was coverage of the Clinton administration's welfare reform plan by Jason DeParle of the *New York Times.* The official said, "It angered people in the administration terribly that he had boiled things down to their nut, which was that welfare reform was going to cost more money, not save it. Most of the time you didn't have to worry about this happening."

166 **"As polls showed":** "Clinton Reaping Political Gain from Raid" by John Aloysius Farrell and John W. Mashek, *Boston Globe,* June 29, 1993.

166 *New York Times* **overnight poll:** "Poll Shows Raid on Iraq Buoyed Clinton's Popularity" by Richard L. Berke, *New York Times,* June 29, 1993.

167 **Harris poll:** The Harris Poll #55, November 1, 1993. Similar findings were reported in *The Gallup Public Opinion Monitor,* July 1993. I am grateful to Peter Loge for obtaining these results.

169 **Predictions of public affairs reporters:** A similar problem occurs in financial journalism. As both Howard Kurtz, in the

Washington Post, and Joseph Nocera, in his book *A Piece of the Action,* have pointed out, the "hottest stocks to buy now" in *Money* magazine and related publications rarely show up on the next year's list of best investments. As Kurtz wrote early in 1995: "In February 1992, a *Money* cover story trumpeted '20 Great Mutual Funds to Buy Now.' A year later, when *Money* touted 'The 12 Funds to Buy Now,' only one of the previous year's hot properties made the list. By February 1994 there were no repeats from the past two years. And last August, not one of *Money's* previous more than 40 recommendations made the cut." *Washington Post,* February 18, 1995.

172 **"the new president":** "Case of Double Jeopardy; Clinton's 2d Setback Over Attorney General Is Calling His Political Savvy into Question" by R. W. Apple, *New York Times,* February 6, 1993. This case was also discussed in an excellent article, "Who Won the Week? The Political Press and the Evacuation of Meaning" by Jay Rosen, *Tikkun,* July 1993.

172 **"Many Democrats Accuse Clinton of Incompetence":** R. W. Apple, *New York Times,* February 16, 1995.

173 **"Get Ready for War":** Charles Krauthammer, *Washington Post,* June 3, 1994.

174 **"Straight 'War Talk' ":** "Korean Conflict II: Straight 'War Talk' Is Needed Now" by William Safire, *New York Times,* June 9, 1994.

176 **"To ask 'who won the week?' ":** "Perspective on the Media: Down with the Weekly Box Score. Making the Presidency a Game That Is 'Won' or 'Lost' Each Week Trivializes Government and the Press" by Jay Rosen, *Los Angeles Times,* June 8, 1993.

178 **"Desperately in Need of Winning Streak, Clinton Finds One":** Todd S. Purdum, *New York Times,* May 7, 1995.

180 **"You can be wrong":** ABC reporter quoted in "The Public Thinks the National Press Is Elitist, Insensitive and Arrogant" by Stephen Budiansky, *U.S. News & World Report,* January 9, 1995.

180 **Reporters' 'attitude' pieces:** An excellent article on this subject was "The New Writers' Bloc: They've Got Attitude, Humor, and an Eye for Detail. But Could Journalism's New Stylists Do More?" by Katherine Boo, *Washington Monthly,* November 1992.

181 **"When the Knicks play the Bulls":** "Who Won the Week? The Political Press and the Evacuation of Meaning" by Jay Rosen, *Tikkun,* July 1993.

5. Getting in the Way

193 **Lack of score-settling during Kennedy administration:** The main exception, as Charles Peters has pointed out repeatedly in the *Washington Monthly,* involved Adlai Stevenson's role during the Cuban Missile Crisis. For reasons never fully plumbed, Kennedy administration officials in general and Robert Kennedy in particular always went out of their way to portray Stevenson, then the U.S. ambassador to the United Nations, as having been too weak, sissylike, and unwilling to stand up to the Soviet threat.

197 **Outguessing reporters:** This is not a new phenomenon. David Shaw of the *Los Angeles Times* wrote in 1989: "Patrick Buchanan, former press aide to Presidents Richard M. Nixon and Ronald Reagan and now a syndicated columnist, says that when he worked in the Nixon White House, he was often able to predict 'every single question . . . and the spin on the questions' that Nixon would face in his next press conference." "Instant Consensus: How Media Gives Stories Same 'Spin'" by David Shaw, *Los Angeles Times,* August 25, 1989.

197 **American press reports on Japan:** This tendency is a principal subject of my previous book *Looking at the Sun: The Rise of the New East Asian Economic and Political System* (New York: Vintage, 1995).

199 **"The cumulative message":** "Role of TV News in Shaping Foreign Policy Under Increasing Scrutiny; Media: Influence May Be Overstated, But Technology Is Requiring Nation's

Leaders to Have New Kinds of Communications Skills and a Clearer Focus" by Thomas B. Rosenstiel, *Los Angeles Times,* July 25, 1994.

202 **Times Mirror Center survey:** "Ordinary Americans More Cynical than Journalists: News Media Differs with Public and Leaders on Watchdog Issues." Washington: Times Mirror Center on the People and the Press, May 22, 1995.

202 **Quotes from Times Mirror report:** "Ordinary Americans More Cynical than Journalists: News Media Differs from Public and Leaders on Watchdog Issues." Washington: Times Mirror Center on the People and the Press, May 22, 1995.

204 **"The results were clear":** "The Media and the Message: Is the messenger to blame, too, for a cynical citizenry?" by Kathleen Hall Jamieson and Joseph N. Cappella, *Atlanta Journal and Constitution,* September 15, 1994.

211 **Health-care alternatives:** Some of the main ones were: "play or pay," in which employers would have to provide insurance for their workers or else pay into a public fund that would cover uninsured workers; "individual mandate," in which people received various tax incentives to provide more insurance for themselves; and simple insurance reforms, which would limit the insurance companies' ability to dump customers they did not want to cover.

211 **Clinton invited proponents to debate:** Ted Marmor, one of the participants in the debate, describes it in "What the Death of Health Reform Teaches Us About the Press" by Tom Hamburger, Ted Marmor, and Jon Meacham, *Washington Monthly,* November 1994.

213 **"ship of fools":** "What Went Wrong: How Wonks and Pols— and You—Fumbled Universal Health Care" by Abigail Trafford, *Washington Post,* August 21, 1994.

213 **"opponents of Clinton-style reform":** "Health Care Reform: The Collapse of a Quest; Clinton's Top Domestic Priority Succumbed to Miscalculation, Aggressive Opposition and Partisanship" by Dana Priest and Michael Weisskopf, *Washington Post,* October 11, 1994.

213 **"Clinton's eager health-care legions"**: from an editorial in *USA Today,* September 27, 1994.

214 **"Clinton Task Force All Ears"**: *Congressional Quarterly,* May 23, 1993.

217 **"Politicians almost unanimously agree"**: *Time,* November 8, 1993.

217 **"The reviews are in"**: *National Journal,* October 2, 1993.

219 **Academic study**: "When Harry Met Louise" by Kathleen Hall Jamieson, *Washington Post,* August 15, 1994.

222 **"A group of reporters"**: Hamburger, Marmov, and Meacham, "What the Death of Health Reform Teaches Us About the Press," *Washington Monthly,* November 1994.

225 **Jamieson's survey**: "Newspaper and Television Coverage of the Health Care Reform Debate, January 16–July 25, 1994," A Report by the Annenberg Public Policy Center, funded by the Robert Wood Johnson Foundation, August 12, 1994.

227 **"The law will prevent"**: "No Exit: What the Clinton Plan Will Do for You" by Elizabeth McCaughey, *New Republic,* February 7, 1994.

229 **Managed care**: Some medical scholars have argued that as more and more people enter managed care, the managed-care system itself becomes more varied and less confining—and that this diversification would have continued under the Clinton plan, which required several different plans (including one fee for service) to be available for each customer to choose from. For example: "Interestingly, most insured Americans (some 70 percent) are already in one or another form of managed care and the effect of that dispersion has been to weaken the controls that managed care has managed. So, for instance, staff-model HMOs represent a small proportion of managed care and the direction of development has been to make most HMO-style bodies more like fee-for-service medical care than the much touted model of Kaiser Permanente." This is from a letter that Theodore R. Marmor and Jerry L. Mashaw of Yale wrote to the *New Republic* complaining about McCaughey's article. It was published on February 14, 1994.

230 **All taxpayers:** Kaus attributed this analogy to Paul Starr of Princeton, one of the principal architects of the Clinton plan. "TRB from Washington: No Exegesis" by Mickey Kaus, *New Republic,* May 8, 1995.

231 **"It would be illegal":** "The Clintons' Lethal Paternalism" by George F. Will, *Newsweek,* February 7, 1994.

232 **"Ms. McCaughey's analysis":** "Editorial Notebook: Fear-Mongering on Health Reform" by Michael M. Weinstein, *New York Times,* February 6, 1994.

232 **"Perhaps she has spent":** "TRB from Washington: Second Opinion" by Michael Kinsley, *New Republic,* February 14, 1994.

232 **"Anyone who reads the bill":** "Correspondence: Round Three" by Elizabeth McCaughey, *New Republic,* February 21, 1994.

232 **Mickey Kaus's reappraisal:** Kaus, "TRB from Washington: No Exegesis," *New Republic,* May 8, 1995.

6. News and Democracy

235 **"Americans debated the connection":** Jay Rosen of the Center for Public Life and the Press at New York University has often stressed the connection between these early twentieth-century debates and the predicament of the press in the 1990s.

236 **"A book called *Public Opinion*":** *Public Opinion* by Walter Lippmann, New York: The Free Press, first published 1922; 1965 edition.

242 **"Hopeless complexity of issues":** *Common Knowledge: News and the Construction of Political Meaning* by W. Russell Neuman, M. R. Just, and A. N. Crigler, Chicago: University of Chicago Press, 1992, p. 111. This passage is cited in *Public Journalism and Public Life: Why Telling the News Is Not Enough* by Davis "Buzz" Merritt, Hillsdale, New Jersey: Lawrence Erlbaum Associates, 1995.

244 **"Study was called *Meaningful Chaos*":** *Meaningful Chaos: How People Form Relationships with Public Concerns.* A Report

Prepared for the Kettering Foundation by the Harwood Group (Bethesda, Maryland), 1993.

249 **"the Harvard philosopher Michael Sandel"**: Sandel's best-known line is: "When politics goes well we can know a good in common that we cannot know alone."

250 **"a series of which the paper"**: The background of the Columbus story is taken from "Journalism as Political Action: The Case of the Columbus (Ga.) *Ledger-Enquirer*" by Jay Rosen, unpublished manuscript, August 1991; and "Community action: sin or salvation? Columbus, Georgia's newspaper, *Ledger-Enquirer* sets up civic movement through public discussions" by Jay Rosen, *The Quill*, March 1992.

251 **"others in the press might follow"**: "Journalism as Political Action: The Case of the Columbus (Ga.) *Ledger-Enquirer*" by Jay Rosen, unpublished manuscript, August 1991; and "Community action: sin or salvation? Columbus, Georgia's newspaper, *Ledger-Enquirer*. sets up civic movement through public discussions" by Jay Rosen, *The Quill*, March 1992.

251 All David Broder quotes are from "A New Assignment for the Press," a lecture by David Broder delivered at the University of California, Riverside, February 12, 1991, Number 26 in the Press-Enterprise Lecture Series.

253 **"It is time for us"**: "Democracy and the Press" by David Broder, *Washington Post*, January 3, 1990.

254 **"chronicling these efforts"**: *Doing Public Journalism* by Arthur Charity (New York: Guilford Press, 1995) is the most comprehensive list of local papers and broadcast stations and the efforts they have made. Buzz Merritt's *Public Journalism and Public Life* describes efforts at papers other than his *Wichita Eagle*.

254 **"talk about the issues in depth"**: "Here's Our Election Bias" by Buzz Merritt, *Wichita Eagle*, September 9, 1990.

256 **"Voters are intensely interested"**: Transcript of the Project on Public Life and the Press fall seminar, American Press Institute, Reston, Virginia, November 10–12, 1993 (Dayton, Ohio: Kettering Foundation, 1995), p. 117.

264 **"toughness is mere self-indulgence"**: Merritt, *Public Journalism and Public Life,* p. 61. In an interview with the author, Merritt elaborated:

> I have come to make an important distinction between "objectivity" and "detachment." Objectivity is a matter of intellectual honesty. Take the example of Jonas Salk. He cared very much whether he found a vaccine for polio, so he was not "detached" about his work. But he had to be completely objective in his research. Other people would be checking the results of his experiments, and if he weren't completely objective the research would be a waste. His objectivity and honesty did not keep him from caring about the results.

265 **"specific action plan for a community"**: In an interview with the author in 1995, Jay Rosen described the difference in perspectives this way:

> The claim that this will just be "advocacy journalism" is the quickest way to discredit public journalism among established journalists. To say this, critics have to ignore the difference between fostering public dialogue and pushing a partisan political agenda.
>
> The mainstream press does all the things they accuse us of—defining the issues, building a stage for public debate. But it does them all in service of its own professional self-aggrandizement. It defines issues in such a way that the press remains at the center of them, with the kind of tactics-expertise that reporters have. It uses a lens on politics that maximizes the dispositive power of the press. It views the world in such a way that the skills reporters and editors want to apply become the relevant skills—handicapping races, assessing tactics, and so on.

268 **creation of *New York Times* op-ed page:** Jay Rosen discussed this phenomenon in "The common problems of the press in Washington and Moscow," *Moscow News,* July 15, 1992.

Acknowledgements

This book is dedicated to two editors, Charles Peters of *The Washington Monthly* and William Whitworth of *The Atlantic Monthly*. They have been my employers—Peters in the early 1970s, Whitworth since 1980—and also my teachers and friends. In personality and in journalistic style they have very little in common, but each has changed journalism for the better through his combination of idealism, dedication, and commitment to excellence. I feel lucky to have been associated with them.

Linda Healey, my editor at Pantheon, was insightful and skillful in showing me how to improve this book. I am grateful again to have worked with her. Sonny Mehta, president of the Knopf Publishing Group, greatly encouraged me with his early support for this project. Altie Karper at Pantheon managed the book production process with both competence and flexibility. Suzanne Herz and Meredith Kahn, also of Pantheon, made this a more successful venture than it would otherwise have been. I am grateful as always to Wendy Weil, my agent, and to Mortimer Zuckerman, Fred Drasner, and Kim Jensen of *The Atlantic Monthly*, who have made it possible for me to write books while working there.

I owe a great debt to Nicholas Lemann, Lincoln Caplan, and Todd Oppenheimer for their comments on an early draft of this manuscript. Frances Kilkenny was loyal and helpful during research stages. Meghan Thompson was a very capable research assistant, and Elizabeth Smith played a crucial role in producing the manuscript. At different stages in this work I got important help from Jason DeParle, Garrett Epps, Jody Greenstone, David Halberstam, Steve Hofman, David Ignatius, Michael Janeway, Matthew Miller, Matt Rohde, Jay Rosen, Steven Waldman, and Jim Wooten. I would also like to thank Greg Allen, Jonathan Alter, Ken Auletta, Stephen Banker, Tom Brokaw, Cole Campbell, Matthew Cooper, Jerome Doolittle, Leonard Downie, David Dreyer, Gregg Easterbrook, Robert Ferrante, Jeff Greenfield, Richard Harwood, Kathleen Hall Jamieson, Charles McCarry, Ellen McDonnell, Buzz Merritt, Ralph Nader, Richard Parker, Walter Shapiro, Alicia Shepard, and Bernard Swain. The press writings of Howard Kurtz in the *Washington Post* and Tom Rosenstiel and David Shaw of the *Los Angeles Times* were of great value.

Tech notes: I am grateful to the software engineers who created the programs on which I relied for this work: OS/2 Warp, the product of many hands at IBM facilities in Austin and Boca Raton; SearchManager/2, from IBM's software center in Germany; Agenda and Magellan, from the Mitch Kapor era at Lotus; DeScribe Word Processor, from Alan Katzen, Bob Caldwell, John Serences, Merrylee Croslin, and other members of the technical and support staffs in Sacramento; and Ask Sam Systems from Perry, Florida.

My wife, Debbie, and my sons, Tom and Tad, were generous and supportive, but of course their support for this book is the least of their virtues in my eyes.